THE BEST BUDDHIST WRITING 2008

THE BEST
BUDDHIST
WRITING
2·0·0·8

Edited by Melvin McLeod
and the Editors of the *Shambhala Sun*

SHAMBHALA
Boston & London 2008

Shambhala Publications, Inc.
Horticultural Hall
300 Massachusetts Avenue
Boston, Massachusetts 02115
www.shambhala.com

9 8 7 6 5 4 3 2 1

First Edition
Printed in the United States of America

⊛This edition is printed on acid-free paper that meets the
American National Standards Institute z29.48 Standard.
Distributed in the United States by Random House, Inc.,
and in Canada by Random House of Canada Ltd

ISBN 978-1-59030-615-4
ISSN 1932-393X
2006213739

Contents

INTRODUCTION   ix

MEETING THE CHINESE IN ST. PAUL   1
Natalie Goldberg

THE NATURAL STATE OF HAPPINESS   12
Chokyi Nyima Rinpoche

A HEART FULL OF PEACE   19
Joseph Goldstein

MY MARITAL STATUS   28
James Kullander

LEARNING TRUE LOVE   43
Sister Chan Khong

NOTHING TO DO, NOWHERE TO GO: PRACTICES
BASED ON THE TEACHINGS OF MASTER LINJI   54
Thich Nhat Hanh

A LITTLE LOWER THAN THE ANGELS:
HOW EQUANIMITY SUPPORTS KINDNESS   69
Sylvia Boorstein

CAVE WITH A VIEW   79
Kate Wheeler

THE JOY OF LIVING   88
Yongey Mingyur Rinpoche

ALWAYS TURN TOWARD, NEVER TURN AWAY   97
Rigdzin Shikpo

THE GREAT WAY   104
John Daido Loori

WHY I HAVE TO WRITE   112
Norman Fischer

THE SUTRAS OF ABU GHRAIB   116
Aidan Delgado

HITTING THE STREETS   131
Lin Jensen

GRATITUDE   137
Joanna Macy

LEARNING FORGIVENESS   148
Noah Levine

THE PRACTICE OF LOJONG: CULTIVATING
COMPASSION THROUGH TRAINING THE MIND   154
Traleg Kyabgon Rinpoche

GRASPING   173
Martine Batchelor

MIND IN COMFORT AND EASE   186
His Holiness the Dalai Lama

WHY BOTHER WITH MEDITATION?   202
Steve Hagen

THE MINDFUL LEADER   205
Michael Carroll

NATURAL ABUNDANCE   220
Frances Moore Lappé

ABOVE THE FRAY   226
R. J. Eskow

CHOOSING PEACE   235
Pema Chödrön

RETREAT AT PLUM VILLAGE   245
Cameron Barnett

GRANDMOTHER MIND   247
Susan Moon

YOGA BODY, BUDDHA MIND   253
Cyndi Lee and David Nichtern

EMOTIONS: WHAT THEY REALLY ARE   267
The Dzogchen Ponlop Rinpoche

NOT OUR BODIES, NOT OURSELVES:
LIFE LESSONS FROM A CADAVER   281
Hannah Tennant-Moore

PAIN BUT NOT SUFFERING   286
*Bhikkhu Bodhi, Darlene Cohen, Shinzen Young,
and Reginald Ray*

WASHING OUT EMPTINESS   300
Sallie Tisdale

PRINCE OF THE ASCETICS: A SHORT STORY   308
Charles Johnson

CONTRIBUTORS   317
CREDITS   327

Introduction

After the Buddha achieved enlightenment, it is said, he sat for another seven weeks under the Bodhi tree trying to decide what to do next. How could he communicate what he had experienced? Should he even try? What words could he choose that would not just create more concepts and grasping, when what he had experienced was the profound simplicity of resting in things as they are, beyond all dualism and struggle?

Buddhism often warns against the seduction of words.

"Words don't cook rice," an old Zen saying admonishes us. "Don't mistake the finger for the moon," warns another. The words Buddhism uses to describe enlightened mind are at best rough approximations of the reality. What else could they be when the very definition of enlightenment is that it is beyond all words and concepts?

Yet, after seven weeks, the Buddha did get up and speak. Thus the religion known as Buddhism was born and over the next 2,500 years it devoted untold words—scriptures, commentaries, poems, songs, logics, treatises—to teaching, parsing, praising, describing, and explaining the inconceivable.

Words don't cook rice, but it does help to have a recipe. The finger is not the destination, but it can point us in the right direction.

The Buddha arose after his seven weeks of doubt and began to teach others what he had discovered. The words he chose reflected his compassion (the imperative to help others was a natural part of his realization) and his skill (he had formulated a path that people could take toward the deep truth he had realized, and found a way to describe it). He saw that as long as we recognize their limits—as long as we don't take the finger for the moon—words can point us toward the wordless.

This book is filled with such words, linear descendants of the Buddha's. The basic truths and practices are the same, for they are beyond time and space, but now they are expressed in the many forms and voices of the modern world. Yes, there are teachings here, the traditional expressions of Buddhism that guide us on our path of personal realization. But there are also people sharing their own journeys through personal stories and memoir, helping us to empathize with others and understand our own lives better. There are people joining the spiritual with the secular by bringing the insight and practices of Buddhism into many different aspects of contemporary life. And there are people using a Buddhist lens to examine the big issues facing life on this planet, looking for the intersection of the personal and the global that could be the key to our future.

The discourse of the teacher to his or her students is the oldest, most basic, and, I would argue, most powerful expression of Buddhism. That's because Buddhism is less an institution than a living lineage of direct transmission from teacher to student.

In this year's edition of *The Best Buddhist Writing*, we have a strong and varied selection of Buddhist teachings. The form is traditional, yes, but the teachings themselves are for contemporary audiences, and they're right up to date. The Tibetan teacher Chokyi Nyima Rinpoche applies the profound teachings of Dzogchen to that most basic question, human happiness, while Vipassana teacher Joseph Goldstein shows how mindfulness practice can change our lives. The great Thich Nhat Hanh and the American Zen teacher John Daido Loori, Roshi, take ancient Zen texts and make them fresh. His Holiness the Dalai Lama uses impeccable logic to help us cut through our false beliefs about the nature of reality, and Traleg Kyabgon Rinpoche and The Dzogchen Ponlop Rinpoche teach us specific Buddhist practices to help with all the challenges and conflicting emotions we experience in interpersonal relations.

Memoir is not a traditional form in Buddhism, yet it is developing in the modern world into a powerful tool of empathy and understanding. You will be inspired and moved, as I am, by the personal stories told in this book. Here, heart and mind are joined in Susan Moon's story of her first grandchild, in James Kullander's journey through a loved one's death, and in Sallie Tisdale's Zen meditation on the frailties of the human body. And you'll smile at the foibles of Natalie Goldberg, Kate Wheeler, and Hannah Tennant-Moore, who are honest about what really happens when we modern people try to take on this ancient path.

It's an interesting thing that Buddhism's impact on modern life has been far out of proportion to the actual number of adherents. Because the basis of Buddhism is working with the mind, its practices and insights have proven to be directly and effectively applicable to many areas of modern life. Buddhism is always "news you can use." In this volume, Buddhist practice is applied to leadership (Michael Carroll), illness (Bhikkhu Bodhi, Darlene Cohen, and Shinzen Young), and ecology (Frances Moore Lappé). Cyndi Lee and David Nichtern show us how we can combine yoga and Buddhist meditation in a complete mind-body practice, and Sylvia Boorstein applies the practice of equanimity to all the vicissitudes of modern life.

In this anxious age, with so many challenges facing us as we look ahead into this century, Buddhism addresses the real root of our problems—greed, aggression, and ignorance, what Buddhism calls the three poisons. We can create all the laws, policies, and technologies we want, but the real solutions are found at a much more basic level—at the level of hate and love, bias and impartiality, revenge and forgiveness, selfishness and selflessness.

Some writers here apply these principles to specific situations: Aidan Delgado to Iraq, Lin Jensen to peace protest, R. J. Eskow to the rough world of political partisanship. Others offer more general teachings on how each of us can bring to our own lives the qualities on which humanity's future depends: Pema Chödrön on the moment when we choose between peace and conflict; Joanna Macy on developing gratitude as the basis of environmentalism;

Noah Levine on the practice of forgiveness that cuts the cycle of revenge and war; Martine Batchelor on the grasping that is the cause of attachment and overconsumption.

Never has it been clearer, never has it been more important to understand, that the personal is the political. It is my hope that this book, which brings together the writing of many wise, caring, and thoughtful people, will benefit you and through you, all others.

I am a Buddhist of one particular lineage. Therefore, I thank first of all my own teachers, the late Chögyam Trungpa Rinpoche and Khenpo Tsultrim Gyamtso Rinpoche. Yet it is my good fortune as editor-in-chief of the *Shambhala Sun* and of *Buddhadharma: The Practitioner's Quarterly* to have met and to read constantly the teachings of many outstanding Buddhist masters, and I have benefited from the teachings of all the great Buddhist schools. I am encouraged about the future of Buddhism in North America because of the many outstanding teachers—Asian and Western, women and men—who are now at the fore of Buddhism here.

I would also like to express gratitude to my colleagues here at the Shambhala Sun Foundation, publishers of the *Shambhala Sun* and *Buddhadharma*. Both Buddhists and non-Buddhists, we are engaged in an ongoing, living exploration of how to manifest our values in our work together and how to best express them through our publications.

The people at Shambhala Publications have been not just colleagues but close friends for years. I would like to thank in particular editor Beth Frankl, assistant editor Chloe Foster, and my good friend Peter Turner, president of Shambhala. I would also like to thank the other publishers represented in this book who play such a vital role in presenting Buddhism to America. In particular, I want to mention my friends and colleagues who specialize in Buddhist publishing at Wisdom Publications, Parallax Press, and Snow Lion Publications. All those interested in Buddhism applaud you for the important job you're doing.

Finally, I'd like to express my gratitude and love for my family: my late parents, Pearl and Jim McLeod, my wife Pam Rubin, and my daughter Pearl. I think that for us in the West, the family is where the real dharma is born and grows. Thank you for letting me try.

MELVIN MCLEOD
Editor-in-chief
The Shambhala Sun
Buddhadharma: The Practitioner's Quarterly

The Best Buddhist Writing 2008

Meeting the Chinese
in St. Paul ◎⟩⟩

Natalie Goldberg

Is Buddhism Eastern or Western? Ancient or modern? It is all of these and none, because its essential truths are beyond time, space, and culture. In modern-day Minnesota, Natalie Goldberg faces the same questions the ancient Chinese masters did, and finds their koans as fresh and relevant as they were a thousand years ago.

As a Soto Zen student I had successfully steered clear of koans for almost my full twenty-five years of practice. They were considered more a part of the fierce Rinzai Zen training and seemed enigmatic and scary. How would I know what the sound of one hand clapping was, as one famous koan asked? Koans were meant to be illogical and stump the student, to kick her into another way of thinking—or not thinking—so that she could have insight into the nature of the universe.

My old Soto teacher said, "Soto is more like the not-so-bright, kindly elder uncle." He admired Rinzai and indicated it was for sharper types.

Despite my reservations, in 1998 I moved up to St. Paul, Minnesota, for two months to dive into koans. I would study of the *Book of Serenity,* an ancient Chinese Zen text of one hundred koans (or cases) depicting situations and dialogues between teacher and student, teacher and teacher, student and student.

Driving in the car through Colorado, Nebraska, Iowa, crossing one state border after another, I repeated to myself, "Yes, I can do it."

My old friend Phil Willkie and I were going to trade homes for this mid-October through mid-December period. We didn't know who was getting the better deal. I would live in his three-bedroom, fourth-floor, walk-up flat on Mackubin in St. Paul, and he would·inhabit my solar beer-can-and-tire house on the mesa six miles outside of Taos.

Phil's apartment was replete with photos of his family, including one of his grandfather, Wendell Willkie, the 1940 contender for the presidency against FDR, and another of an aunt sitting in the backseat of a convertible with Dwight Eisenhower. Best of all, a former boyfriend of Phil's lived in the back bedroom. He too was studying Zen at the time. At night we'd often share a simple dinner of steamed broccoli and rice. He was a modest fellow, saving all the plastic yogurt containers and calling them his fine Tupperware collection. We had known each other years before, when he and Phil visited me in the Southwest.

During the day, I had little to do but wrestle with these Chinese ancestors who embodied the koans. I wanted to understand what was meant by their interchanges.

> Luoshan runs into Yantou and asks, "When arising and vanishing go on unceasingly, what then?"

A perfectly good question, if you were thinking about the nature of the universe. We often ask, "What should I do with my life?" Usually it's asked in despair: I'm lost. Help me. We want a concrete answer: Become a dentist and everything will be all right. But there is a deeper cry in the question. How should I live knowing the world is a confusing place?

First, Luoshan asked Shishuang his question: "When arising and vanishing go on unceasingly, what then?"

Shishuang replied, "You must be cold ashes, a dead tree, one thought for ten thousand years, box and lid joining, pure and spotlessly clear."

Luoshan didn't get it. Too complicated an answer. He only became more confused trying to figure it out. He went seeking Yantou and asked his question again, "When arising and vanishing go on unceasingly, what then?"

Yantou shouted and said, "Whose arising and vanishing is it?"

Maybe the shout would have been enough. Imagine that you're an earnest student going from teacher to teacher, saying, "Please clarify this," and one of the renowned, respected ones screams in your face. Maybe then you'd step back and see yourself. But Yantou offers more than his shout. He asks, "Exactly who are you that is experiencing this coming and going?" This time Luoshan is enfolded into his own question. Engulfed in radical nonseparation, he wakes up.

I understood what was happening to Luoshan. But my understanding wasn't good enough. The koan wouldn't come alive until I demonstrated that understanding. There is an old adage in writing: don't tell, but show. I could tell you what happened in the koan, but to show it, I had to become Luoshan and exhibit his—and my—insight. That's how I would pay true homage to the lineage of old Chinese practitioners I'd come to love, by making their work and effort alive and vital in me right now. To stay Natalie Goldberg from Brooklyn, with her usual collection of needs and desires, pains and complaints, wouldn't work. Becoming some idea of Chinese—or Japanese—wouldn't work either. These koans might have come through a particular culture, but what they are aiming at is the core of human nature. Who are we really? What is this life about? I had to learn to become a fool, a barbarian, the moon, a lamppost, a fallen leaf—any angle necessary to answer the questions posed by these ancient fellows. But I couldn't get stuck, not even as a single, perfect plum blossom. My mind had to become greased in its skull, a pearl rolling in a silver bowl. No settling; no abiding; no fixed residence.

The koan mind does not dwell; instead, it is alive—and empty—like a dust mote in a ray of sun. In other words, I had to let go and to see fresh, like a blind donkey. Tell me, how can something sightless see?

I paced St. Paul's streets, past Scott Fitzgerald's old home on Summit, the vast houses on Crocus Hill, the River Gallery, and the Harvest Bread Bakery. I crossed the bridge on the mighty Mississippi, reveling in the long, slow display of burnt leaves that marked the coming of the dark season. I wanted to know who these Chinese brothers—and the occasional Chinese sister, such as Iron-Grinder Lui, the woman of Taishan, and the teacake seller—were. I was used to studying Western literature, full of elaborate stories, subplots, metaphors, and flashbacks. These Chinese tales were so digested that only a few lines were enough.

Leaning over our supper plates one evening, Phil's old boyfriend from the back room beseeched me, "So Aunt Natalie, tell me a bedtime koan before we drop off." It was his second year of practice, and his early enthusiasm met my old determination.

I lunged into the koan about Luoshan. I described the rough road, the jagged mountain where I imagined the interchange had taken place. I fleshed out the two men's ragged dress, their recent meal—"For sure, it was not hot dogs on a bun." I wanted to plant a deep impression in my faux nephew's mind so he would never forget these crazy, wild ancestors. I made faces, with lips turned out, eyes raised to the ceiling; I howled, groaned, drooled, clawed at Yantou. I demanded a response to rising and vanishing. We both went to bed tired and giddy that night to wake at 4:30 A.M. and drive the mile and a half to the zendo.

Later that morning I unfolded on my bedroom floor a glossy map of the whole Zen lineage from 532 C.E. to 1260 C.E. and knelt over it, running my finger from Matsu to Pai-Chang to Kuei-shan. These were all characters in the *Book of Serenity*. I relished the link between teacher and student and how the student of the next generation became the teacher in the next. Below all the dates and Chinese names was a drawing of an immense fork-tongued dragon sprouting out of the clouds. He was a feral force in the orderly map of connections.

The original *Book of Serenity* was lost after it was first compiled by Wansong in northern China, but it was reconstructed by Wansong at the urging of one of his disciples, Yelu Chucai. He was one of a group of Chinese statesmen desperate to save their provinces from destruction by the ravaging army of Genghis Khan, and they wanted to study the text as a way to illuminate their minds and come up with a fresh solution. Through their work, they eventually softened the harshness of the Mongol ruler.

Studying these cases brings one more fully and deeply into the structures that underlie conventional life. The cases were not created to help people disappear into a mist high on a mountain. The terrible truth, which is rarely mentioned, is that meditation doesn't lead us directly to some vaporous, glazed-eyed peace. It drops us right into the personal meat of human suffering. No distant, abstract idea of distress; instead, we get to taste the bitter pain between our own twin eyes. With practice we settle right down into the barbed-wire nest, and this changes us. Working with koans creates a bigger heart; a tender, closer existence; a deeper seeing.

Near the end of November, I turned to page 108, case number twenty-five. "Rhinoceros Fan" was the title. My mind froze. That's my usual tactic: when anything new comes along, I brake, clutch, and stop dead. What do I know about a rhinoceros? Aren't they African? I later found out that China did have rhinos and that their horns were carved into fans.

What stumped me more was the juxtaposition of these two words: *rhinoceros,* that huge, forceful animal, probably as close to a dinosaur as we are going to find now on earth, placed beside the word *fan,* something light, used to create a breeze, a stirring of wind to refresh court ladies or Southern belles.

I moved on from the title to the actual case:

One day Yanguan called to his attendant, "Bring me the rhinoceros fan."

The attendant said, "The fan is broken."

Yanguan said, "If the fan is broken, then bring me back the rhinoceros!"

The attendant had no reply.

Zifu drew a circle and wrote the word *rhino* inside it.

Yanguan was an illustrious disciple of Matsu. After his teacher's death, he had wandered until he became the abbot of Fayao Temple. This was a monastery situation. The attendant was not paid staff, but Yanguan's student. As an attendant, the student had the great opportunity of extra time with his teacher. In this particular story, the student is anonymous. All the better; he could be any of us—John or Sue or Sally, you or me.

I was not sure who Zifu, who appears at the end, was. I would look him up later. But for now I'd stay with the teacher-and-student interaction.

More than likely, their interchange takes place in a quiet moment when Yanguan has a little time to put his attention on this monk. He's going to test him, poke him: Are you there? Yanguan and the attendant are in kinship. They had both probably lived in the monastery for many years, but Yanguan couldn't turn around to the attendant and say something simple like, "Do you love me?" or "Are you happy here?" Instead, there is decorum. One person is made the attendant, the other the Zen master. Of course, one has been practicing longer than the other. Out of time we create hierarchy, levels, positions. In the large space of this true book, we eventually let go of these criteria, but we also play along.

So Yanguan asks for a fan. The fan is the excuse for an exchange, though it could also have been one of those unbearable hot summer days. Bring me some relief. Where's the fan?

The attendant replies that the fan is broken.

"He can't find another one?" I'm thinking. "What was going on here?"

That evening after I read this case, I couldn't sleep. I tossed and turned.

The night became a deep and endless thing. My mind wandered over much terrain: a particular apple orchard, a young boy who died. I remembered an old friendship I once had. This line ran through my head: the relationship is broken.

Broken! I sat up in bed. That is the word the attendant used. I jumped up, ran to the shelf, and opened the book. I took a leap: The attendant was saying he himself was broken, even if he referred to a fan. He was the fan.

But that didn't stop Yanguan, his teacher. Hell, if the fan—the product—was shattered, then bring back the whole rhinoceros. What a stunning concept! If the paper is torn, bring the enormous tree into the living room.

Yanguan was asking this of his student (and of us): Take a tremendous step—not forward but backward—into your essential nature. Manifest your original face. Don't get stuck on something broken—a heart, a wish. Become the rhinoceros—reveal your full self, go to the source, nothing hidden.

And this is what I loved the most: "The attendant had no reply." What do we do when a rhino is charging us, when a bear of a teacher is storming us? We run for our lives. In no other case that I had studied so far was there such an abrupt stop. No action, nothing. The attendant had already given his all when he said the fan was broken, when he revealed he was not whole.

It's a naked thing to show we are fractured, that we do not have it all together. Broken all the way through to the bottom. What freedom that is, to be what we are in the moment, even if it's unacceptable. Then we are already the rhinoceros.

Think about it. We are always doing a dance—I'm good, I'm bad, I'm this, I'm that. Rather than the truth—I don't know who I am. Instead, we scurry to figure it out. We write another book, buy another blouse, exhaust ourselves. Imagine the freedom to let it be, this not-knowing. How vulnerable. This is why I love the attendant. He said who he was—a broken man, a shattered fan derived from the concentrated point of a fierce beast. When his teacher asked for more, the monk didn't do a jig to win him over. There was no more. Usually we will do anything to cover up a reality so naked.

I know the relief, and ensuing shame or terror, of making that kind of simple statement. When I was in the middle of a divorce, I visited my parents in Florida. My father was on the first day of a new diet. He was looking forward to dinner. We were going out to a steakhouse for the early-bird special. My father made fun of my huarache sandals when I stepped out of the bedroom, ready to go.

"What are those, horse hooves?"

I was touchy and tired of his putdowns. I twirled around and marched back into the bedroom. "I'm leaving," I screamed. I threw clothes into a suitcase and charged out the front door and onto the nearby turnpike. I was walking on the divider line, headed for the airport fifteen miles away. A car pulled up beside me and drove the speed of my walking pace. I looked straight ahead.

"Nat." My father pulled down his window.

I burst out crying.

"Wait, stay here. I'll go get your mother. Do you promise not to move?"

I nodded, leaning against the guard rail.

Moments later my parents pulled up together. My mother ran out of the car. "Natli, what's the matter?"

I uttered three words: "I am lost." I had no energy for a cover-up. Those words came from my core.

Everything halted. My mother stood with her hands at her sides. My father looked straight ahead, his face frozen, his arm hanging over the door of the car.

Nothing was to be done. It was a huge, unbearable opening between us. My parents became embarrassed. So did I. We'd never been so naked with each other.

After a long, excruciating time, my father's head turned. "Now can we go eat? I'm starving."

The monk did not have this distraction. No restaurant for him. My experience was that the monk stood his ground for all time. He did not reply after he showed his naked face. But like the rabbis making commentary on the Torah, later Zen teachers responded to koans, and in this case disagreed over the monk's state of mind. Maybe the attendant in his silence had emptied his depths, so that the rhinoceros, the source, stood there radiantly, painfully alive in his no reply. Or maybe he was just dumbfounded and petrified, thinking, "What should I do now in front of my teacher?"

In the next sentence, in steps Zifu. He draws a circle and writes the word *rhino* inside it. I imagine that he picked up a nearby stick and drew the circle in the dirt or in the air and then wrote the Chinese character boldly in the center.

I found out that Zifu was a Zen master who lived at least a hundred years after the interchange between Yanguan and the monk. These stories, passed on generation to generation, were kept splendidly alive. Sitting in his monastery, Zifu heard the situation and plunged in. Zifu's dust circle was a stamp of approval. His response radiated back through a century and screams forward to us now.

"Attendant, I see you," Zifu calls out.

"Yes," Zifu is saying, "this exchange between student and teacher is complete. Nothing is left out." Even if the attendant was immobilized rather than inexpressively present, Zifu catches the whole thing and brings it to completion, enlightening the attendant, the rhino, the teacher, folding us all into the great circle.

I spent the autumn of my fiftieth year roaming through these Chinese minds. I began to see everything as a koan. The news announced that bread burned in someone's kitchen in Blue Earth and the house went down in flames. Everything now was related. The house, the bread, the town in southern Minnesota presented a koan. How could I step into those flames and burn too? Life became a revolving story. No matter from what age or country, it met me where I was.

I watched my friend Wendy, an old practitioner and the gardener for twenty years at Green Gulch, a Zen farm outside of San

Francisco, answer questions after a reading from her forthcoming book, *Gardening at the Dragon's Gate.*

"How big is your garden?" one of my students queried.

Wendy was struck silent for a full minute. The audience fidgeted in their seats. I realized what was happening.

"Wendy," I leaned over, "this is not a koan—she's not challenging your whole being. She just wants to know, in feet, the area you garden."

Wendy snapped back. "Many feet are cultivated." Then she went on to speak of once putting a dead deer in the compost heap, and a month later nothing was left but hooves and bones.

In the *Book of Serenity,* Guishan asks Yangshan where he comes from, and Yangshan replies, "the fields." There are many fields to come from—playing fields, plowing fields, the upper or lower field, or the dharma field spread out before us.

Soon after I returned home to Taos, I had a week of teaching with my good friend Rob Wilder. He is sharp and has a generous heart. Little goes by him. We sat together at dinner the second night of the workshop. I was eager to share where I had been. I told him about koans, then I told him about the last one I had worked on. I laid out the case, how I entered it, what I understood. He was listening intently, the way only a writer can from years of developing an attunement to story and sound. He nodded often. I felt encouraged.

I went to bed that night happy. I had been afraid, coming home from St. Paul, that no one would understand where I had been.

The next morning was a silent breakfast. Almost everyone had already cleared out of the dining room when Rob sidled up next to me. "Nat," he said in a low voice, "I was thinking how amazing it is. We can know each other so well. We can be such good friends, and I had no idea what you were talking about last night."

My head snapped back. What's going on here? The fan of our communication was fractured?

A student walked in and we shut up.

I gulped down some water to swallow the ball of cornflakes that sat in my mouth. I felt almost lonely, walked to the brink of isolation. Rob was on one side of the old adobe dining room and I on another. Suddenly something in front of my eyes shattered. The rhino emerged glistening. I abruptly started to laugh, big eruptions through my entire body. This was one whole world. Rob Wilder was my relation. We had plunged right into the lineage together. No one left out. The water glass, the spoon, the flowers in the vase—all glimmered and shook. Who was laughing? Hours melted in my hand. The walls of the building dissolved. Everyone and no one lifted the spoon to take the next bite of cereal.

The Natural State of Happiness ☯

Chokyi Nyima Rinpoche

*The basic fact of our lives is that we all want to be happy, but so few
of us really are. This problem is called the First Noble Truth, and all
of Buddhism exists only to solve it. As the outstanding Tibetan teacher
Chokyi Nyima Rinpoche explains, the key is to look inside, discover the
goodness of our true nature, and eliminate the negativities that obscure it.*

The basic nature of our mind is essentially good. The Buddha
taught that all beings are buddhas covered by momentary obscurations; when those obscurations are removed, they are real buddhas.
The true identity of every sentient being, not just human beings, is a
state of unconditioned suchness. This is the basic nature as it is, pure
and perfect. We have an inherent capacity to care for others and to
understand; it's not a product of education or upbringing. To practice the dharma means simply to develop and nurture these intrinsic qualities. That is our task, our responsibility.

According to the Buddhist approach to spirituality, the ability to
care includes both loving-kindness and compassion. We aim to cultivate loving-kindness and compassion until they are boundless, totally free from partiality. The ability to understand, when developed

to its utmost, is called "the wisdom that realizes egolessness," an insight that sees the fact that the self, or the personal identity, has no real existence.

There are many conventional methods for infinitely expanding our kindness and compassion and realizing the true view. *Contentment,* for instance, is a valuable asset not only for so-called spiritual people but for everyone. Discontentment ruins every chance for happiness and well-being, but true happiness is immediately present in a moment of feeling content and satisfied. From today on, no matter what, try to appreciate whatever you have: the comfort of your home, the pleasure of your possessions, and the goodness in the people close to you. Happiness is already present and accessible to each and every one of us.

Often when imagining what it takes to make us feel happy, we see some other place or object that we haven't managed to possess: "I'm just about to. I'm on my way there. I can achieve it, I simply haven't yet." As long as fulfillment is at a distance, we will remain unfulfilled. When we do not get what we want, we are not happy. Ironically, once we do get what we seek, it's not that satisfying and we still are not happy. The grass is always greener on the other side.

We all know that those who have nothing suffer. It is understandable; they are hungry and they have lots of other problems. They may be too hot or too cold. But who is truly happy?

We need to seriously investigate whether people who have fame, power, and wealth are happy and whether those who have nothing are always unhappy. When we look into this, we see that happiness is not based on objects but on one's mental state. For that reason, those who are truly happy are the ones who appreciate what they have. Whenever we are content, in that moment, we are fulfilled. The teachings of the Buddha are common sense.

On one hand, it's very simple: we are all searching for happiness. How do we become happy without a big effort? Whenever we appreciate what we have, we are happy. That effort is an intelligent technique. We might have a very simple life, but still we can think, "This flower is lovely," or "This water is good." If we are too picky, thinking,

"This is wrong," and "That's wrong," then nothing is ever perfect. We need to learn how to be content so that whatever we have is precious, real, and beautiful. Otherwise, we might be chasing one mirage after another.

The second noble quality is *rejoicing*. Our basic goodness is obscured by negative emotions. The Buddha said that there are eighty-four thousand types of negative emotions, but among these, there are two in particular that often cause problems because they are quite difficult to notice: pride and envy. Envy is one of our biggest, most unnecessary types of mental suffering. If someone else's life is better than ours, we become jealous, angry, and disappointed. It can sometimes make us very uneasy; our food loses its flavor, we have trouble sleeping, and our blood pressure can go up. Rejoicing is the second intelligent remedy to all this useless self-torture. We can mentally share in other people's happiness. Is there any easier way to attain happiness?

The third noble quality is *forgiveness,* which is very important. Pride can be quite powerful. Even in moments when we are loving and caring, if we're not getting along with someone and our heart is saying, "The best thing to do is just forgive," behind that voice there is another one saying, "No, don't. You are right. You did nothing wrong." Pride constantly prevents us from forgiving others, an act that is so healthy and beautiful.

Forgiving and apologizing have the power to completely heal rifts, but we need to understand how and when to apply them. If we try too early, the situation might still be volatile. We need to find the proper moment, and once we've done that, we should be careful about the words we choose, the tone of our voice, and even the physical gestures and facial expressions we make. Each of these has a lot of power, and if one of them is off, we won't be that effective. If, on the other hand, we can express an apology in a heartfelt way, we will always be able to achieve peace, respect, and mutual understanding.

Most important of all is to have a *good heart,* which is the fourth noble quality. Like everything else, in order to have a good heart, we need to investigate until we are clear about what true well-being actually is, in both the temporary and the long-term sense. The source of happiness and well-being is not only loving-kindness and compassion, but also an insight into the true view of reality, because someone who fully recognizes reality becomes a *tathagata,* or "fully awakened one." Conversely, the source of suffering is hate, craving, and close-mindedness. These three are the roots from which all our troubles grow.

By "true view," I mean knowing the nature of things exactly as it is: the basic, essential nature of what is. This insight has to do with how we experience things. Everything that appears to us seems real and solid but in fact is only a mere impression of something that occurs as a result of causes and conditions. In and of themselves, things do not possess even a shred of solid existence. This is why the Buddha taught that all phenomena are emptiness while occurring in dependent connection. Hence, it is good to study the twelve links of dependent origination, both external and internal. This will enable us to see that mind is of primary importance; everything depends on it. Whatever is experienced, felt, or perceived is dependent on mind—on an experiencer experiencing it, observing it, knowing it.

Why would the Buddha say that all sentient beings are confused or bewildered? Was it because sentient beings really are confused? It could be that the Buddha was mistaken and that all sentient beings are not confused. We need to investigate this point, because one of the two parties is definitely mistaken. The Buddha also said, "Don't take my words at face value." If they are wrong, then we should speak up. We are allowed to examine the Buddha's words for ourselves and to question whether or not he was wrong.

Let's take an example. The Buddha said that all formed things are impermanent and unreal. However, we have the instinctive feeling that things are actually real and permanent. He really challenged us. He said that we haven't bothered to look closely; we haven't questioned our own beliefs. When we do, we discover that things are not really as they seem. Things are re-formed again and again, moment by moment, by causes and circumstances. When we start to carefully investigate and dissect objects, we also see that they are made out of smaller and smaller parts: molecules, atoms, more and more minute particles. If people bothered to explore in this way, they would find that even the atom does not really exist.

In *The Root Verses of the Middle Way,* the great master Nagarjuna wrote that since the formed cannot be found to exist, the unformed couldn't possibly exist either. He also said that samsara is merely our thinking. When we are free of thought, that is real freedom.

The discovery of the unconditioned natural state involves a process of learning, reflection, and meditation training. The most important of these three is meditation. We hear about all different styles of spiritual practice—such as meditating, visualizing, and reciting mantras—but we must understand that there is only one purpose to all these endeavors: improving ourselves. This means allowing our basic goodness to manifest.

To achieve this we need to apply the teachings in daily life. The first step toward developing kindness is *mindfulness,* making our minds as calm and clear as possible, which is the fifth noble quality. This is something we can practice every day, wherever we are, whatever we are doing. We need to be aware each and every moment. What are we saying? What are we thinking? How are we moving about? Be aware moment by moment, before moving the body, before speaking, and also while moving and speaking; then afterward remain aware, asking, "What did I say or do?"

There are many types of meditation training, but they all fall into one of two categories: the first is deliberate meditation with effort, and the second is the practice of being completely effortless, free of conceptual focus. The most profound and truest meditation is the training in complete effortlessness, but it is not our habit to be that way. We are pretty much in the groove of being deliberate, in using effort, whether mental, verbal, or physical. Unconditioned suchness, which is our natural state, transcends every type of mental construct and is effortless. Learning, reflection, and meditation are very important because we need to recognize our true basic state. Through listening and learning we become familiar with the teachings, and through reflection we become convinced of their truth and develop certainty. Learning and reflecting are definitely deliberate and require a lot of effort, but they are essential.

In order to be brought face-to-face with unconditioned suchness, our basic nature exactly as it is, there are two factors that are very helpful, but they are not easy to acquire. One is boundless love and compassion; whenever love is almost overwhelming, when kindness and compassion are unwavering, there is a moment available for you to realize the unconditioned natural state. The other is sincere devotion to and unshakeable pure perception of the unconditioned natural state. From this spontaneously arises a respect for and pure perception of those who have realized the unconditioned natural state and have the capacity to reveal it to others. This also includes a pure appreciation of anyone who really practices and trains in the Buddhist teachings.

In a nutshell, the real Buddhist practice is to try our best to bring forth in all beings the true sources of happiness and well-being—boundless love and compassion and the unmistaken realization of the natural state, the unconditioned innate nature—while at the same time removing the causes of suffering, which are craving, hate, and close-mindedness. That is what it really means to have a good heart.

Love and compassion can be expanded until they become boundless, genuine, and impartial, making no distinctions between friend, enemy, and stranger. We must continue in our efforts until we have removed even the slightest obstacle to our love and compassion. Only when our love and compassion have become boundless will they be truly effortless.

Meanwhile, our perseverance should be joyous and spontaneous. Such perseverance springs from our awareness of the unconditioned natural state; therefore, it is not merely an admiration, a yearning, or a longing. As your comprehension of the profound nature becomes stronger and grows deeper, you develop a confident trust. Spontaneous, effortless compassion begins to blossom as you continue to train after having truly recognized the natural state as it actually is. Sincere compassion radiates from the deepest part of your heart. You can't help it; it just naturally springs forth.

Before becoming aware of this natural state, we are bewildered, creating painful states all the time, but by continually training in this, we recognize that beneath everything is an unconditioned natural state. We start to notice that every selfish emotion begins to soften and subside of its own accord. As pain and worry diminish, our confused way of experiencing subsides more and more. Then we begin to really understand how other beings feel. You may ask yourself, "What can I do to help them? If I don't help them, who will?" This is when real compassion overtakes you and a sincere, unchangeable devotion begins to grow within you. We call this the dawn of irreversible or unshakeable confidence.

True confidence begins with a trust in the instruction that reveals this nature. Once you have experienced firsthand that it works, of course you feel confident. This also is directed to the source of the instructions, the one from whom you received them. You are grateful to him or her, as well as to the entire lineage of transmission through which the instruction came to be passed on to you. That is true devotion. These two—effortless compassion and unchangeable devotion—join forces so that your training quickly grows deeper and deeper. Your practice is strengthened to the point that it is unshakeable, like when a strong gust of wind causes a huge fire with plenty of firewood to blaze even higher.

The great master Atisha wondered what it meant to be really learned and concluded that real wisdom is to understand egolessness. True ethics are to have tamed or softened your own heart; whenever that is the case and somebody actually cares, is watchful and conscientious, that is real ethics. What is the foremost virtue? Atisha said it is to have a profound sense of caring for the benefit and well-being of others. What is the foremost sign of success or accomplishment? Not clairvoyance or miraculous powers, but to have fewer selfish emotions. These may sound like just a few simple sentences, but they are very profound and of great benefit when you take them to heart.

A Heart Full of Peace

Joseph Goldstein

*If the cause of suffering is ignorance, then the solution must be wisdom—
direct, experiential knowledge of how things really are. Fortunately, there
is a path to wisdom, which is to train and deepen the mind's natural
awareness so we can see through the discursiveness, conflicting emotions,
and conceptual errors that ensnare us. This is the basic Buddhist practice
called mindfulness, and one of the best teachers of it is Joseph Goldstein
of the Insight Meditation Society.*

Mindfulness is the key to the present moment. Without it, we cannot see the world clearly, and we simply stay lost in the wanderings
of our minds. Tulku Urgyen, a great Tibetan Dzogchen master of the
last century, said, "There is one thing we always need, and that is the
watchman named mindfulness—the guard who is always on the
lookout for when we get carried away by mindlessness."

Mindfulness is the quality and power of mind that is deeply
aware of what's happening—without commentary and without interference. It is like a mirror that simply reflects whatever comes before it. It serves us in the humblest ways, keeping us connected to
brushing our teeth or having a cup of tea.

Mindfulness also keeps us connected to the people around us,
so we don't just rush by them in the busyness of our lives. The Dalai

Lama is an example of someone who beautifully embodies this quality of caring attention. After one conference in Arizona, His Holiness requested that all the employees of the hotel gather in the lobby, so that he could greet each one of them before he left for his next engagement.

Mindfulness is the basis for wise action. When we see clearly what is happening in the moment, wisdom can direct our choices and actions, rather than old habits simply playing out our patterns of conditioning. And on the highest level, the Buddha spoke of mindfulness as the direct path to enlightenment: "This is the direct path for the purification of beings, for the overcoming of sorrow and lamentation, for the disappearing of pain and grief, for the attainment of the Way, for the realization of nirvana."

I began to practice meditation when I was in the Peace Corps in Thailand. At the time I was very enthusiastic about philosophical discussion. When I first went to visit Buddhist monks, I arrived with a copy of Spinoza's *Ethics* in my hand, thinking to engage them in debate. Then I started going to discussion groups for Westerners, held at one of the temples in Bangkok. I was so persistent in my questions that other people actually stopped coming to the groups. finally, perhaps out of desperation, one of the monks said, "Why don't you start meditating?"

I didn't know anything about meditation at the time, and I became excited by the prospect of what I saw as an exotic Eastern practice. I gathered all the paraphernalia together, sat myself down on a cushion, and then set my alarm clock for five minutes. Surprisingly, something important happened even in those few minutes. For the first time, I realized there was a way to look inward; there was a path for exploring the nature of my mind.

This realization is a turning point in everyone's spiritual life. We reach a certain point in our lives when something connects, and we acknowledge to ourselves, "Yes, I can do this." All of this was so new and interesting to me that, for a while, I'd invite my friends over to watch me meditate. Of course, they didn't often come back.

The Practice of Mindfulness

We can start the practice of mindfulness meditation with the simple observation and feeling of each breath. Breathing in, we know we're breathing in; breathing out, we know we're breathing out. It's very simple, but not easy. After just a few breaths, we hop on trains of association, getting lost in plans, memories, judgments, and fantasies. Sometimes it seems like we're in a movie theater where the film changes every few minutes. Our minds are like that. We wouldn't stay in a theater where the movies changed so rapidly, but what can we do about our own internal screening room?

This habit of wandering mind is very strong, even when our reveries aren't pleasant and, perhaps, aren't even true. As Mark Twain put it, "Some of the worst things in my life never happened." We need to train our minds, coming back again and again to the breath and simply beginning again.

As our minds slowly steady, we begin to experience some inner calm and peace. From this place of greater stillness, we feel our bodies more directly and begin to open to both the pleasant and unpleasant sensations that might arise. At first, we may resist unpleasant feelings, but generally they don't last that long. They are there for a while, we feel them, they're unpleasant—and then they're gone and something else comes along. And even if they come up repeatedly over a period of time, we begin to see their impermanent, insubstantial nature and to be less afraid of feeling them.

A further part of the training is becoming aware of our thoughts and emotions, those pervasive mental activities that so condition our minds, our bodies, and our lives. Have you ever stopped to consider what a thought is—not the content, but the very nature of thought itself? Few people really explore the question, "What is a thought?" What is this phenomenon that occurs so many times a day, to which we pay so little attention?

Not being aware of the thoughts that arise in our minds, nor of the very nature of thought itself, allows thoughts to then dominate our lives. Telling us to do this, say that, go here, go there, thoughts often drive us like we're their servants.

Once, when I was teaching in Boulder, Colorado, I was sitting quite comfortably in my apartment. Thoughts were coming and going, when one arose in my mind that said, "Oh, a pizza would be nice." I wasn't even particularly hungry, but this thought lifted me out of the chair, took me out the door, down the stairs, into the car, over to the pizza place, back into the car, up the stairs, and into my apartment, where I finally sat back down to eat the pizza. What drove that whole sequence of activity? Just a thought in my mind.

Obviously, there is nothing wrong with going out for pizza. What does merit our attention, though, is how much of our lives is driven by thoughts. Unnoticed, they have great power. But when we pay attention, when we observe thoughts as they arise and pass away, we begin to see their essentially empty nature. They arise as little energy bubbles in the mind, rather than as reified expressions of a self.

Just as there was no all-powerful wizard behind the curtain in *The Wizard of Oz,* the only power our thoughts have is the power we give them. All thoughts come and go. We can learn to be mindful of them and not be carried away by the wanderings of our minds. With mindfulness, we can exercise wise discernment: "Yes, I will act on this one; no, I'll let that one go."

WORKING WITH EMOTIONS

In the same way, we can train ourselves to be mindful of emotions, those powerful energies that sweep over our bodies and minds like great breaking waves. We experience such a wide range of emotions, sometimes within quite a short period of time: anger, excitement, sadness, grief, love, joy, compassion, jealousy, delight, interest, boredom. There are beautiful emotions and difficult ones—and for the most part, we are caught up in their intensity and the stories that give rise to them.

We easily become lost in our own melodramas. It's illuminating to drop down a level and look at the energy of the emotion itself. What is sadness? What is anger? Seeing more deeply requires looking not at the emotion's "story," but at how the emotion manifests in our minds and bodies. It means taking an active interest in discovering the very nature of emotion.

The America monk Ajahn Sumedho expressed this kind of interest and investigation very well. He suggested that in a moment of anger or happiness, we simply notice: "Anger is like this," "Happiness is like that." Approaching our emotional lives in this way is quite different than drowning in the intensity of feelings or being caught on the rollercoaster of our ever-changing moods. To do this takes mindfulness, attention, and concentration. We need to take care, though, not to misunderstand this practice and end up suppressing emotions or pushing them aside. The meditative process is one of complete openness to feelings. From the meditative perspective, the question is, "How am I relating to this emotion? Am I completely identified with it, or is the mind spacious enough to feel the grief, the rage, the joy, the love without being overwhelmed?"

THE PRACTICE OF LETTING GO

As you meditate, keep bringing your attention back to what is happening in the moment: the breath, a feeling in the body, a thought, an emotion, or even awareness itself. As we become more mindful and accepting of what's going on, we find—both in meditation and in our lives—that we are less controlled by the forces of denial or addiction, two forces that drive much of life. In the meditative process we are more willing to see whatever is there, to be with it but not be caught by it. We are learning to let go.

In some Asian countries there is a very effective trap for catching monkeys. A slot is made in the bottom of a coconut, just big enough for the monkey to slide its hand in, but not big enough for the hand to be withdrawn when it's clenched. Then you put something sweet in the coconut, attach it to a tree, and wait for the monkey to come along. When the monkey slides its hand in and grabs the food, it gets caught. What keeps the monkey trapped? It is only the force of desire and attachment. All the monkey has to do is let go of the sweet, open its hand, slip out, and go free—but only a rare monkey will do that. And similarly, the twentieth-century Japanese Zen teacher Kosho Uchiyama speaks of "opening the hand of thought."

Another quality that develops in meditation is a sense of humor about our minds, our lives, and our human predicament. Humor is essential on the spiritual path. If you do not have a sense of humor now, meditate for a while and it will come, because it's difficult to watch the mind steadily and systematically without learning to smile. Someone once asked Sasaki Roshi whether he ever went to the movies. "No," he replied. "I give interviews."

Some years ago I was on retreat with the Burmese meditation master Sayadaw U Pandita. He is a strict teacher, and everyone on the retreat was being very quiet, moving slowly, and trying to be impeccably mindful. It was an intense time of training. At mealtime, we would all enter the dining room silently and begin taking food, mindful of each movement.

One day, the person on line in front of me at the serving table lifted up the cover on a pot of food. As he put it down on the table, it suddenly dropped to the floor making a huge clanging noise. The very first thought that went through my mind was, "It wasn't me!" Now where did that thought come from? With awareness, one can only smile at these uninvited guests in the mind.

Through the practice of meditation we begin to see the full range of the mind's activities, old unskillful patterns as well as wholesome thoughts and feelings. We learn to be with the whole passing show. As we become more accepting, a certain lightness develops about it all. And the lighter and more accepting we become with ourselves, the lighter and more accepting we are with others. We're not so prone to judge the minds of others, once we have carefully seen our own. The poet, W. H. Auden, says it well: "Love your crooked neighbor with all your crooked heart." Spacious acceptance doesn't mean that we act on everything equally. Awareness gives us the option of *choosing wisely;* we can choose which patterns should be developed and cultivated, and which should be abandoned.

Just as the focused lens of a microscope enables us to see hidden levels of reality, so too a concentrated mind opens us to deeper levels of experience and more subtle movements of thought and emotion. Without this power of concentration, we stay on the surface of things. If we are committed to deepening our understanding, we need to practice mindfulness and gradually strengthen concentration. One of the gifts of the teachings is the reminder that we can do this—each and every one of us.

PRACTICING IN DAILY LIFE

In our busy lives in this complex and often confusing world, what practical steps can we take to train our minds?

The first step is to establish a regular, daily meditation practice. This takes discipline. It's not always easy to set aside time each day for meditation; so many other things call to us. But as with any training, if we practice regularly, we begin to enjoy the fruits. Of course, not every sitting will be concentrated. Sometimes we'll be feeling bored or restless. These are the inevitable ups and downs of practice. It's the commitment and regularity of practice that is important, not how any one sitting feels. Pablo Casals, the world-renowned cellist, still practiced three hours a day when he was ninety-three. When asked why he still practiced at that age, he said, "I'm beginning to see some improvement."

The training in meditation will only happen through your own effort. No one can do it for you. There are many techniques and traditions, and you can find the one most suitable for you. But regularity of practice is what effects a transformation. If we do it, it begins to happen; if we don't do it, we continue acting out the various patterns of our conditioning.

The next step is to train ourselves in staying mindful and aware of the body throughout the day. As we go through our daily activities, we frequently get lost in thoughts of past and future, not staying grounded in the awareness of our bodies.

A simple reminder that we're lost in thought is the very common feeling of *rushing*. Rushing is a feeling of toppling forward. Our minds run ahead of us, focusing on where we want to go, instead of settling into our bodies where we are.

Learn to pay attention to this feeling of rushing—which does not particularly have to do with how fast we are going. We can feel rushed while moving slowly, and we can be moving quickly and still be settled in our bodies. Either way, we're likely not present. If you can, notice what thought or emotion has captured your attention. Then, just for a moment, stop and settle back into your body: feel your foot on the ground, feel the next step.

The Buddha made a very powerful statement about this practice: "Mindfulness of the body leads to nirvana." This is not a superficial practice. Mindfulness of the body keeps us present, and therefore, we know what's going on. The practice is difficult to remember but not difficult to do. It's all in the training: sitting regularly and being mindful of the body during the day.

To develop deeper concentration and mindfulness, to be more present in our bodies, and to have a skillful relationship with thoughts and emotions, we need not only daily training, but also time for retreat. It's very helpful, at times, to disengage from the busyness of our lives for intensive spiritual practice. Retreat time is not a luxury. If we are genuinely and deeply committed to awakening, to freedom—to whatever words express the highest value we hold—a retreat is an essential part of the path.

We need to create a rhythm in our lives, establishing a balance between times when we are engaged, active, and relating in the world and times when we turn inward. As the great Sufi poet Rumi noted, "A little while alone in your room will prove more valuable than anything else that could ever be given you."

At first this "going inside" could be for a day, a weekend, or a week. At our meditation center, we also offer a three-month retreat every year, and at the new Forest Refuge, people have come for as long as a year. We can do whatever feels appropriate and possible to find balanced rhythm between our lives in the world and the inner silence of a retreat. In this way we develop concentration and mindfulness on deeper and deeper levels, which then makes it possible to be in the world in a more loving and compassionate way.

My Marital Status 🌀

James Kullander

*All the Buddhist talk of mind and meditation can sound pretty abstract.
But the traditional term for enlightenment actually means "awakened
heart-mind," and Buddhism is really more lived than practiced, more
heart than mind. In this moving story by James Kullander, we witness
honesty, openness, and compassion lived in the most trying of times.*

Six years after the event, I still cannot say for sure whether I am divorced or widowed. The question comes up whenever I am filling
out a form that wants to know my marital status. All the other questions I can answer in seconds, but this one—which asks that I check
"single," "married," "separated," "divorced," or "widowed"—always
stumps me. I'll pause there at the dentist's office, insurance company, or bank, and while the clock ticks and other people's children
scamper at my feet, I'll reflect on what it really means to be married.

The event I refer to is the death of the woman who used to be my
wife. Wanda was not my wife when she died in December 2001 at the
age of forty-two. Not legally, anyway. She and I had met in the summer of 1980, married in the summer of 1984, and divorced in the
summer of 1994. Before we'd gotten married, I'd made it clear to
Wanda that I did not want children, and she'd told me that she could
accept this. Yet throughout our years together, it seemed she never
put her longing to rest. I watched her study the infants our friends

and family brought into the world, as if silently hoping I would change my mind. I didn't. I couldn't see the sense in my becoming a parent and said so. Wanda's mother, with her affable proddings, would ask me why I'd married her daughter if we weren't going to have children. That, she would say, did not make sense to her.

The discontent Wanda and I felt about each other's intractable positions eventually spread into the rest of our marriage and soured it. What Wanda's mother kept saying began to make sense to me: why stay married if I wasn't going to give Wanda the child she wanted? I was forty; Wanda was thirty-four—still plenty of time for her to have a child with someone else. I talked to Wanda about it, we put ourselves through a year of psychotherapy, and finally the two of us sadly agreed that things just weren't working out.

After we'd split, our lives suddenly took far different turns, as if we'd been spring-loaded to take off in new directions. I began studying Buddhist meditation; went on retreats in Nepal, Thailand, and here in the States; and found myself at the feet of dozens of spiritual sages who invariably spoke of the impermanence of everything. I knew about impermanence, having ended a marriage that was supposed to last as long as we both would live. But somehow hearing it spoken by teachers I considered wise gave me solace. I also put myself through Union Theological Seminary in New York City and earned a master's in divinity.

Meanwhile, Wanda launched herself into physical pursuits, becoming a luminary in the local contra dance, zydeco, and swing-dance community—a scene the two of us had never set foot in when we'd been together. She occasionally invited me to dances at a local parish hall or rec center near our homes in upstate New York. Sometimes, when I missed her, I'd show up. I'd pick her out of the crowd and wave, and she'd scoot over and guide me onto the floor, where I'd hobble along under her patient instruction as some of her suitors looked on. I can keep in step to rock and roll, but to this music I was like a rusty engine that's reluctant to turn over. Wanda and I would laugh at how clumsy I was. Then I'd watch her dance with another man, the two of them seeming to glide across the floor.

The remorse I'd felt about initiating the divorce diminished when I saw Wanda enjoying life on her own. From time to time we'd talk on the phone and trade stories about our latest romantic escapades. It turned out she and I were better friends than we'd been spouses: happier, more candid with each other, and less prone to bickering.

I had not seen Wanda for several months when she phoned me in April 2001 to tell me she was having surgery to remove a large mass in her abdomen. As I penciled in the date on my calendar, she told me not to worry, said it was nothing. And off she went with her latest beau to a Cajun-music festival in New Orleans.

I have always liked Wanda's family, and they have always liked me. Even after the divorce, I was invited to holiday dinners, birthday picnics, and Christmas services at their church. Wanda was Chinese American: her father had emigrated from Beijing and her mother from Shanghai in the 1940s, both fleeing the Communist takeover. They'd met in New York City, married, and moved to suburban New Jersey, where I met Wanda while working at a newspaper. I was a young reporter, and she was an intern in the paper's graphic-design department. A middle-class, Connecticut-raised WASP, I was charmed by Wanda's Asian beauty. Although she and her two siblings were as American as I was, her parents were still very Chinese, and their culture seemed exotic to me. Her mother spoke with an accent I found hard to understand. Her father showed me sawtooth-edged black-and-white photos of the house where he'd grown up; a palatial estate in Beijing that had been confiscated by the Communist regime and turned into a barracks for the People's Liberation Army. Wanda and her family seemed less tormented by the guilt, worry, and conflict that droned on in my family and friends, and this held a certain allure for me.

On the day of Wanda's operation, I joined her mother, father, older sister Frieda, and brother-in-law Peter at the hospital. Wanda maintained her silly, often droll sense of humor throughout the pre-op. As the nurses rolled her on the gurney into the operating room, she held up the hand not tethered to the IV and cranked it side to side, like Queen Elizabeth waving from her Rolls-Royce. Several hours later we met with her surgeon. We learned that a softball-sized pelvic mass had been removed in a total hysterectomy. He appeared disconcerted; the tissue, he said, would be sent to a lab for a biopsy, and the results would take a couple of days. Wanda would remain in the hospital to recover.

One evening a few days later, I walked into her room after a stressful day at the office. Wanda was on the phone, snapping at the hospital-switchboard operator—unusual behavior for her; Wanda was usually courteous to a fault. And she was glaring at the foot of her bed. The way I figured it, she had just been sliced open and was in pain. Of course she was irritable. Seeing me, she hung up and started to cry.

"I don't have good news," she said.

Whatever had bothered me at work that day fell away, and I rushed to her bedside and cupped one of her hands in mine. I imagined some infection, or perhaps she would need another operation.

"What is it?" I asked, caressing her long, black hair.

"It's cancer," she said.

Ovarian. And it was serious.

I laid my head on Wanda's lap and sobbed.

In the years we'd been apart, Wanda and I had each had several lovers who'd come and gone, but neither of us had remarried, nor were we seeing anyone at that time. This gave us the freedom to be with each other without competing love interests at the margins. I spent hours with Wanda in the cramped living room of her apartment, which adjoined her parents' house, an hour's drive from mine in New York State, where they had moved a few years before. A hospital bed her maternal grandmother had used in her final years was set up there. I also accompanied Wanda and her sister on trips to Boston's Dana-Farber/Brigham and Women's Cancer Center, where Wanda was treated with punishing, nauseating rounds of chemotherapy that kept her down for days. It was an aggressive regimen. She had a rare and virulent form of cancer—clear-cell—and it was at stage IV, which meant that the cancer had gotten into the liver. Stage IV can be treated but is terminal; few live beyond five years. In the aftermath of these treatments, Wanda would sometimes call me for comfort or to gripe about the pain, often weeping.

I tried to appear strong in the face of Wanda's weakening condition and, to some extent, my own. I visited her, ran errands for her, and sometimes cooked for her while the earth tilted us into summer and then fall. The September 11 attacks left Wanda and her sister stranded in Oregon, where they had spent a week learning *qigong* from a renowned Chinese master, hoping this ancient healing practice might help Wanda get well again. A few days later, when Peter and I drove to the Newark airport to pick them up, we could see, across the New Jersey tidal marshes, clouds of smoke from the still-smoldering remains of the Twin Towers. With all the death and dying in the air, I was elated to see Wanda alive at the gate. We hugged, and for a moment I had the idea that everything was going to be fine.

For most of October, Wanda's condition remained relatively stable; her oncologist seemed encouraged by her response to the experimental brew of chemotherapy he'd prescribed, and perhaps to the qigong. Then one November morning, Frieda called me.

"Something bad is happening with Wanda," she said, her voice distant from the poor cell phone connection. Peter had gone into the apartment to get Wanda, she said, and found her lying upstairs on a stripped bed in a spare bedroom, disoriented and barely cognizant. An ambulance was on the way.

"Jim's here!" exclaimed Frieda, when I parted the baby blue privacy curtain at the emergency room. Wanda, stretched out on a gurney, looked at me. There was no spark of recognition. Her head stayed tilted to the left, and her eyes were wide, as if she were shocked by the condition in which she found herself. The sole movement in that tight space was Wanda's left arm, which slowly rose and fell like a machine, as if to push back from her face the thick, black hair she'd once had. Doctors say hearing is the last of the senses to go, and I wondered if Wanda was listening as her family and I discussed her condition. I passed my hand lightly over her head to let her know I was there.

Wanda was admitted for observation and a battery of tests to determine what exactly had gone wrong with her brain. I spent my days and nights at the hospital, while a handful of office colleagues took on a good portion of my work. I had barely noticed the changing of the seasons that year, and when I did finally notice, it was through the sealed, grimy window of Wanda's fourth-floor room. The tops of the trees had gone bare, and the people on the broken sidewalks had thick clothes on, their shoulders hunched against the cold and puffs of steam coming from their mouths. I wanted so much to be out in the world; I wanted Wanda to be out there too—on the street, making plans, living life.

Wanda had a room to herself, and the night nurses let me stay past visiting hours. With the very real possibility of death hovering near, the world outside the window became increasingly irrelevant. The lines between day and night, the known and the unknowable, were beginning to blur. Even the fact of our divorce seemed to get erased.

I tried to get some rest in two tangerine-colored chairs I'd pushed together, but I never could sleep sitting up. To distract myself, I slipped on the headphones of the portable cassette player we'd brought for Wanda. (We'd thought music might comfort her.) I pushed the PLAY button. Van Morrison's "Carrying a Torch" came on.

Wanda had made the tape, labeled "Mellow Music," several weeks earlier. She'd put the Van Morrison song on it, she'd told me, because it reminded her of us. Sometimes we'd joked that when we got old and feeble, we'd shack up together in a nursing home. Now, delirious from insomnia, I gazed at Wanda's wasted form in the pale gray light and listened to Van Morrison beseech his lost lover to "reconnect and move further into the light." It was as if everything under me—the earth itself—had been pulled away, and I was plunging through a dark space, nowhere to go but down. I felt that by not wanting children and initiating the breakup of our marriage, I'd committed a heinous crime, and now I was being punished. Selfish bastard that I was, I'd stayed involved with Wanda even after we'd split up, perhaps thwarting her chances to get remarried and have the child she wanted. I'd read that not having children can increase a woman's risk of ovarian cancer—so that too was my fault.

Early the next morning, I was awakened by the sound of Wanda gurgling on vomit. After being admitted, she'd been given a morphine patch to ease her pain. I'd voiced a mild objection, having been told that, because she was "narcotic naive"—Wanda hardly even took aspirin—morphine could make her nauseous. Now I ran down the waxed hallway to tell the nurse that "my wife" was throwing up. It was the first time I had called Wanda "my wife" since we'd separated. I wanted the nurse to take my plea for help seriously, and somehow I thought that using the word *wife* would do the trick. But there was another, less calculated, reason: as I had vowed nearly twenty years before, I still cherished Wanda as if she were my wife, in sickness and in health.

The nurse came and wiped green bile from Wanda's chin, and despite my misgivings, I agreed Wanda should keep the morphine patch on. A few minutes later, though, just as I thought Wanda had drifted back to sleep, she started heaving again. I called the nurse back, and this time I took it upon myself to peel the morphine patch off Wanda's pale, blue-veined chest.

"She doesn't want morphine," I snarled, as if it were the nurse's fault it had been put there in the first place.

I'd been awake barely a half-hour, and already the day had taken its toll on me. Left alone in the room, I climbed into bed with Wanda. I thought that if she couldn't see or hear me, perhaps she could feel me. The rubber-coated mattress crinkled under my weight. Her emaciated form lay still as I curled against her, fetal-like, and nuzzled her neck. Wanda fell back to sleep, and after a few moments, so did I. It was the first time we'd been in the same bed together in eight years, and in a strange way, it felt like home. When her family doctor showed up later that morning, I was startled awake and felt intruded upon, as if he'd barged into our bedroom.

A couple of days later, tests revealed that the cancer cells had wormed their way into Wanda's skull, causing the brain tissue to swell. The neurologist described the condition as "impossible to treat."

So that was that. Her words were like a door gently closing, the lock quietly clicking into place. Wanda's family and I were drained of all the hope that had buoyed us through the previous six months—and there'd been plenty, I realized the moment it was snatched away. Wanda was brought home in an ambulance and put back in her grandmother's hospital bed to die.

I don't know when the idea first occurred to me, but I began to consider asking Wanda's family if we could hold a remarriage ceremony. I could not give Wanda back her life or undo the divorce. I couldn't even offer my help: the errands had all been done; the trips to Boston were over. Love was all I had left to give, and the ceremony would be a declaration of that. It would not be a legal marriage; Wanda was incapable of consenting. But I believed she would have wanted it. There had remained a sort of low blue flame of love between us, the kind Van Morrison sings about in the song on Wanda's tape. Wanda and I—and also her family and I—still carried that torch for each other.

At first I was reluctant to make my request, for fear her family might be upset. But the idea of us carrying to our graves the broken promise I had made to Wanda in our first marriage ceremony—to be together "till death do us part"—troubled me. When I timidly mentioned the idea to her family, they were thrilled; they'd been thinking the same thing but couldn't bring themselves to ask me.

The family's minister came to the apartment to perform the ceremony. I spoke of the love that had kept Wanda and me and her family connected through the years. The minister read from the Song of Solomon ("Love is strong as death") and Ecclesiastes ("For everything there is a season"). Then he read some vows for me to respond to with "I will" and "I do." I wondered whether Wanda heard any of it. Could she see the small circle of friends and family members who had gathered round us? When it was over, Wanda's mother opened her arms to me, and we held one another tight, both of us weeping. Wanda's younger brother, whom I hardly knew, suddenly embraced me and said, "Welcome back."

During the night, I kept vigil, sleeping fitfully and dreamlessly in a twin bed perpendicular to Wanda's. Her breathing had grown labored and painful to listen to—somewhere between a snore and a wheeze. Each night her condition deteriorated, and she often gasped as if being strangled, which maybe she was, as death tightened its grip.

In the predawn hours of December 6, five days after we'd brought her home from the hospital, Wanda's labored breathing awakened me, louder than ever. Spit that looked like strained peas pooled in the corners of her mouth and on the collar of the thin cotton hospital gown. Normally squeamish about bodily excretions, I'd tended to Wanda's without a second thought. Her mother and I had already changed Wanda's soiled undergarments several times, both of us noticing how her right foot was turning ever deeper shades of purple from lack of circulation. I had little reaction to all of this. Perhaps I had closed down, or perhaps I was opening up. Buddhists speak of how, if you can train the mind not to get attached to human suffering, you can benevolently enter any "hell realm" of existence like a swan with wings spread, swooping down on a lake. I now got up and wiped Wanda's chin with a handful of tissue, then passed my hand over her head, trying to comfort her. Her eyes were wide and fixed on something beyond me, beyond all of us.

I climbed back into my bed and fell asleep. When I woke again, a cold, gray December dawn was showing through the tops of the skeletal trees outside the windows. This time it was not Wanda's breathing that had awakened me; it was the silence.

I rose, felt my bare feet hit the shag carpet, slipped on some clothes over my briefs and bare chest, and knelt by her bed. She was cold and hard to the touch; rigor mortis was already setting in. It seemed she was still staring at whatever she'd been staring at earlier, and I had to put a hand over her eyes to close them because her eyelids kept going up like the weighted eyes of a doll. When I lifted her left arm—the one she had repeatedly passed over her head—to put it under the covers, it felt as stiff as a downed tree limb. I slipped from the stubborn fingers of Wanda's right hand a set of sandalwood Buddhist *mala* beads I'd given to her as a talisman against evil spirits. I stuffed the beads into the left front pocket of my jeans; I would carry them always as a way to remember her. Then I read aloud the Twenty-third Psalm, as I had planned to do, from the Bible that I'd used in my years as a seminarian: "The Lord is my shepherd, I shall not want . . ."

I slipped into Wanda's parents' kitchen to deliver the news, feeling like some dark angel. Her mother was making coffee and didn't hear me coming. As I floated toward her, I uttered the heaviest, gravest words I've ever said to anyone: "Wanda's dead."

"Oh, OK," she replied. That was it. I'd expected her to fall apart, but she didn't. Nor had I, come to think of it. We hugged lightly, as if I might have been going off to a day at the office. I think we were in shock. No matter how close someone you love is to death, there is nothing so final as a corpse in your midst.

A couple of hours later, a gray panel van arrived from the funeral home, and two men lumbered out to retrieve Wanda's body. If I'd had any sense, I would have backed off and let the men do their job, but I was not yet ready to abdicate my responsibilities to Wanda. I helped lift her body off the hospital bed and onto a gurney, bedsheets and all. I'd prepared to lift a heavy weight, but Wanda's frame was so insubstantial, so eaten up by cancer, I could have picked her up by myself. One of the men had put a pale blue corduroy body bag on the gurney, and I zipped it up over Wanda the way you would a child's parka on a winter day. Wanda disappeared, and I realized that this would be the last time I'd ever see her.

As I helped wheel the gurney out to the van, I suddenly insisted that the body be moved headfirst, and the driver obliged. Years ago I'd read about an ancient Hindu tradition: you carry a body feet first at the start of its trip to the funeral pyre, so the spirit can remember its earthly life; for the second half of the journey, you turn the body headfirst, to help facilitate the spirit's departure from its material existence. After the van had pulled away, I turned to Susan, a friend of Wanda's and mine whom I'd called that morning, and I collapsed into her arms and fell apart.

Later that day at the funeral home, as we prepared the death certificate and obituary, I asked whether I could accompany Wanda's body to the crematorium. Wanda's family wanted her cremated so that, come spring, we could gather and each fling a handful of her ashes from the sharp, gray shoulders of Shawangunk Mountain, which you can see in the distance from the back deck of Wanda's apartment. I knew it was an unusual request, but I didn't know what else to do except see my grief through to the end, if there was one.

Consent was granted, and Susan accompanied me. No special arrangements were made for us. In fact, we were treated as a minor inconvenience. In my car, Susan and I trailed the funeral-home van past strip malls, warehouses, and office buildings to a lovely cemetery with a palatial mausoleum. The crematorium, however, was a square, squat, cinder-block building at the end of a narrow paved road, where you'd expect to find a maintenance shed. Inside, a huge black furnace stood like the machinery of Oz. The van backed up to the open garage door, and I was shocked to see a long corrugated-cardboard box emerge. Two attendants indecorously dressed in jeans and T-shirts—they were maintenance workers, after all—clumsily hoisted the box onto an assembly line of rollers about chest high. Before Susan and I caught up to what was going on, the furnace door was lifted, and the box with Wanda in it was gliding toward its open maw. Susan and I reached out just in time to tap the box good-bye before it rolled away. The furnace door was lowered, a switch was thrown, and the woman I'd loved in the flesh for twenty-one years went up in smoke.

As Wanda was efficiently transported into the ether, a man in a dark suit—he must have been management, perhaps showing up as a last-minute courtesy—told us the heat inside the furnace could reduce a corpse to ash in minutes. Was this supposed to be some sort of comfort? My mind reeled. I tried to reconcile this small, shabby scene with photos I'd seen of the towering, flower-strewn funeral pyres along the Ganges River in India and all their ancient, complex rituals for honoring the dead. While the man prattled on, Susan and I stared at each other with raised eyebrows and finally, by some silent agreement, decided that it was time to go.

On the busy road at the edge of the cemetery, cars and trucks streaked by, windshields glinting in the morning sun. Susan and I started toward my car, but something made us look back, as if the tips of our noses were tethered to the grim place we'd just left. We both saw in the windless blue sky above the crematorium chimney a blurry streak of heat and ash: Wanda's ashes. It should have shattered me, but instead I was struck by the bizarre collision of events—these final moments of Wanda's corporeal existence, the gruff handling of her remains by the maintenance workers, the blathering of the manager about the furnace heat—and I began to laugh. Susan joined in, and soon we were both pitched over, warm tears wetting our cold cheeks. The two of us nearly fell on the frozen pavement, so disjointed by the pain and hilarity of it all that we could hardly stand. We caught ourselves on the trunk of my car, bent over like a couple of marathon runners, come at last to the end of a long and exhausting race. I knew then I was going to be all right. I felt Wanda laughing with us, the three of us gathered in the arms of the big, fat, grinning Buddha, howling at the absurdity of this mortal coil, as if that was all there was to us. And even if it was, so what?

For weeks afterward, I was awakened on dark winter mornings by the smell of bacon frying in my house, where I live alone. Some

Sunday mornings, in the home Wanda and I had shared, she'd cooked bacon for breakfast. Waking up now to the smell of bacon when no one was cooking anything was eerie but comforting. I considered all the rational explanations for the phantom aroma, but my nearest neighbor was hundreds of feet away, and all my windows were sealed against winter's cold. Maybe I was just imagining it. No matter, I thought. When it came to coping mechanisms, an imaginary one would do just fine.

One hot summer night a few months before Wanda had died, I'd shown up at a dance fund-raiser her friends had put together to help pay her medical expenses. Wanda and I were outside the parish hall on the lawn. We could hear the band playing a Cajun reel through the open windows, and Wanda asked if I wanted to dance. I said, as usual, that I didn't know how. She took my hands and placed them on her shoulder and waist and showed me the steps. It seemed like trigonometry to me, and when it became clear that I was never going to get it, we fell into each other's arms for a long hug.

When I smelled bacon cooking in my house, it felt as if Wanda and I were still doing some sort of dance, and she was still taking the lead.

A part of me died with Wanda, a part I was glad to see go: my resistance to love. I'd often put distance between myself and others as a way to keep from feeling trapped or getting hurt. I'd delivered wearying criticisms of people I thought were less than perfect, as if I were any better than them. Living like that had been a long, hard battle with many casualties, the most wounded sometimes being me. I think that during all those silent meditation sessions; in all the time I'd spent listening to the wisdom of renowned teachers, theologians, and sages; in all the millions of words I'd read in profound spiritual tracts, I'd been trying to learn how to love. But no amount of meditation or yoga or studies of scriptures could have given me that. Wanda's death put me in touch with one of the highest orders of human existence: to love others as though we are all dying all the time, because the plain truth of the matter is that we are. For a long time I didn't know how to articulate this new feeling, even to myself. Then a couple of years ago I heard k.d. lang sing a Leonard Cohen song in which love is described as "a cold and broken hallelujah." And I thought, "Yes, that's it." In this love I found rest from a sort of homesickness that had afflicted me all my life.

It was not long before my days reassembled themselves into a more or less familiar shape, which was a sort of relief. But I began to forget how, in my hour of grief, I'd cherished my existence and the people around me. Years later, it sometimes feels as if I have to reach across a great psychic distance to get in touch with the way I felt then, as though it lies beyond the curve of the earth.

I have not remarried. From time to time, I wonder if I will ever again feel for anyone else what I felt for Wanda in our final months together. And if not, then what? Sometimes someone will ask me if I regret not having children. No, I say. And yes. I don't know whether being a father would have sustained the love I felt as Wanda died. Parents I know have told me that this is what having children does to you: it opens your heart. One mother said that what you feel bringing a person into the world is akin to what you feel seeing someone out of it. Perhaps I didn't have children with Wanda because I was afraid of feeling too much; I don't know. What I do know is that I miss Wanda's features—her brown eyes, round face, delicate frame, and silly sense of humor—some of which appear in the children of her siblings, some of which would no doubt have been replicated in our children. And maybe if Wanda and I had brought a child or two into the world, it wouldn't be such a struggle for me now to recollect the love I felt when she was dying.

So my pen hovers over the little boxes on those forms. My own internal compass tells me I'm widowed. Even if we'd never had that remarriage ceremony, I still would have felt married to Wanda when she died. Our divorce did not end our relationship, and for me, her death made it even more lasting and unfathomable.

For a while after she died, I checked "widowed," hoping the clerks would notice it and tease a story out of me. It was like a little flag I waved. I wanted sympathy, to be seen as more than just another client, customer, patient, student. I was also hoping to trigger a discussion of a similar loss on their part so we could commiserate, like strangers in a snowstorm, and I could give voice to the huge, uncertain emotions swirling inside me.

Legally, however, I am not widowed. So reluctantly I check the "divorced" box. But what is a marriage if not the depth of feeling you have for each other? It's only the love between two people that's real, that lasts. Everything else just comes and goes.

Learning True Love

Sister Chan Khong

*Thich Nhat Hanh is one of the most revered Buddhist teachers in the
world. Less well-known is his invaluable lieutenant, the courageous and
formidable Sister Chan Khong. She has been by his side since the first days
of his campaign for peace and social justice during the Vietnam War, when
the Engaged Buddhism movement was born. We witness in her memoir of
those terrible days a selflessness and heroism I can only describe as saintly.*

In France, I had written loving letters to my mother each week,
telling her how much I missed her. But when I got back to Vietnam,
I spent all my days with the poor in the pioneer villages and the
slums. Sometimes, Mother would tell me, "You say you love me, but
then you spend all your days working for the poor and come to see
me only late at night." I gently comforted her, "Please think of me as
married—not to a man, but to my ideal of life. If I had married a
man, I would have to spend my days and nights with him, bringing
happiness only to him. But because I am married to my ideal of life,
I can bring joy to many people, and I can also return home at night
to be with you." My mother understood, and since that day she has
always supported my work.

Among the young professionals who joined our social work in
the pioneer villages, one talented and humble physician, Tran Tan
Tram, fell in love with me. I enjoyed working beside him, helping the

peasants in Thao Dien and Cau Kinh, but I was devoting all my energy to these projects, and twice I declined to marry him. He waited two years and finally, under pressure from his parents, married another woman. For a Vietnamese woman, her wedding day is supposed to be the most wonderful day of her life, and on the day of Tram's wedding, I felt very sad. Looking back at my sadness, I can see that it was not because I was losing him to another woman, but because I realized I would never marry. Getting married meant taking special care of one's husband and his family and one's children, and I realized that if I did that, I could not also take care of the "wild" children in the slums and remote areas who desperately needed help, nor could I devote myself to building pioneer villages as models for social change in the country. I had seen many friends who, after getting married, became caught in endless family obligations, and I knew that my life was not for the effort of bringing happiness to one person, but to thousands. Because I was so active during this period, in a short time my sadness was transformed into joy in service, and I felt a great renewal of energy as I came to appreciate more and more the freedom to do the work I cared about most.

In late 1964, there were huge floods in Vietnam. More than four thousand people were reported dead and thousands of homes washed away. The whole nation was mobilized to help the victims, but the investigation team sent by our Van Hanh Student Committee for Flood Relief reported that victims in villages near the Ho Chi Minh Trail, where the fighting was escalating, were suffering the most. Other relief efforts concentrated on helping victims near big cities like Da Nang and Hoi An, so we decided to go to the most remote areas that no one else dared visit.

Creek bottoms there were filled with rocks, and after many days of heavy rain, these rocky gorges overflowed so quickly that it was impossible for the inhabitants to escape the floods in time. In one hour, water levels in some places increased more than twenty-five meters. (The same kind of flooding occurred again in 1992.) Thay Nhat Hanh [Thich Nhat Hanh] joined us on our mission. We took seven boats filled to the brim with food supplies, and we went up the Thu Bon River, crossing Quang Nam Province and going high up into the mountains, through areas of intense fighting. Many times we saw soldiers shooting at each other across the river.

For five days and nights, we stayed high up in the mountains. We had no mosquito netting or drinkable water. We had to filter and boil river water before cooking or drinking, which was not easy in these conditions. But going with Thay made things easier. Everywhere we went, former students of his, including some high monks trained by him at the An Quang Pagoda in the 1950s, supported us, and on some occasions, it was thanks to the presence of these monks that we experienced some safety and respect from both warring parties. One time we were stopped and searched by nationalist soldiers and then allowed to go. Thay asked them, "What if we are stopped by the other side and given their propaganda literature? We could not refuse." "You may receive it, but when you get to the stream again, throw it into the water," the soldiers responded. Thay asked, "What if we don't have time to throw it in before we are caught again by people like you?" The soldiers did not answer.

When they saw us, old men and women who had been devastated by the floods knelt down in prayer before us, as if they were in the presence of Avalokitesvara. They could not believe that humankind still existed after what they had experienced. Many had lost sons, daughters, grandchildren, homes, livestock, and everything they owned. One old man had lost his entire family and belongings except for one water buffalo, which he floated on as the water rose. Wherever he went, the water buffalo accompanied him like a son.

We stopped at the most devastated villages, distributed gifts, and stayed the day with people. At night, we slept on our boats after a simple meal of plain rice. The smell of dead bodies was everywhere, horribly polluting the air. Although this was a remote mountain area, there was fighting between the nationalists and the guerrillas even up here. When we saw wounded soldiers from either side, we helped them without discrimination.

Seeing such immense suffering, Thay Nhat Hanh cut his finger and let a drop of blood fall into the river: "This is to pray for all who have perished in the war and in the flood." Thay wrote this poem, "Experience," to describe some of the suffering we witnessed during that trip:

I have come to be with you,
to weep with you
for our ravaged land
and broken lives.
We are left with only grief and pain,
but take my hands
and hold them, hold them.
I want to say
only simple words.
Have courage. We must have courage,
if only for the children,
if only for tomorrow.
During the month after the flood,
the young man received only two pounds of rice
from the emergency aid.
Tonight he is eating areca tops and rotten corn.
And he is one of so many children,
jaundiced, with bloated faces.

He had dysentery for a week
with no medicine
and no hope.

The flood carried off
his father,
his mother,
and his brother.
This innocent child's brow
wears no mourning band.

But from the scorched and gutted fields,
a sickly ray of sun
comes to envelop my soul
in its ghoulish sheet.

Please come here
and witness
the ordeal of all the dear ones
who survived the flood of the Year of the Dragon.

Take this bleeding child in your arms.
She is the only member of her household
whose misfortune was to survive.

A young father
whose wife and four children died
stares, day and night, into empty space.
He sometimes laughs
a tear-choked laugh.

Please come and see
his white-haired elder,
left alone for days on a barren, weedy patch of land.
He kneels before a startled boy
and offers him some rice.
He is kneeling in love
while the boy weeps,
"O Grandfather, don't kneel in front of me.
I am the age of your grandson."

The message of love has been transmitted.
Again, I put my faith in tomorrow.

Her husband is dead,
her children dead;

her land ruined;
her hearth cold.
There is no spark to light a fire,
for death is here
on a patch of earth sucked dry.

Nothing remains,
not even her resignation,
the last one left.

She curses aloud her existence.
"How fortunate," she says,
"those families who died together."

I tell her, "We are not alone.
There are others,
and we must help still their cries
on this endless road.
Let us walk on with our heads bent."

The villager looks me over.
Agonized yet fearless,
he answers,
"I hate both sides.
I follow neither.
I only want to go
where they will let me live
and help me live."
O life! What misery!

On this high place by the Thu Bon River,
I cut my finger
and watch the blood drip
and mix with the water.
O be at rest,

you who are lost.
O be at peace!

To you who have drowned, I speak,
and to you who have survived,
and to the river—
having heard all space reverberate
with the infants' screams.
Tonight
I've come to stand midway
between these sheer mountains,
and to watch them bend over the river,
and to listen
to their eternal tales.

Here is the impermanent
and yet continuously flowing world.
Let us stand together for future generations.

Each tiny bodhisattva,
with bowed head and hidden tears,
student's ink still on her hands,
holds a shovel or a mattock
and throws up earth for a bridge
or for burying the bloated dead.

Under palm-leaf hats,
brown-clothed and barefoot,
are they not Quan Yin in all her glory,
her charity, her fearlessness?

The small, bare feet walk over stones,
the sharp stones of pain and grief.
The bare feet enter shacks
built hastily on ash,

that they may approach the living
who have reached the limits of their lives.

While I watch their hands,
as gentle as heavenly silk,
outstretched to infants,
the crying stops,
and the mother's eyes,
staring at cans of milk,
glow like precious stones.

And still I sit
before the Gates of Heaven
tightly shut
with bowed head, waiting.

In the old garden, I wonder,
could one feel the fragrance
of areca blossoms?

O here,
why is there such silence here?—
such silence,
when even the birds of our stricken land
have vanished.
O speak out now,
speak audibly again,
so hearing you in far corners
the birds will return;
our waters be like jewels again;
our land like brocade.

O sing,
sing loud
so True Being may follow the Word.

This poem inspired many young Buddhists to join our efforts to help victims of the war.

During the war with the French, Thay had contracted malaria and dysentery, and during this trip to the remote mountain areas, both diseases recurred. Despite that, his presence was very inspiring for our whole team. Thay reminded us to be mindful of everything—the way Thay Nhu Van, a high monk who was very popular with both sides, talked to the officers of both sides; the way Thay Nhu Hue organized the local Buddhists; and the way the rowers of our boat ate in mindfulness. We observed the steep canyon of the Thu Bon River and were aware of the icy mountain wind and the homeless victims of the flood on the verge of death. The atmosphere of death permeated our whole trip—not only the death of flood victims, but our own risk of dying at any moment in the ever-present cross fire.

As we were leaving the area, many young mothers followed us, pleading with us to take their babies, because they were not certain the babies could survive until our next rescue mission. We cried, but we could not take these babies with us. That image has stayed with me to this day.

After that, as I went to Hue every two months to lecture on biology, I never failed to organize groups of students, monks, and nuns to help people suffering in these remote areas. We began with the daylong journey from Hue to Da Nang, where we would sleep in a temple and then travel to Quang Nam and Hoi An. In Hoi An, we rented five midsize boats to carry nearly ten tons of rice, beans, cooking utensils, used clothing, and medical supplies.

One night, we stopped in Son Khuong, a remote village where the fighting was especially fierce. As we were about to go to sleep in our boat, we suddenly heard shooting, then screaming, then shooting again. The young people in our group were seized with panic, and a few young men jumped into the river to avoid the bullets. I sat quietly in the boat with two nuns and breathed consciously to calm myself. Seeing us so calm, everyone stopped panicking, and we quietly chanted the *Heart Sutra,* concentrating deeply on this powerful chant. For a while, we didn't hear any bullets. I don't know if they actually stopped or not. The day after, I shared my strong belief with my coworkers: "When we work to help people, the bullets have to avoid us, because we can never avoid the bullets. When we have good will and great love, when our only aim is to help those in distress, I believe that there is a kind of magnetism, the energy of goodness, that protects us from being hit by the bullets. We only need to be serene. Then, even if a bullet hits us, we can accept it calmly, knowing that everyone has to die one day. If we die in service, we can die with a smile, without fear."

Two months later, while on another rescue trip, bombs had just fallen as we arrived at a very remote hamlet, about fifteen kilometers from Son Khuong village. There were dead and wounded people everywhere. We used all the bandages and medicine we had. I remember so vividly carrying a bleeding baby back to the boat in order to clean her wounds and do whatever surgery might be necessary. I cannot describe how painful and desperate it was to carry a baby covered with blood, her sobbing mother walking beside me, both of us unsure if we could save the child.

Two years later, when I went to the United States to explain the suffering of the Vietnamese people and to plead for peace in Vietnam, I saw a woman on television carrying a wounded baby covered with blood, and suddenly, I understood how the American people could continue to support the fighting and bombing. The scene on the television was quite different from the reality of having a bleeding baby in my arms. My despair was intense, but the scene on television looked like a performance. I realized that there was no connection between experiencing the actual event and watching it on the TV screen while sitting at home in peace and safety. People could watch such horrible scenes on TV and still go about their daily business—eating, dancing, playing with children, having conversations. After an encounter with such suffering, desperation filled my every cell. These people were human beings like me; why did they have to suffer so? Questions like these burned inside me and at the same time inspired me to continue my work with serene determination. Realizing how fortunate I was compared to those living under the bombs helped dissolve any anger or suffering in me, and I was committed to keep doing my best to help them without fear.

Nothing to Do, Nowhere to Go: Practices Based on the Teachings of Master Linji

Thich Nhat Hanh

Here we see the fundamental unity between Thich Nhat Hanh's peace activism and his Buddhist teachings. He begins with a discourse on the famous Chinese master Linji (better known in the West by his Japanese name, Rinzai) and his famous doctrine of the "businessless person," as Thich Nhat Hanh translates it. Thich Nhat Hanh then offers us some of his own gathas, short meditations we can do throughout our day. They teach us that peace begins with every step and breath we take.

Many students of Buddhism are the children of Master Linji, even if they don't know his name. In the Zen tradition, the spirit of Master Linji is in everything we're taught and everything we do.

Master Linji lived during the Tang dynasty in China. He was born in western Shandong Province, just south of the Huang Ho (Yellow) River, sometime between 810 and 815 C.E. When he was still young, he left his family and traveled north to study with Zen Patriarch Huangbo in his monastery near Hongzhou in Jiangxi Province, just south of the Yangzi River. It was a time of political instability in China. There was government repression of Buddhism, which culminated in a decree, issued in 845 by the emperor Tang Wu Zong, ordering all monks and nuns to disrobe and return to lay life. Many temples and statues were destroyed, particularly in the cities. Monasteries in outlying areas were less affected.

After several years, the young Linji was sent by his teacher to study briefly with the reclusive monk Dayu, after which time he returned to live with the monks at Patriarch Huangbo's temple. Later he had his own temple in Zhengzhou, Hebei Province, where he taught in his signature direct and dramatic style. As was the custom in China at the time, he took his name, Linji, from the name of the mountain on which he lived and taught. He resided there until he passed away in 867. He never wrote down his teachings, but his students recorded and compiled them in *The Record of Master Linji*.

As a young monk, Linji studied diligently and gained a deep and extensive knowledge of the Tripitaka, the three baskets of the Buddhist teachings: the sutras, commentaries, and Vinaya (monastic precepts). He noticed that although many monks studied very diligently, their studies didn't influence their understanding and transformation. They appeared to be seeking knowledge only to increase their fame or position in the temple. So Master Linji let go of his studies in order to follow true Zen practice.

Many of us have spent our whole lives learning, questioning, and searching. But even on the path of enlightenment, if all we do is study, we're wasting our time and that of our teacher. This doesn't mean we shouldn't study; study and practice help each other. But what's important is not the goal we're seeking—even if that goal is enlightenment—but living each moment of our daily lives truly and fully.

Master Linji had a solid knowledge of the Buddhist canon, but his teaching method was based on his confidence that human beings need only to wake up to their true nature and live as ordinary people. Master Linji didn't call himself a Zen master. He called himself a "good spiritual friend," someone who could help others on the path. Master Linji called those who had insight to teach "the host," and the student, the one who comes to learn, "the guest."

In Master Linji's time, some Buddhist terms were used so often they became meaningless. People chewed on words like *liberation* and *enlightenment* until they lost their power. It's no different today. People use words that tire our ears. We hear the words *freedom* and *security* on talk radio, television, and in the newspaper so often that they've lost their effectiveness. When words are overused, even the most beautiful words can lose their true meaning. For example, the word *love* is a wonderful word. When we like to eat hamburger, we say, "I love hamburger." So what's left of the deeper meaning of the word *love*?

It's the same with Buddhist words. Someone may be able to speak beautifully about compassion, wisdom, or nonself, but this doesn't necessarily help others. And the speaker may still have a big self or treat others badly: His eloquent speech may be only empty words. We can get tired of all these words, even the word *Buddha*. So to wake people up, Master Linji invented new terms and new ways of saying things that would respond to the needs of his time.

For example, Master Linji invented the term the "businessless person," the person who has nothing to do and nowhere to go. This was his ideal example of what a person could be. In Theravada Buddhism, the ideal person was the arhat, someone who practiced to attain enlightenment. In Mahayana Buddhism, the ideal person was the bodhisattva, a compassionate being who, on the path of enlightenment, helped others. According to Master Linji, the businessless person is someone who doesn't run after enlightenment or grasp at anything, even if that thing is the Buddha. This person has simply stopped. She is no longer caught by anything, even theories or teachings. The businessless person is the true person inside each one of us. This is the essential teaching of Master Linji.

When we learn to stop and be truly alive in the present moment, we are in touch with what's going on within and around us. We aren't carried away by the past, the future, our thinking, ideas, emotions, and projects. Often we think that our ideas about things are the reality of that thing. Our notion of the Buddha may just be an idea and may be far from reality. The Buddha outside ourselves was a human being who was born, lived, and died. For us to seek such a Buddha would be to seek a shadow, a ghost Buddha, and at some point our idea of Buddha would become an obstacle for us.

Master Linji said that when we meet the ghost Buddha, we should cut off his head. Whether we're looking inside or outside ourselves, we need to cut off the head of whatever we meet and abandon the views and ideas we have about things, including our ideas about Buddhism and Buddhist teachings. Buddhist teachings are not exalted words and scriptures existing outside us, sitting on a high shelf in the temple, but are medicine for our ills. Buddhist teachings are skillful means to cure our ignorance, craving, anger, as well as our habit of seeking things outside and not having confidence in ourselves.

Insight can't be found in sutras, commentaries, or dharma talks. Liberation and awakened understanding can't be found by devoting ourselves to the study of the Buddhist scriptures. This is like hoping to find fresh water in dry bones. Returning to the present moment, using our clear mind which exists right here and now, we can be in touch with liberation and enlightenment, as well as with the Buddha and all his disciples as living realities right in this moment.

The person who has nothing to do is sovereign of herself. She doesn't need to put on airs or leave any trace behind. The true person is an active participant, engaged in her environment while remaining unoppressed by it. Although all phenomena are going through the various appearances of birth, abiding, changing, and dying, the true person doesn't become a victim of sadness, happiness, love, or hate. She lives in awareness as an ordinary person, whether standing, walking, lying down, or sitting. She doesn't act a part, even the part of a great Zen master. This is what Master Linji means by "be sovereign wherever you are and use that place as your seat of awakening."

We may wonder, "If a person has no direction, isn't yearning to realize an ideal, and doesn't have an aim in life, then who will help living beings be liberated, who will rescue those who are drowning in the ocean of suffering?" A buddha is a person who has no more business to do and isn't looking for anything. In doing nothing, in simply stopping, we can live freely and true to ourselves, and our liberation will contribute to the liberation of all beings.

PRACTICES BASED ON *THE RECORD OF MASTER LINJI*

Master Linji taught that each one of us has a bright and shining mind. If we can find our way back to that bright mind, then we can be as the Buddha and the bodhisattvas are. When our shining mind is dulled, that means it's covered by afflictions. With the practice of mindfulness, we can restore our bright mind. Our mind is a garden, and our garden has been ignored for a long time. The soil is hard, and brambles and wild grasses are growing everywhere. To practice is to come back and care for our garden. We are the gardener, our mind is the earth, and in the soil there are good seeds.

When we want to train a wild horse to pull a cart or carry a rider, one method we use is to put a rope around its neck so we can hold the horse. The horse will struggle, but it can't get free. Slowly the horse calms down and we can train it to become useful. Our mind is the same way. Our mind is the wild horse, and the practice of mindfulness is the reins that hold it so it can be tamed gradually and we can master it. We have many methods for grasping and holding on to the mind. The first method is mindful breathing—mindfulness of the in-breath and the out-breath. There's also the practice of mindful walking in which we maintain awareness of the breath and the steps. If we practice for a few weeks, we'll see the situation change. We have to practice continuously and not just superficially. It can't be done halfheartedly. We have to be determined to grasp our mind. A period of continuous diligent practice will surely lead to transformation.

If we don't return to the mind, take hold and master it, we cause suffering to ourselves and those around us. Mastering our mind brings great benefit and happiness. To master the mind, we first of all have to grasp the body. The body and the mind go together. The breath belongs to the body, just as the two feet and legs belong to the body. If we can grasp the breath and be in touch with the breath and the steps, then we'll slowly get hold of the mind. The mind contains the body, and the body contains the mind. Don't think this practice takes too much time. We can practice in all our daily activities. When we drive to the market, cook a meal, or wash the dishes, we can practice getting hold of the mind. Using *gathas* in our practice makes it easy and enjoyable. Gathas are Zen poems that we can memorize and recite silently to ourselves as we practice mindfulness of breathing. Gathas are simple and can be used to accompany any activity.

Taking Refuge in the Island of Self

Breathing in, I go back
to the island of myself.
There are beautiful trees,
There is water, there are birds,
There is sunshine and fresh air.
Breathing out, I feel safe.

This is a wonderful gatha. We can use it when our mind is confused, when we don't know the right thing to do, when we're in a dangerous situation or beginning to panic. When we come back to the breath, breathe mindfully, and recite this gatha, our mind will be calmed immediately. Once we feel stable, we'll be able to see clearly what we should and should not do in order to improve the situation.

Coming back to take refuge in the island of self is the teaching the Buddha gave when he was eighty years old. He knew that after he entered nirvana there would be many disciples, both monastic and lay, who would feel lonely and that they'd lost their place of refuge. So he taught that inside us there's an island where we can take refuge. When we feel lost, lonely, sad, hesitant, in despair, when we don't know what the correct thing to do is, we can come back to that island and have safety. That island is our stable mind. That island is not a place outside us. One breath can bring us back to that island immediately. In each person there are the seeds of stability, freedom, and nonfear. It's these seeds that make a place of refuge for us and protect us. When we take refuge in our island, we're taking refuge in something real, not in some abstract idea or a vague notion about the future. We can use this gatha when we do sitting meditation or walking meditation. Whether we're sitting, standing, walking, or lying down, we can practice coming back to take refuge. Breathing in, we can say, "Coming back to take refuge." Breathing out we can say, "In the island of myself."

> Coming back to take refuge
> in the island of myself.

Or we can say,

> Coming back
> Taking refuge
> The island
> Of myself.

Breathing In, Breathing Out

> Breathing in, breathing out,
> I am blooming as a flower.
> I am fresh as the dew.
> I am solid as the mountain.
> I am firm as the earth.
> I am water reflecting
> what is real, what is true.
> I am space, I am free.
>
> Buddha is my mindfulness
> Shining near, shining far.
> Dharma is my breathing

guarding body and mind.
Sangha is my skandhas
working in harmony.
Taking refuge in myself,
coming back to myself,
I am free.

This is another gatha for taking refuge. When we come back to our island, what will we meet? First, we will meet the Buddha. Buddha is neither outside of us nor something abstract. Buddha is mindfulness. Outside of mindfulness, we can't have the Buddha. When someone breathes in and out with awareness, they give rise to the energy of mindfulness. Without the substance of mindfulness, the Buddha cannot be called Buddha; therefore mindfulness is the Buddha. So when we come back to our island, we will meet the Buddha immediately. We breathe in and know that we're breathing in. We take a step and we know that we're taking a step. Mindfulness is the light. When we drink water and we know we're drinking water, that's the light. When we drink water without knowing we're drinking water, that's darkness. Mindfulness means to recognize what's happening, and that recognition is the shining light. When there's light shining, we aren't afraid anymore.

"Dharma is my breathing / guarding body and mind." When a person breathes in with awareness and breathes out with awareness, this is called mindfulness of breathing. This isn't our usual way of breathing. Every day, all of us breathe in and breathe out without stopping. But that isn't the dharma. When we breathe in and know that we're breathing in, when we breathe out and know that we're breathing out, that is the dharma. This isn't the spoken or written dharma, but the true living dharma. The living Buddha is mindfulness and the living dharma is mindfulness of breathing. When there's mindfulness of breathing, this living dharma can protect our body and mind. When we're frightened or startled, when we've received bad news, when we're about to go crazy, then we come back to the breath and practice this gatha. We breathe in and breathe out with mindfulness. Then that in-breath and out-breath will bring us into a state of safety.

"Sangha is my skandhas / working in harmony." The five skandhas are the members of the sangha in our body. When we practice mindfulness of breathing, the breath begins to regulate and harmonize our five skandhas by recognizing and embracing the body, feelings, perceptions, mental formations, and consciousness. Our skandhas may be dispersed, opposed to one another, or in chaos. With mindful breathing, the living dharma, the five skandhas begin to come together in a harmonious rhythm, a harmonious state. In just five or ten minutes, that harmony will bring about peace and stability of the body and the mind. We come back to take refuge in the three jewels and use their strength to protect us. The three jewels are not only Buddhist, they're universal. They aren't objects of worship or devotion, but real energies. In one of his previous lives, when the Buddha was still looking for the path, he met a demon who said, "I know a gatha about the true dharma, but I'll only read it to you if you agree to let me eat you afterward." And the body of the previous life of the Buddha said, "Yes, if you tell me that right dharma, then I will allow you to eat me." And it was this gatha on taking refuge that the Buddha learned. So this gatha is worth us exchanging our life to hear it.

This gatha is valuable in all situations. No matter how difficult, chaotic, upside-down the situation is, if we know how to come back to the breath and practice this gatha, then we'll have security. But we don't have to wait until there's a real difficulty to use this gatha; we can use it at any time during the day. We can practice this gatha while we're eating; we can chew with the rhythm of this gatha. If we chew for the entire length of the gatha, the food will become very soft in our mouth, and it will be easily digested. Instead of talking about this and that while we eat, thinking about this or that person's business, thinking about this or that place, we just dwell in this gatha while we eat. I have eaten so many times with this gatha. It's very enjoyable.

We can also enjoy using this gatha for walking meditation. In walking meditation, we slow down and become mindful of each step. When we walk alone, we can do very slow walking meditation. How slow? That depends on us, but there must be enough time in each step for us to live deeply, thoroughly. In each step we see that we have returned, that we have come back, that we are taking refuge, that we are truly on our own island, and that we are deeply in touch with reality. Until we're in touch with this inside, we won't lift up the other leg. It's like when we press a seal onto a piece of paper. We press it down firmly, strongly, at all angles, so the ink can imprint on the paper properly, completely; then we lift the seal. Our steps are the same way. When we aren't completely with the present moment, our walking has the characteristic of being chased by a ghost. When we do walking meditation by ourselves, we have the opportunity to walk as slowly as we want so we can properly imprint our seal. When we walk together with the sangha, we might walk at a more ordinary pace.

We can use the words *now* and *here* as meditation words. We take a step and say, "Now." We don't just say the word. We have to be in touch with the now, and then we can take another step and say, "Here," like the seal imprinting itself on the paper. Only when we're satisfied do we take another step. And if we're unable to be in touch with it, then we just let it be like that until we can be in touch. Only when we're able to be truly in touch, deeply and stably, do we take the next step. During those steps our mind is completely under our observation. The rope of the mind is tied properly, but it's very pleasant. We can walk alone in an oak grove or along a busy street. We can practice all we want. With each step like that, we step into reality and not a dream.

In, Out, Deep, Slow

In,
Out,
Deep,
Slow,
Calm,
Ease,

Smile,
Release.
Present moment,
Wonderful moment.

This gatha is also valuable for holding the mind. This is a very simple gatha that we can practice at any time of the day, in sitting as well as walking meditation. "In, Out" means "Breathing in, I know that I'm breathing in. Breathing out, I know that I'm breathing out." "In, Out" is just a short way of saying it. When we breathe in, we know that the in-breath is happening; our mind doesn't think about other things, our mind holds on to the breath. Holding on to the breath, grasping the breath, means having control over the mind. The mind doesn't run anymore. The mindful breath is a rope that holds on to the mind, and by practicing this one line, we can take hold of the mind. "Breathing in, here is my in-breath." We recognize the in-breath as the in-breath. When I'm breathing in, I know that I'm breathing in, and when I'm breathing out, I know that I'm breathing out.

This gatha is based on the first four exercises taught by the Buddha in the *Anapansati Sutra* (*The Sutra on the Full Awareness of Breathing*). "Deep, Slow" means "The in-breath has become deep, the out-breath has become slow." If we practice awareness of our in- and out-breaths for one or two minutes, then we've already succeeded, and naturally the in-breath will have become deeper and the out-breath will have become slower. It's not that we are breathing in and trying to make the in-breath become deeper—this is something we should never force. Before we practice, the in-breath and the out-breath are short and shallow. But when we practice even for half a minute or a minute, then the in-breath becomes lighter, deeper, calmer, slower, and there begins to be space and calm in the body and the mind. When there's calmness and lightness in the breath, then there will also be lightness, calmness in the body and in the mind. The breath is the medium connecting the body and the mind. Breathing in, I feel a sense of well-being.

"Breathing in, my mind is calmed. Breathing out, I feel at ease. Breathing in, I smile. Breathing out, I release. Dwelling in the present moment, I know it is a wonderful moment." We have only one moment to live, and that is the present moment. If we come back to the present moment, we'll be in contact with innumerable wonders in us and around us. I guarantee that after a few weeks of practicing this gatha, you'll see a transformation.

When we have a strong feeling, we can practice this gatha and the feeling will be calmed; this is called calming the mind. Practicing this gatha will bring about relaxation of the body and the mind. The mind can't be relaxed if the body isn't relaxed and vice versa. This gatha can be practiced in any position—when we're sitting, standing, lying down, or walking. This gatha is no less valuable than a koan. It's worth more than a thousand blocks of gold.

We can use this gatha with walking meditation. In walking meditation, we match the steps to the breath. If, for example, we're taking three steps during each in-breath, we say, "In, in, in." And if for each out-breath we're taking three steps, we say, "Out, out, out." After we've practiced with "In, Out" for some time, we go on to "Deep, deep, deep. Slow, slow, slow." We have to truly experience the "In, Out" and the "Deep, Slow." We breathe with our two feet.

Of course it's possible not to use any gatha at all and still step into reality and dwell in mindfulness in each step. But when our mind is still a wild horse, we need to use a rope to pull the mind back. But the rope is very pleasant. When a horse is already trained, we don't need to use the rope anymore. When we have practiced well, each step becomes a seal on the land of peace and freedom. With each step, we dwell in mindfulness, and we leave the seal of our peace and happiness on the land.

Here Is the Pure Land

Here is the Pure Land
The Pure Land is here
I smile in mindfulness
and dwell in the present moment.

Buddha is the autumn leaf,
Dharma is the floating cloud,
Sangha is everywhere,
My true home is here.
Breathing in, the flowers bloom.
Breathing out, the bamboo sways.
My mind is free.
I enjoy every moment.

This gatha is good to use with walking meditation when we are taking four steps for each in-breath and four steps for each out-breath. This gatha can bring us a lot of happiness.

If in the present moment we can't be in touch with the Pure Land, then we can't hope that in the future there will be a Pure Land. If we can be in touch with the Pure Land in the present moment, then with certainty there will be the Pure Land in the future. The wonders that we come back to be in touch with in the present moment, all of them belong to the Pure Land. Our own body belongs to the pure land; it is something wonderful, miraculous like the Pure Land. The Pure Land isn't something that's outside of our body and mind. How and what do you use to step into the Pure Land? Mindfulness, because mindfulness dispels oblivion. It dispels chaos, and it brings about wisdom and understanding. Understanding and wisdom allow us to have insight and to know that in the present moment we're living a wonderful moment in the Pure Land that's in and around us.

"I smile in mindfulness and dwell in the present moment." This isn't a social or coquettish smile, but it's a smile of mindfulness. Why do we smile? Because life is so wonderful. There needs to be only one light breath, and all the miracles manifest. The birds are singing, the pines are singing, the flowers are blooming; the blue sky and the white clouds are all there. Living like this is truly the art of living, and we can do it now.

Right now we can be in touch with the three jewels. Practicing this gatha is also taking refuge. The Buddha, the dharma, and the sangha are inside us and everywhere around us, in the leaves and the clouds. The sangha isn't just human beings, but also the trees, the birds, the stream. Our true home is the present moment, right here and right now. We don't need to look for happiness anywhere else. The swaying bamboo and the flowers blooming are all the wonders of life. Breathing in and out like this, our mind is free, not attached, not in bondage to anything.

We can use this gatha when we eat. We don't seek a Pure Land and happiness somewhere else. We have the chance to sit and eat in mindfulness. We're also eating with the Buddha and the original sangha. They're not in the past; they're present with us right now. The Buddha is mindfulness, so there is no moment that we cannot spend with the Buddha.

I Have Arrived, I Am Home

I have arrived
I am home
In the here
In the now.
I am solid,
I am free.
In the ultimate
I dwell.

When we practice this gatha, happiness can be there right away. If we don't have happiness, it's because we haven't succeeded in arriving and coming home. Once we have arrived, once we've come home, then we're successful, and we have happiness right away. To be solid and free means we have stability and we're not pulled away by the past or the future; we have freedom. Stability and freedom are the two characteristics of happiness and of nirvana. Coming back to take refuge means coming back to the present moment and taking refuge in the island of self. This island is our mindfulness, our breathing, and our steps. Mindfulness of our breath and our steps is something very concrete that we can take refuge in.

Please write these eight words and hang them somewhere you will see them: "Wherever you are, you are your true person." You can write them on a small piece of paper, the size of a credit card, that you put in your wallet to take out as a reminder. If you can practice these eight words, you are worthy of being Master Linji's student and his continuation. Master Linji taught us that we have to use our bright shining mind to come back to the present moment and enter the world of the ultimate, the realm of the Buddha, the Pure Land. With mindful breathing, mindful walking, and these gathas to help us come back to our true self, we can be the businessless person with nothing to do but hold the hand of the Buddha and roam.

A Little Lower Than the Angels: How Equanimity Supports Kindness ◑⟩⟩

Sylvia Boorstein

With her kind smile and twinkling eyes, Sylvia Boorstein could be American Buddhism's Jewish grandmother. (That's not just a metaphor— she really is a Jewish grandmother). Her kindness is natural, yet it's also the product of a serious study and practice of Insight Meditation, of which she is a prominent teacher. Boorstein illustrates Buddhist principles with the kind of warm, wry, and wise stories that families share around a dinner table.

*B*rahmaviharas is the Buddhist name for the set of four emotional states that includes equanimity and its direct derivatives—impartial goodwill, spontaneous compassion, and genuine appreciation. A *vihara,* in Pali, the language in which the oldest Buddhist scriptures are written, is a dwelling place. *Brahma* is the word associated with divinity. Classic texts translate the term *brahmaviharas* as "divine abodes" and name the four basic ones: *metta* (friendliness), *karuna* (compassion), *mudita* (empathic joy), and *upekka* (equanimity). I love the term "divine abodes," and I think of these four states as wonderful conditions of human consciousness in which the mind can rest, feeling at ease, as if at home.

Equanimity, it seems to me, is the ground out of which the other three flavors of benevolent mind arise. Everything depends on it. Equanimity is the capacity of the mind to hold a clear view of whatever is happening, both externally and internally, as well as the ability of the mind to accommodate passion without losing its balance. It's the mind that sees clearly, that meets experience with cordial intent. Because it remains steady, and thus unconfused, it is able to correctly assess the situations it meets.

This correct assessment brings with it what the texts call "clear comprehension of purpose," the sure knowledge of what response is required and what is possible. Clear comprehension creates a response, sometimes in action, sometimes just in thought. And because we are humans and have empathy built into our brain structure, when we are touched by what we encounter—and when our minds are balanced—we respond with benevolence. With friendliness or compassion or appreciation. It's a beautiful truth about the potential of human beings. "A little lower than the angels . . ." is the phrase that comes to my mind. Or maybe not lower. Perhaps divine.

Here is how it works. I'll explain it using traditional Buddhist psychology, and I'll include examples of how this works in my life. As you read, see if these centuries-old postulates about the natural responses of the mind are true for you as well.

There are three possible valances of emotional response to every experience: pleasant, unpleasant, and neutral. (Here you might think for a moment about how many times in a day, or even in an hour, you think, "Oh, good!" or "Oh, phooey!" or even "Boring day. Not much happening.") The Buddha taught that these different flavors of experience are normal, just the facts of life, and that they aren't, by themselves, problematic. They do, however, have the potential to create unhappiness. If they are not recognized and acknowledged, they create thoughts that carry an imperative for change. "I *need* more of this." "I *must* get rid of this!" "I can't *stand* this." The imperative agitates the mind into confusion.

If, on the other hand, there is enough equanimity in the mind to fend off confusion, wisdom can prevail. Then the mind can respond to ordinary (neutral) situations with goodwill, to frightening (unpleasant) situations with compassion, and to beguiling (pleasant) situations with relaxed, untroubled appreciation.

Here are three examples that come from my living in France several months each year and traveling back and forth between San Francisco and Paris frequently. The first is about ordinary goodwill, friendliness, which is what the Pali word *metta* means. Perhaps I understate it by calling it ordinary friendliness. It is closer to intentional, omnipresent, devout friendliness based on the awareness that everyone, including oneself—because life is complicated and bodies and minds are often uncomfortable—needs to be working hard all the time just to keep things okay. Here's an example.

The overnight flight from San Francisco to Paris takes more than ten hours, and in the time between midnight and morning, the hours seem longer and the space between the seats in the coach section seems shorter. When I get up to stretch and perhaps walk down an aisle, I see men and women, old and young, large and small, all unknown to me, some traveling with young children, all trying to figure out how to be comfortable. I see them wrapped up in airplane blankets, scrunched up into whatever position of repose they can organize for themselves, leaning on each other if they are traveling together or trying not to lean on each other if they aren't. Often a man or a woman is patrolling the aisle across from me, holding an infant against his or her chest and moving in the rocking gait that often soothes a baby's distress. I feel a pleasant intimacy with them. I too am trying to stay comfortable. I'm not frightened for them or for me, because I'm relaxed about flying and I assume we will land successfully, but I wish them well. I enjoy the feeling of my own goodheartedness. In fact, in that moment of mental hand-holding, all those people look a bit more familiar than ordinary strangers. That moment of easy, impartial, benevolent connection—metta—buoys up my mind. I feel better as I sit back down in my seat.

Compassion is a variation of metta. It's different from relaxed friendliness because it's hard for the mind to stay relaxed and friendly when it encounters a painful, unpleasant situation. In fact, it's normal, and often helpful, for human beings to startle at the awareness of distress. The startle is an instinctive response, a signal to the mind: "Uh oh. Something is wrong, and you might need to do something." Sometimes, when the startle is strong enough to frighten the mind into confusion, there is a period of unease as the mind tries to cope, either by accommodating the experience or distracting itself if it can't. In contrast, when the mind is able to stay steady, it moves immediately to act, in thought or in deed, in consolation. Traditional Buddhist texts say, "The heart quivers in response."

A man died suddenly in the middle of a flight I was on from Paris to San Francisco. I didn't see it happen, but I knew something was wrong because the plane icon on the TV map on the screen in the back of the seat in front of mine reversed direction. Soon after that, while the people all around me were showing one another the map and discussing what might be happening, the pilot announced that there had been a medical emergency and requested that any medical personnel come forward to assist. My husband, Seymour, responded, as he had on previous flights when there had been a call for a physician, and was gone for an hour.

The flight continued as if nothing were awry. Flight attendants served lunch. People watched movies. The icon on the TV turned westward again, and I assumed (correctly, I later learned) that the person had died and that landing for emergency medical care wasn't necessary. I wondered who the person had been, whether he or she had been traveling alone, how his or her family would learn the news. I thought about how my family would feel if it were I or Seymour who had died. I thought, "I hope I don't die in a plane," but then I realized that at the center of my startled mind was the awareness that I can't choose when or where I'll die. No one can. Seymour told me later that as the flight personnel carried the dead man's body down the length of the plane to the front galley, where they made the requisite CPR attempts, people turned themselves in their seats and averted their eyes to avoid seeing what was happening. I'm imagining many of those people were thinking, as I was, "That could be me."

I knew that I was too unnerved to read or watch a movie, and I did not want lunch. I sat quietly, and after some few minutes, I heard my mind, on its own, beginning to recite wishes of consolation. "May the dead person's consciousness, wherever it is now, be at ease. May that person's family, on this plane or wherever they are, be strengthened in their loss. May the memory of this person be a blessing to them. May all the people on this plane who have been frightened feel at ease. May I feel at ease. May we land safely." There are traditional Buddhist karuna phrases, but I didn't say them. I rarely do, because they don't feel natural to me. I make up my own. But the traditional ones and the ones I make up mean the same thing: I am aware of painful feelings in me as a result of what is happening to you (or to me), and even though I know that everything passes, now is a suffering time. I hope we all have the strength to endure what is happening without creating extra turmoil. I don't say all that as a prayer! Much too unwieldy. I say, "May I be at ease," or "May you be at ease," or "May you [I, we, all beings] come to the end of suffering." I say words that are regular speech, like something I might actually say to a person. Saying prayers of consolation always makes me feel better. And it settles my mind. I thought, "This plane is like a small city. Three hundred people. Lots of new babies. Lots of old people. All ages of people in between. People eating, people sleeping, people working, people dreaming. And one person who just died. It's like regular life." I felt sad for the family of the dead person, but I felt okay.

Seymour came back to his seat. He'd spent some time talking with the wife and daughter of the man who had died. His death hadn't been a surprise to them. He'd been very ill. Still, it was a shock, happening all of a sudden in midflight and among strangers. They seemed to appreciate, he told me, having someone to talk to. We noticed that members of the flight crew took turns sitting with them for the rest of the flight, talking. It might be part of standard airline training, but I think it is, anyway, the instinctive response of human beings to pain. We console. (The heart quivers in response.)

And here's the third story, an example of how the mind (surprisingly) needs equanimity when it meets pleasant situations. It seems as if pleasant situations should leave the mind unruffled. Not true. If an experience inspires yearning, when a moment before, yearning did not exist . . .

On the last day of a winter month spent in France, Seymour and I drove to Les Angles, a ski resort two hours from where we live. We had enjoyed seeing the snow on the peaks of the Pyrenees from our deck, but this was our first time up close. The resort was full of Christmas holiday skiers, and we stood at the bottom of the easiest beginner lift and watched people learning to ski. I was feeling particularly glamorous in my new high-heeled, fake fur–lined boots and purple tweed cap and scarf that my friend Toni had knitted for me. I thought about all the years Seymour and I had skied and all the trails we'd raced each other down before we'd stopped skiing, ten years previously.

"We could ski again," I said. "This is an easy hill. Next year, let's ski."

"No, we can't. It's not worth the risk. We're old. We could break something."

"Look, though. This is so easy. It would be such fun to put on skis again. We'd choose a sunny day, like today."

"Forget it. It would be ridiculous. Your back isn't so good. You have bursitis in your shoulder. Last year you pinched a nerve in your neck. Let's go have lunch on the deck. We'll watch the skiing from there."

I caught a glimpse of myself reflected in a window as we walked to the restaurant. I looked shorter and plumper, definitely less glamorous, than I had imagined. We ordered lunch. I felt my mind, mired in nostalgia, dragging itself along, seeming to arrive at the table after I did. I thought momentarily of sulking, pretending to be peeved at what I had perceived as a peremptory dismissal. I realized, though, that what I was peeved about was being old. Then I noticed two women sitting at the table adjacent to ours, not unlike me in size and age, carefully made up, coiffed, wearing brightly colored, warm (nonski) jackets and big, beautiful earrings. They were eating hearty lunches, talking and laughing as they ate. I thought they looked marvelous. I looked down at my boots and was glad about the high heels. Later on, before we left, I took some great photos of what I guessed was a three-year-old girl in a pink snowsuit, balanced on her skis with their tips crossed, trying to get her pole straps over her wrists. She looked marvelous too.

The mind wobbles when it discovers it can't have something it wants, and then when it catches itself, it appreciates. This wobble was a small one, easily overcome. Other yearnings are much more painful. The cycles, though, of "Oh, a pleasant thing"; "I want it"; "I lament not being able to have it. I feel sad"; and "This is the way it is. It can't be other now," are the same regardless of whether the yearning is trivial or tremendous.

In the end, relief comes in two stages. The first is the moment when the mind stops struggling and says, "I wanted something different, but this is what I have." The second is the ability to rejoice with other people, delighting in their pleasure. "May you two beautiful women enjoy this lunch and many others." "May you, lovely little girl in pink who reminds me of my own children and grandchildren, grow up to enjoy skiing and also your whole life." (The Pali word for the capacity to fully appreciate and bless is *mudita*.)

And here is one final piece of Buddhist theory that I can add, now that I've told these three stories of what seem to me to be the natural goodwill responses of the mind balanced by wisdom. The responses of friendliness, compassion, and appreciation that I felt in these three situations—all situational permutations of basic goodwill—depended on my mind's being relaxed and alert enough to notice both what was happening around me and what was happening as my internal response. In each case, even though the situation included challenge, my mind had enough equanimity in it to allow me to stay connected with affection. My refuge was my own good nature, available for expression.

And it might have been otherwise. If my mind, in the long overnight flight, had been preoccupied with stories of my life, past or anticipated, or had been agitated by fears about flying, or even if I had simply been too tired to pay attention to the scene around me, I would have missed it. I would not have been able to recognize the fundamental truth about human beings—that we do our best to keep ourselves comfortable, in orderly ways so as not to disturb others, in whatever situations we find ourselves—and I would have missed the opportunity to be touched by human courage. Instead of feeling warmly connected to the other people on my flight, I would have been indifferent. On the outside, I would have looked the same. On the inside, I would not have felt nearly as good.

And I really don't know if my mind could have stayed balanced enough to rest in consolation if someone had taken ill or died in the row next to mine. I might have felt frightened about not having the skills to help. I've been with friends as they died, but I wanted to be there and I wasn't surprised. Perhaps on a plane and caught off guard, I'd be wishing that it weren't happening or that I were somewhere else. I don't know. If my mind had been overwhelmed by resentment or fear, the wisdom that reminds me that these things happen—people take ill, and die, according to conditions beyond their control, just as I will someday—would not have been available to comfort me. I might have forgotten to pray.

And perhaps if I had been less happy than I was on the day at Les Angles, I would have fallen prey to envy or jealousy, and to avoid recognizing those feelings, I might have started a quarrel about being spoken to peremptorily. As it turned out, I had enough wisdom available to me to think, "Things change. That was then. Now is now. There are other pleasures I can enjoy. Everyone takes turns being able to do this or that in life. We can for a while, and then we can't. May everyone, including me, enjoy this moment."

Indifference, pity, envy, and jealousy are what the Buddha called the "near enemies of the brahmaviharas." Indifference, for example, might masquerade as equanimity, looking very balanced and even, but representing, in fact, the very opposite of emotional connection. (Think of the expression "I couldn't care less," which I've always heard as having a sad ring to it.) Pity looks a little like compassion, because it acknowledges suffering, but it is still an arm's-length awareness of the pain and carries some aversion in it. "It's too bad this is happening to you," the mind thinks, without remembering, "This, or some other painful thing, will sometime happen to me or my kin. May all beings always be comforted in their suffering." And without balancing awareness in the mind, delight and affection morph into envy and jealousy when other people's joys are joys we covet or when we require something in return for our friendship. All of the near enemies are unhappy, tense states. The brahmaviharas all establish connections that nourish and enliven the moment. The near enemies create distance and isolation.

What keeps me connected to the world outside myself, as well as to my own natural goodness, is wishing others well in moments of both bad and good fortune, and acting with ordinary benevolence toward people as they go about their regular business of life—of appreciation, consolation, and friendliness.

Both those perspectives act as safety nets for me. Staying alertly connected to the world outside myself keeps me from falling into the limitations of self-absorption from which no reality check into wisdom is possible. And the reconnection with my own benevolent nature, each time it happens, protects me from the despair of feeling that nothing I (or anyone else) could do can make a difference. Safely connected to my life, and reassured of my essential goodness, I feel at ease, at home, really in the most sublime of homes.

And here's one more detail from the traditional accounts of the Buddha's enlightenment experience that—because the Buddha sounds so human in it—is particularly inspiring to me. He is reported to have hesitated before starting out to teach, thinking of the enormity of the task before him. Some legends say that heavenly messengers appeared to him, urging him on, reminding him of what benefit his news about ending suffering would be to those people who heard it. The Buddha's decision to teach was, presumably, the result of hearing those heavenly messengers.

I know that in situations where I am hesitating about doing something—something I know will be helpful—my own kindness pushes me to do it. I anticipate how bad I'll feel if I don't act. I think it was the same for the Buddha. "Heavenly messengers," I think, are our impulses of natural kindness.

Cave with a View

Kate Wheeler

Kate Wheeler's long-awaited chance to meditate in a cave in India wasn't what she expected, what with the hot meals, electric lights, and frequent visitors. But the kind Tibetan nuns who took care of her were as great an example of dedication and realization as any high lama or renowned yogi.

I sit in a pink plastic lawn chair in front of my borrowed meditation cave. The afternoon is perfect, a warm cedar-scented breeze sighing through the branches of the deodar cedars on the hill. Tiny birds chirp in the underbrush. My rosary drops onto my lap, my mantra recitation slurs to a halt.

Past my bare toes is a gulf of bluish, haze-softened air. Far below, the sacred lake glints like dull-green jade. The high Himalayas are visible today, low and pale across the horizon.

I've wanted to meditate in a cave ever since reading those first hyperbolic yoga books as a teenager. But I thought I'd be eating weeds, fighting off leopards and even a demon or two. Privation and loneliness would be the whole enlightening deal. I'd end up luminous and scrawny, wearing nothing but a diaper.

Reality, here, is quite the opposite. I'm getting fatter by the day. By the time I go home, after a month, I will have gained eight pounds. My cave has electricity and linoleum on the floor, keeping dust at bay. It's not exactly a cave, but rather an overhang under a cliff, beefed up with a front wall, door, and curtains on the windows. The effect is reminiscent of a rustic stone house you might see in the Alps, but with bigger spiders.

Yes, I'm surrounded by minibeings. Spiders, centipedes, flies, mosquitoes, beetles, silverfish, moths, and cockroaches. Through the pitch-black night, I hear them crunching in each other's jaws, plus the scufflings of rats, mongooses, feral cats, and snakes, fighting and mating in the crevices of the roof. Not to mention the living presence of the mountain, dropping the occasional clod onto my bed as she takes another baby step toward the sea.

These things all provide occasion for forbearance and a tale of hardship I can tell the folks back home. But vermin and the danger of collapse aren't the main duress of being here. It is accepting the extraordinary love I'm being given.

One night I dream of my mother, alive. She died in 1983, but I know what the dream means. I haven't been cared for like this since I was an infant.

Three weeks ago, armed with introductions and a few small gifts, I arrived in Rewalsar, as the Indians call the lake and town a thousand meters below this cave (for Tibetans, it's Tso Pema, "Lotus Lake"). Ani Choe Lhamo was the first person I contacted. She is a nun, about forty, and speaks a little English. We hung out. "You and me, same!" she said, laughing, the day she learned we shared a root guru, the late Dzogchen master Nyoshul Khenpo Rinpoche. A few days later she offered me her cave. I'd mentioned envying her, but honestly, I didn't mean it as a hint.

"If you or I meditate in my cave, what difference?" Then she laughed maniacally again.

But I'm cautiously in agreement that we may have been sisters in some forgotten past life. It's a feeling. Laughing together, lying side by side on a bed, eating mango sprinkled with Chunky Chat spice powder, I feel inexplicably close to her. Rationally, I tell myself this is simply what it's like to hang out with someone who practices being unselfish, compassionate, and wise every day for years. Still, being here seems like stumbling into the arms of a long-lost, alternate family. Or maybe I don't even have to call it alternate. It's real, with resonances deep as blood.

"I will miss you," she said, and walked off around the shoulder of the hill.

So my cave is full of her absence, an austere, demanding gift in its own way. I'm sleeping in her bed, sitting in her pink lawn chair gazing out at this view—while she shares a room with her eighty-year-old great-uncle at a monastery down the hill.

And this is only half the story. For the cave is a duplex, and another nun lives next door: rotund, gossipy Ani Choenyi, sixty-one years old.

"My" side of the cave is slightly bigger than hers. Still, from the bed, where I usually meditate, I can reach everything without un-crossing my legs. Book, teacup, incense, light switch. It is delightful to be snuggled into the mountain's dark stone belly, upheld by the sturdy rhythms of Ani Choenyi's practice.

I love listening to her drum and bell, the strange wail of her thighbone trumpet that wriggles through the air as soon as darkness swallows the mountain. She is practicing *Chöd,* offering her body to demons, hungry ghosts, and presumably the human being next door. I know she thinks I'm hungry, given the way she feeds me dur-ing the day.

I've been fantasizing a lot about my life unrolling forward from here, especially when it rains and the outer world literally vanishes behind low, rolling clouds the color of dirty rags. Or when morning light comes in the window. And even when dozens of spiders spiral around the walls. Of course I know this is like a dream. I won't be here long—very soon, my karmic debt to this community would go from overwhelming to disgraceful. Like the *New Yorker* cartoon of a wife coming to retrieve her husband from a similar mountaintop: "Sheldon!"

For now, it's obvious that love is the practice I am meant to be doing here. Especially since this lake is where Guru Rinpoche—the

yogi who converted Tibet to Buddhism, also known as Padmasam-
bhava—fell in love twelve hundred years back.

A few hundred yards from where I sit, he and Princess Mandarava disappeared into the stony bowels of this mountain. Though
her mind was freed by their tantric practice, it's hardly surprising
that her father, the king, got upset. There are still some pretty wild
ascetics wandering around India. Just a week ago, down by the lake,
I got creeped out by the coals at the bottom of a pair of eyes I'd made
the mistake of looking into. I wouldn't want my daughter running
off with him!

The king tried to burn Guru Rinpoche alive, but the saintly magician turned the pyre into a lake, and as in all such stories, the king
bowed down as a disciple.

The actual lake is kind of small, but around here, the mythical
proportions of things are more important. There is an island said to
migrate around the lake; I finally figured out it was a tiny mat of
reeds, decked with old, white offering scarves.

Tso Pema is in the Mandi district of Himachal Pradesh, a region
known for its prosperity. Indeed, the foothills seem less deforested
than elsewhere and the villages better off: ample stone houses with
slate roofs, a few satellite dishes. Each hamlet is rich in invisible
wealth too. Veritable armies of yogis have reached enlightenment in
these green hills. Some have been famous, like the Buddhist saints
Naropa and Tilopa, but many more are anonymous practitioners in
a luminous tradition that continues to the present day. When I arrived with my list of folks to contact, some were unavailable, in *tsam,*
"sealed retreat." Old folks meet daily to pray and circumambulate; in
the monastery dorm, many rooms have curtains drawn across the
doors, indicating the tenant is in retreat.

You can't miss it. Everybody feels it. A sweet energy dances in the
air. How to absorb it? Do you just sit there? It's fun, but weirdly
difficult. Love, surrender, openness are clearly key points, but I keep
bumping up against neurotic guilt and self-doubt.

Another dream: I'm in a Hindi spy movie, full of paranoid in-
trigue, but wake up just as I'm finding out everything's actually okay.

Luckily I have two career cave yoginis showing me how it's done. I can see they are not living in any outward paradise. Both of them have medical issues and rely on sponsors in far-off countries to send them the forty dollars a month they need to live on. Ani Choe Lhamo has stuck a Buddha image in the biggest ceiling crack, presumably to ward off a collapse of the entire cliff above.

What I notice is that they don't let their minds get the better of them: Ani Choenyi hates the bugs in her cave, but she'd never kill them. "What? And ruin the blessings?" The longer I am here, the more people I hear the two of them are helping with their monthly forty dollars.

One day, Ani Choe Lhamo shows up to check on me, but I think she wants her cave back and offer to move out. She scowls good-humoredly—I'm being tiresome. The next time she comes, I can't resist offering again. The truth is, I can't imagine moving out of my house in Boston for her.

That was the night I had my Hindi spy dream.

As for Ani Choenyi, she's been waiting on me hand and foot. Buttered chapatis at breakfast, stir-fried vegetables at lunch, piping hot corn porridge at dinner. "Eat, eat," she cries, ladling a third helping onto my plate. Tea—I must be swilling forty cups a day. Sweet, milky Indian tea, Tibetan butter tea, plain black tea (*suja, pocha,* and *ngakja* in Tibetan). Every afternoon she comes with a cup of suja and a cookie, in case I'm hungry and tired from all my practice.

I have to receive this love. What else am I going to do, go home early and pay a penalty to the airlines?

Ani Choenyi is a Chaucerian character, stout, honest, with a face as rough as the earthen walls. We spend mealtimes laughing, having elaborate conversations in a blend of pantomime and baby-talk Tibetan. She's taught me many of the things a mother would teach her child. The names and uses of my fingers, for example. first finger: eating finger. Middle finger: ring finger. Third finger: secret finger. Fourth finger: little finger. Sticking her two secret fingers into her nostrils, she tells me this is a foolproof method of easing childbirth.

The baby will pop right out, she assures me, nodding vehemently with her fingers still stuck in.

And as it often used to happen in those romantic old spiritual books, she's teaching me things I could learn in no other way, the rhythms of a practitioner who's in it for the long haul: wake up between 3:00 and 4:00 A.M. and practice until 8:00 A.M.; take the rat you trapped last night and release it far away (the supply of rats is endless); enjoy a leisurely breakfast, then meditate until lunchtime; after lunch you nap, do chores, or perhaps receive a visitor. Then, what? More meditation; dinner is small; then practice until late—10:00 P.M.

Ani Choenyi saw her mother and sister killed by the Chinese. "I went to my teacher, Golok Ani, and I said, 'Let's go.'" Golok Ani, the nun from Golok, was her teacher for thirty years, but Ani Choenyi never learned her personal name. The two of them took trains and walked to India. They stopped in Sikkim to see the Nyingma master Dudjom Rinpoche, then in Bodh Gaya, arriving here in 1962.

Back in the old days, the hill was "empty," natural. Villagers said the deep, narrow cave at the top of the mountain was where Guru Rinpoche and Mandarava practiced. She and Golok Ani joined the great meditator Wangdor Rinpoche, living in small caves (*phuk-pa chum-chum*) among the piled rocks. Snow would blow in. Golok Ani died, sitting up in meditation; then Ani Choe Lhamo came along, a new cavemate.

After Wangdor Rinpoche emerged from his practice, temples were built around him. More refugee practitioners keep arriving. Now there are at least fifty people up here. Most are young nuns from Derge, Wangdor Rinpoche's region of Tibet. He supports the community as best he can, bringing money back from teaching tours to the United States and Europe. He installed electricity and water pipes and donated furry blankets to everyone. But now he's seventy-two and finds it more difficult to travel. Some of the foreign sponsors got tired of sending money to people they'd never seen. And now that caves are chockablock, the local villagers are reportedly resisting new arrivals.

Back in the old days, Ani Choenyi tells me, it was better, not so crowded. But certainly less convenient. They lugged water from a spring an hour's walk downhill and begged for food in the villages.

It makes me cry when she talks about how the Indian people helped Tibetans. In the early days, a locket bearing the Dalai Lama's image was a train ticket, meal ticket, and room for the night. "We owe them everything," she says simply. Soon I learn from a tea-shop owner that Ani Choenyi put him through school and is now paying for his children's education. Then there's Malka, the sad, homeless widow who roams the hillsides, kicked out by her family. She keeps a change of clothes in Ani Choenyi's woodshed. When the milk seller's husband gets drunk and beats her, she too pours out her heart to Ani Choenyi.

But Ani Choenyi is no fool; she has what in the West we call "good boundaries." Time to meditate? She kicks out her friends and locks the gate. One day the tea-shop owner invites her to the christening of a new baby, and Ani Choenyi comes toddling home from the party after half an hour. They were drinking alcohol, she grouses. A nun has no business lingering at that sort of party.

She's confided in me her opinion of Westerners. The ones she's met are a little cuckoo. Emotional. "Should I do this practice or that practice?" she mimics, guffawing. I wince with recognition.

Today the only reason I'm alone, out on this veranda, is that she's chanting in a ceremony downtown—a feast offering for an un- successful itinerant clothing vendor. Afterward she'll go to the mar- ket and buy food for the two of us.

It's actually funny—I am secretly relieved she'll be away so I can finally skip a meal and eat the chocolate Luna bar I've been saving. I tell her not to arrange a lunch, and she slyly pretends to agree. As soon as I've gobbled the Luna Bar, there comes a shy knock at the blue metal gate. I unbolt it and sure enough, there stands Ani Nge- jung from two caves down, holding an enamel plate piled high with rice and eggplant curry. She sits and watches me eat, then silently takes the plate away.

After she leaves, I try to meditate indoors. But it's mid-July, hot season in India. Stuffed and drowsy, I come out where it's cooler. A flock of warblers dips in and out of the bushes. Soon the mongoose slinks out from behind the water tank, liquid and silent as the snakes it feeds on. Seeing me, it slinks back. Alas, if I am to embody a tantric deity, it will be a distracted one.

Downhill a house is being built. Stonemasons' hammers clink, each blow clear but tiny. Fainter still is the tumult of the pilgrim town. Bus motors grinding, dogs yapping, laughter, shouts, an occasional temple bell. The thousand-meter drop provides a contemplative distance my unruly mind cannot. The worried world looks doll-house-sized. Leaning forward, I can see the town rimming a button-sized lake. Tibetan *gompas* with yellow corrugated roofs; the Sikh *gurdwara's* powder-blue dorm, the fat white spire of the Hindu *mandir.*

A shoulder of the mountain hides the new statue of Guru Rinpoche, still mostly imaginary. He grows larger slowly as pilgrims' coins drop into donation boxes. The completed statue will be eighty-seven meters tall, adding to the magnetism of the lake.

The mayor, who also runs the dry-cleaning shop, tells me that fully half of the local population consists of pilgrims, a stable flux of six thousand. This supports local farmers and shopkeepers. July is the high season, plains dwellers heading for the hills, bringing their children before school has started. All the passes down from Ladakh are open too. Huge Sikh families are continually disgorged from SUVs, cameras ready to point and shoot at any Westerner. Busloads of Ladakhis—indescribably dirty and devout—come to prostrate in all the gompas. Not to mention the trickle of new Tibetan refugees arriving day by day. And the odd foreigner, like me.

Who *must* force herself to go back to visualizing her wrathful deity.

He's squashing me under his big toe. "Rulu, Rulu!" he roars, then disappears into space.

"Why do people practice in caves?" I ask Tenzin Wangyal Rinpoche, the Bön Buddhist lama, a month after I return to the United States.

He laughs and says that back in Tibet, if you didn't want to be a nomad or a town dweller any more, the caves were right there. Free housing.

I press him. "Is there an energy in the earth?"

"Yes," he says, making a circular gesture in front of his belly. "But hardly anybody knows how to work with it. Sacred energy is easier— the energy from previous meditators. Your efforts enter a kind of multiplying circuit, enhanced and eased by those who came before you."

It sure feels that way.

Hundreds of colorful prayer flags flutter in the gentle breeze like laundry of the gods. Their shadows dart jerkily, unpredictably in the thin, dried-up thorn branches that edge the nuns' terrace. This homemade security fence has seemed threatening and unaesthetic up to now, with its inch-long thorns poking through damp, grubby laundry, trapping food crumbs from the dishwater Ani Choenyi tosses down the nearly vertical hillside. Suddenly the fence reminds me of a sculpture I saw once in a gallery: a room-sized, impossibly fragile construction made of toothpicks by a Polish artist. Hers lacked the element of movement, this mesmerizing flitting from depth to surface, point to point. I fantasize shipping the whole caboodle to New York, then lapse into a purer contemplation of the ephemeral movements of light. Is anything actually moving? Does the light inherently exist? Is it different from the shadow that follows it so closely?

Finally I hear a rattling at the blue gate. Ani Choenyi coming home. I straighten my back, begin to move the *mala* through my fingers. I've missed her; I wouldn't want her to think I'm slacking off.

In a few days I will leave this sacred place and time. Ani Ngejung will insist on carrying my suitcase on her head all the way to the bus stop. Ani Choenyi will accompany me down to a restaurant where I'll treat her and Choe Lhamo to meat *momos*.

"Come back in two years!" they'll say. "We'll set you up in a sealed retreat. Now that we know you, we can really help you!"

The Joy of Living

Yongey Mingyur Rinpoche

If Buddhism is a science—and many people think of it that way—then it is a science of mind. Buddhist meditators have been examining and mapping the inner, subjective experience of mind for thousands of years. What they have discovered about the basic nature of mind is epitomized in the Tibetan tradition called Dzogchen, whose profundity Western science is only beginning to appreciate.

One of the first things I learned as a Buddhist was that the fundamental nature of the mind is so vast that it completely transcends intellectual understanding. It can't be described in words or reduced to tidy concepts. For someone like me, who likes words and feels very comfortable with conceptual explanations, this was a problem.

In Sanskrit, the language in which the Buddha's teachings were originally recorded, the fundamental nature of the mind is called *tathagatagarbha*, which is a very subtle and tricky description. Literally, it means "the nature of those who have gone that way." "Those who have gone that way" are the people who have attained complete enlightenment—in other words, people whose minds have completely surpassed ordinary limitations that can be described in words.

Not a lot of help there, I think you'll agree.

Other, less literal translations have variously rendered *tatha-gatagarbha* as "buddhanature," "true nature," "enlightened essence," "ordinary mind," and even "natural mind"—none of which sheds much light on the real meaning of the word itself. To really understand tathagatagarbha, you have to experience it directly, which for most of us occurs initially in the form of quick, spontaneous glimpses. And when I finally experienced my first glimpse, I realized that everything the Buddhist texts said about it was true.

For most of us, our natural mind or buddhanature is obscured by the limited self-image created by habitual neuronal patterns— which, in themselves, are simply a reflection of the unlimited capacity of the mind to create any condition it chooses. Natural mind is capable of producing anything, *even ignorance of its own nature.* In other words, not recognizing natural mind is simply an example of the mind's unlimited capacity to create whatever it wants. Whenever we feel fear, sadness, jealousy, desire, or any other emotion that contributes to our sense of vulnerability or weakness, we should give ourselves a nice pat on the back. We've just experienced the unlimited nature of the mind.

Although the true nature of the mind can't be described directly, that doesn't mean we shouldn't at least try to develop some theoretical understanding about it. Even a limited understanding is at least a signpost, pointing the way toward direct experience. The Buddha understood that experiences impossible to describe in words could best be explained through stories and metaphors. In one text, he compared tathagatagarbha to a nugget of gold covered with mud and dirt.

Imagine you're a treasure hunter. One day you discover a chunk of metal in the ground. You dig a hole, pull out the metal, take it home, and start to clean it. At first, one corner of the nugget reveals itself, bright and shining. Gradually, as you wash away the accumulated dirt and mud, the whole chunk is revealed as gold. So let me ask: which is more valuable—the chunk of gold buried in mud or the one you cleaned? Actually, the value is equal. Any difference between the dirty nugget and the clean is superficial.

The same can be said of natural mind. The neuronal gossip that keeps you from seeing your mind in its fullness doesn't really change the fundamental nature of your mind. Thoughts like "I'm ugly," "I'm stupid," or "I'm boring" are nothing more than a kind of biological mud, temporarily obscuring the brilliant qualities of buddhanature or natural mind.

Sometimes the Buddha compared natural mind to space, not necessarily as space is understood by modern science, but rather in the poetic sense of a profound experience of openness one feels when looking up at a cloudless sky or entering a very large room. Like space, natural mind isn't dependent on prior causes or conditions. It simply *is*: immeasurable and beyond characterization, the essential background through which we move and relative to which we recognize distinctions between the objects we perceive.

NATURAL PEACE

> In natural mind, there is no rejection or acceptance, no loss or gain.
> —THE THIRD GYALWANG KARMAPA, in *The Song of Karmapa: The Aspiration of the Mahamudra of True Meaning*, translated by Erik Pema Kunsang

I'd like to make it clear that the comparison between natural mind and space as described by modern science is really more of a useful metaphor than an exact description. When most of us think of space, we think of a blank background against which all sorts of things appear and disappear: stars, planets, comets, meteors, black holes, and asteroids—even things that haven't yet been discovered. Yet despite all this activity, our idea of the essential nature of space remains undisturbed. As far as we know, at least, space has yet to complain about what happens within itself. We've sent thousands— millions—of messages out into the universe and never once have received a response like, "I am so angry that an asteroid just smashed into my favorite planet," or "Wow, I'm thrilled! A new star has just come into being!"

In the same way, the essence of mind is untouched by unpleasant thoughts or conditions that might ordinarily be considered painful. It's naturally peaceful, like the mind of a young child accompanying his parents through a museum. While his parents are completely caught up in judging and evaluating the various works of art on display, the child merely sees. He doesn't wonder how much some piece of art might have cost, how old a statue is, or whether one painter's work is better than another's. His perspective is completely innocent, accepting everything it beholds. This innocent perspective is known in Buddhist terms as "natural peace," a condition similar to the sensation of total relaxation a person experiences after, say, going to the gym or completing a complicated task.

As with so many aspects of natural mind, the experience of natural peace is so far beyond what we normally consider relaxation that it defies description. In classical Buddhist texts, it's compared to offering candy to a mute. The mute undoubtedly experiences the sweetness of the candy but is powerless to describe it. In the same way, when we taste the natural peace of our own minds, the experience is unquestionably real yet beyond our capacity to express in words.

So now, the next time you sit down to eat, if you should ask yourself, "What is it that thinks that this food tastes good—or not so good? What is it that thinks it recognizes eating?" don't be surprised if you can't answer at all. Congratulate yourself instead. When you can't describe a powerful experience in words anymore, it's a sign of progress. It means you've at least dipped your toes into the realm of the ineffable vastness of your true nature, a very brave step that many people, too comfortable with the familiarity of their discontent, lack the courage to take.

The Tibetan word for meditation, *gom*, literally means "becoming familiar with," and Buddhist meditation practice is really about becoming familiar with the nature of your own mind—a bit like getting to know a friend on deeper and deeper levels. Like getting to know a friend, discovering the nature of your mind is a gradual process. Rarely does it occur all at once. The only difference between meditation and ordinary social interaction is that the friend you're gradually coming to know is yourself.

GETTING TO KNOW YOUR NATURAL MIND

> If an inexhaustible treasure were buried in the ground beneath a poor man's house, the man would not know of it, and the treasure would not speak and tell him, "I am here!"
> —MAITREYA, in *The Mahayana Uttaratantra Shastra*, translated by Rosemarie Fuchs

The Buddha often compared natural mind to water, which in its essence is always clear and clean. Mud, sediment, and other impurities may temporarily darken or pollute the water, but we can filter away such impurities and restore its natural clarity. If water weren't naturally clear, no matter how many filters you used, it would not become clear.

The first step toward recognizing the qualities of natural mind is illustrated by an old story, told by the Buddha, about a very poor man who lived in a rickety old shack. Though he didn't know it, hundreds of gems were embedded in the walls and floor of his shack. Though he owned all of the jewels, because he didn't understand their value, he lived as a pauper—suffering from hunger and thirst, the bitter cold of winter, and the terrible heat of summer.

One day a friend of his asked him, "Why are you living like such a pauper? You're not poor. You're a very rich man."

"Are you crazy?" the man replied. "How can you say such a thing?"

"Look around you," his friend said. "Your whole house is filled with jewels—emeralds, diamonds, sapphires, rubies."

At first the man didn't believe what his friend was saying. But after a while he grew curious and took a small jewel from his walls into town to sell. Unbelievably, the merchant to whom he brought it paid him a very handsome price, and with the money in hand, the man returned to town and bought a new house, taking with him all the jewels he could find. He bought himself new clothes, filled his kitchen with food, engaged servants, and began to live a very comfortable life.

Now let me ask a question. Who is wealthier—someone who lives in an old house surrounded by jewels he doesn't recognize, or someone who understands the value of what he has and lives in total comfort?

Like the question posed earlier about the nugget of gold, the answer here is both. They both owned great wealth. The only difference is that for many years they didn't recognize what they possessed. It wasn't until they recognized what they already had that they freed themselves from poverty and pain.

It's the same for all of us. As long as we don't recognize our real nature, we suffer. When we recognize our nature, we become free from suffering. Whether you recognize it or not, though, its qualities remain unchanged. But when you begin to recognize it in yourself, you change, and the quality of your life changes as well. Things you never dreamed possible begin to happen.

BEING YOU

> We need to recognize our basic state.
> —TSOKNYI RINPOCHE, in *Carefree Dignity,* translated by
> Erik Pema Kunsang and Marcia Binder Schmidt

According to the Buddha, the basic nature of mind can be directly experienced simply by allowing the mind to rest as it is. How do we accomplish this?

Let's try a brief exercise in resting the mind. This is not a meditation exercise. In fact, it's an exercise in "nonmeditation"—a very old Buddhist practice that takes the pressure off thinking you have to achieve a goal or experience some sort of special state. In nonmeditation, we just watch whatever happens without interfering. We're just interested observers of a kind of introspective experiment, with no investment in how the experiment turns out.

Of course, when I first learned this, I was still a pretty goal-oriented child. I wanted something wonderful to happen every time I sat down to meditate. So it took me a while to get the hang of just resting, just looking, and letting go of the results.

First, assume a comfortable position in which your spine is straight, your body relaxed, and your eyes open. Once your body is positioned comfortably, allow your mind to simply rest for three minutes or so. Just let your mind go, as though you've just finished a long and difficult task.

Whatever happens, whether thoughts or emotions occur, whether you notice some physical discomfort, whether you're aware of sounds or smells around you, or whether your mind is a total blank, don't worry. Anything that happens—or doesn't happen—is simply a part of the experience of allowing your mind to rest.

So now, just rest in the awareness of whatever is passing through your mind . . .

Just rest . . .

Just rest . . .

When the three minutes are up, ask yourself, "How was that experience?" Don't judge it; don't try to explain it. Just review what happened and how you felt. You might have experienced a brief taste of peace or openness. That's good. Or you might have been aware of a million different thoughts, feelings, and sensations. That's also good. Why? Because either way, as long as you've maintained at least a bare awareness of what you were thinking or feeling, you've had a direct glimpse of your own mind just performing its natural functions.

So let me confide in you a big secret. Whatever you experience when you simply rest your attention on whatever's going on in your mind at any given moment is meditation. Simply resting in this way is the experience of natural mind.

The only difference between meditation and the ordinary, everyday process of thinking, feeling, and sensing is the application of the simple, bare awareness that occurs when you allow your mind to rest simply as it is—without chasing after thoughts or becoming distracted by feelings or sensations.

It took me a long time to recognize how easy meditation really is, mainly because it seemed so completely ordinary, so close to my everyday habits of perception, that I rarely stopped to acknowledge it. Like many of the people I now meet on teaching tours, I thought that natural mind had to be something else, something different from, or better than, what I was already experiencing.

Like most people, I brought so much judgment to my experience. I believed that thoughts of anger, fear, and so on that came and went throughout the day were bad or counterproductive—or at the very least inconsistent with natural peace! The teachings of the Buddha—and the lesson inherent in this exercise is nonmeditation—is that if we allow ourselves to relax and take a mental step back, we can begin to recognize that all these different thoughts are simply coming and going within the context of an unlimited mind, which, like space, remains fundamentally unperturbed by whatever occurs within it.

In fact, experiencing natural peace is easier than drinking water. In order to drink, you have to expend effort. You have to reach for the glass, bring it to your lips, tip the glass so the water pours into your mouth, swallow the water, and then put the glass down. No such effort is required to experience natural peace. All you have to do is rest your mind in its natural openness. No special focus, no special effort, is required.

And if for some reason you cannot rest your mind, you can simply observe whatever thoughts, feelings, or sensations come up; hang out for a couple of seconds; and then dissolve and acknowledge, "Oh, that's what's going on in my mind right now."

Wherever you are, whatever you do, it's essential to acknowledge your experience as something ordinary, the natural expression of your true mind. If you don't try to stop whatever is going on in your mind, but merely observe it, eventually you'll begin to feel a tremendous sense of relaxation, a vast sense of openness within your mind—which is, in fact, your natural mind, the natural, unperturbed background against which various thoughts come and go. At the same time, you'll be awakening new neuronal pathways, which, as they grow stronger and more deeply connected, enhance your capability to tolerate the cascade of thoughts rushing through your mind at any given moment. Whatever disturbing thoughts do arise will act as catalysts that stimulate your awareness of the natural peace that surrounds and permeates these thoughts, the way space surrounds and permeates every particle of the phenomenal world.

Always Turn Toward,
Never Turn Away

Rigdzin Shikpo

*Rigdzin Shikpo (Michael Hookham) was an early British disciple
of the young Chögyam Trungpa Rinpoche, who went on to become one
of the most important Buddhist teachers in the West. Trungpa Rinpoche's
accessible but uncompromising teachings still largely define how we
understand Buddhism today, and Rigdzin Shikpo does an outstanding
job presenting their essence.*

If you asked Trungpa Rinpoche for the essence of the Buddha's
teaching, he would say, "It is very simple. It is simply the teaching of
openness, complete openness."

Trungpa Rinpoche's approach was simply to be open and to
minimize the projections we make on our experience. His great saying was, "Turn toward everything." Even if we don't know what to do
or how to handle a situation, we just turn toward it. What comes to
us might be quite painful, but it is always better to turn toward. It is
a very simple choice, although it might be a painful choice sometimes. We can either turn toward or we can turn away, and Trungpa
Rinpoche said you should *always* turn toward and *never* turn away.

We may find, having turned toward a situation, that we don't know what to do. That might be embarrassing, but it's an interesting kind of embarrassment.

Empty-Handed

A martial arts teacher once explained to me that the word *karate* means to have "an empty hand." We don't need what he called a "secret sword"; in fact, we train to give up all such secret swords. From a Buddhist point of view, we all have a number of secret—and maybe not so secret—swords that we use to handle difficult circumstances, when all we really need is to be empty-handed, to come nakedly into situations.

We could almost call this the path of embarrassment. Ordinarily, we free ourselves from embarrassment in difficult situations by having some contrived method up our sleeves. But the only method that really helps in the end is simply to turn toward and experience things clearly. We have to overcome the embarrassment of not always knowing how to handle ourselves. We have to let go of our habits, projections, and other easy, familiar devices that don't really work.

We don't need to be especially brave to practice dharma. It is more like we reach a situation where there is only one road to take; it's almost the wisdom of despair. We have tried everything else, so why not try this? If we thought we had another option, we might not try anything so radical. Maybe we are irritated with our ordinary ways of reacting to situations. Perhaps there is a simpler way of dealing with existence, something more radical than simply "handling" things.

This approach is actually more real than radical. There is something very wholesome about turning toward things completely and openly. It is very sharp and uncontrived and feels genuine in a way that our ordinary projections and ways of handling things never do. But we will never know this unless we do the practice, because we will have nothing to compare it to.

By turning toward situations as openly as possible, we get the raw data of our experience. This is just the first stage, but that first stage is crucial and carries us a long way.

SEEING THINGS AS THEY ARE

The next stage is more at the level of insight. We might discover, for example, that our sense of self is not as solid as we thought. Or we could have some genuine realization of what we dismissively call "just change." Experiencing a moment of nonego sounds like more of a discovery because it is such an unfamiliar experience. But everyone knows things change. What is there to discover in that? Well, actually there is a great deal to discover, because we have only a conceptual understanding of change. Intellectually, of course, we all know that things change. But we never feel the significance of change in our hearts and in our guts.

It is obvious that ordinary things change. We can see this as we walk into a room and switch on the television, or leave the house to go shopping. We think that this is just how things work, and its significance doesn't hit us. But when our bodies change—especially if the change is dramatic or sudden—then this has a much greater emotional impact. An accident or the sudden discovery that we or someone close to us has a life-threatening disease feels much more invasive. But again, we often miss its significance. Instead, we think about visiting a doctor, and as our beauty fades, we wonder about face creams. Meanwhile, the significance of aging and change still doesn't hit us.

As Buddhist practitioners, we train to see the significance of impermanence at every level: at the seemingly insignificant level of everyday things like shopping and watching television, as much as the dramatic and emotionally compelling level of old age, sickness, and death.

Some people feel Buddhism is pessimistic. But really it is neither optimistic nor pessimistic. It is just seeing things as they are. Buddhist practice is about becoming more open, clear, and sensitive. There is nothing gloomy about that. Of course, this makes our experience clearer and sharper, and we might not like that. We may feel uncomfortable when our seemingly solid world becomes "more transparent" and "not so easily grasped at," as Trungpa Rinpoche used to say. But it is hardly pessimistic to see that the world of our experience is potentially a much brighter, vaster place than we ever thought possible.

It reminds me of being taken to the seaside when I was very small. Looking at the sea for the first time, I burst into tears and ran away. The sea seemed so very big and I was so small. The sea scared me, but that was no reason for pessimism. I was just seeing clearly what was there before me, and I had to overcome my fear with the help of parents and friends.

THE TRUTH OF SUFFERING

The Buddha's first truth, the truth of suffering, is not saying that everything is miserable. It's saying that suffering, or *dukkha,* is inherent in the very nature of existence and in the basic structure of all sentient beings. Now Western books on Buddhism often give the impression that the Buddha taught this to everyone he met. But evidence suggests that the Buddha would teach very differently if his audience wasn't ready to discover this universal—if hidden—truth of the nature of things.

The term *dukkha* cannot be fully understood by our ordinary idea of suffering. Technically, its meaning has three aspects: the suffering of suffering, the suffering of impermanence and change, and the suffering of the *skandhas.*

The first is fairly easy to understand. Suffering and dissatisfaction are unfair, in the most obvious sense. The fact that we may already be suffering doesn't insure against more suffering. This is what Trungpa Rinpoche described as the "suffering of suffering." The example he gave to me was that having cancer is no insurance against being run down by a car.

The second, more subtle aspect of suffering is the dukkha of *anitya,* or the suffering of impermanence and change. Sooner or later, due to the dynamic of change, the things we grasp at and want to continue will fall apart. If we cling to them and have a vested interest in their permanence, we will be forever disappointed and will suffer for that reason.

Of course, it could be argued that if we're already suffering, any change in our circumstances would be a good thing. But this is more subtle than our ordinary notions of liking or disliking; it is the fact that the instability, the collapse, and the finishing of things is painful in itself. We wish for stability and permanence, and this is forever denied us, irrespective of whether we are talking about pain or pleasure. It is something we want but can never get.

The third and most subtle kind of suffering is the dukkha of the five skandhas. These are the very constituents of our existence: the form of our bodies, our feelings of pleasure and pain, our sense perceptions, the contents of our minds and hearts, and our consciousness. The skandhas are not only the constituents of our personal existence, they also involve our perception of the external world and the things we hold on to in that world.

The extra subtlety here is that the skandhas are themselves a false creation. Since they don't correspond to what is truly there, we find ourselves emotionally involved in false projections and distortions of reality. Our seeming reality is fundamentally false, and we are absorbed into that falseness, which is painful. This is the most subtle kind of dukkha: the suffering of our very existence.

Taken at face value, most of us in the West would dispute the truth of suffering. Not everything in our lives and in the world is suffering. Yes, there is much suffering in the world—both mental and physical—and life is often unsatisfactory. We are not going to live forever, so there is always that uncertainty hovering over us. But on the scale of suffering, some of us seem to suffer less than others, and on occasion, we all rather enjoy ourselves. Of course, we are talking here about something that points to a much deeper level of experience. But while it is all very well to say this, most Western people still can't relate to it.

In traditional cultures, where there is more respect for the buddhadharma and the teaching itself has great charisma, people tend to accept the truth of suffering, whether they understand it or not. It has a cultural meaning for them, and they can go on to train to see the truth of it. Lacking that background, we might easily think that Buddhism must be intrinsically depressing and certainly not life-affirming.

Early Western commentators, looking at the first translations of Buddhist texts, sometimes portrayed Buddhism as being negative and pessimistic. I feel there is no point in pressing on that particular nerve. The Buddha's teaching contains many things, and while the nature of dukkha is fundamental, we can let it emerge gradually, if it does. Who knows? Maybe we will find that, in some deep and profound way, life is wonderful after all, even from a Buddhist perspective.

The most important thing is to experience the nature of our worlds as directly as we can. I say, "worlds," because our seemingly common world is made up of all of our very different emotions, ideas, and projections. We can at least aspire to become free of notions and projections about how the world should be and try to experience things as they are.

That simple act of aspiring to be free, to be free insofar as we can be free, is more important than we might think.

Imaginary Barriers

Trungpa Rinpoche decided that the best way to express the Buddha's teaching was in terms of openness. The word *open* has an immediate meaning for us. We speak of people being open or closed. Being closed is associated with claustrophobia and a narrowed outlook or vision. Being open suggests we are open to many different possibilities and ways of thinking and feeling. We are open to others, allowing them to rub up against or even strike us at times, without immediately blocking them off. Openness is a way of learning about the world that enables us to relate to things properly and to act skillfully.

Trungpa Rinpoche occasionally spoke to me about absolute or complete openness. This is something more than openness in the ordinary sense. Rinpoche suggested it was possible to experience the world free of any ego-contrived barriers whatsoever. Moreover, this state of absolute openness is completely natural. We don't have to construct it, or indeed, deconstruct it, as we say these days. We don't have to pull down a burning wall in our minds and hearts. Such walls exist only in our imagination. That imagination, however, is as powerful as a magical enchantment.

Waking from a Spell

The power of our false view of the world is like an enchantment. The great fourteenth-century master Longchen Rabjam spoke of it in these terms. *Enchantment* is a good word for it. It's as if we are under a spell, or "glamour," that causes us to see things that aren't there and fail to see things that are. This false view makes up the world as we know it.

This spell is not cast upon us by some evil magician; in a sense, we create it ourselves. Through our practice of openness and awareness, we become convinced that we are under an enchantment. A gradual sense of disenchantment—in the positive sense—arises. Now you might think that this would come as a great relief, but not so, unfortunately. The biggest shock often comes as the spell dissolves, and we find ourselves saying, "Where has my world gone?"

Suddenly we realize that the universe is a much vaster place than we ever imagined. We see what a parochial view we had before. We may yowl that we don't want to go there! We don't want it to be so vast and open! But it's just a sign that we need to straighten ourselves out.

Fortunately, it's not fundamentally that difficult. Many others have done so before, and so can we. This is the Buddhist view and the path of openness, which is certainly not pessimistic.

The Great Way

John Daido Loori

It's maybe the best single-sentence summary of Buddhist practice: "The Great Way is not difficult. It only avoids picking and choosing." So easy to say, yet it overturns every conventional principle by which we lead our lives. Here is a commentary on this seminal Zen text by the eminent American roshi John Daido Loori.

The Great Way is not difficult;
It only avoids picking and choosing.
When love and hate are both absent,
Everything becomes clear and undisguised.
Make the smallest distinction, however,
And heaven and earth are set infinitely apart.
If you wish to see the truth,
Then hold no opinions for or against anything.
To set up what you like against what you dislike
Is a disease of the mind.
When the deep meaning of things is not understood,
The mind's essential peace is disturbed to no avail.
The Way is perfect like vast space,
Where nothing is lacking and nothing is in excess.
Indeed, it is due to our choosing to accept or reject
That we do not see the true nature of things.

Live neither in the entanglements of outer things
Nor in inner feelings of emptiness.
Be serene in the oneness of things
And such erroneous views will disappear by themselves.
To deny the reality of things
Is to miss their reality;
To assert the emptiness of things
Is to miss their reality.
The more you talk and think about it,
The further astray you wander from the truth.
Stop talking and thinking
And there is nothing that you will not be able to know.

This passage is from *The Faith Mind Sutra: Verses on the Unfailing Source of Life* by Master Sengcan (J. Sozan). It deals with faith in mind, faith in how the mind really functions. Later in the sutra, Master Sengcan says,

One thing, all things,
Move among and intermingle without distinction.
To live in this realization,
Is to be without anxiety about nonperfection;
To live in this faith is the road to nonduality,
Because the nondual is one with a trusting mind.

"One thing, all things, / Move among and intermingle without distinction" points to the unfailing source of life that Sengcan mentions in the subtitle. It refers to the metaphor of the Diamond Net of Indra. Everything throughout space and time is interconnected, and at each connection—at each point—is a diamond that reflects every other diamond, so that in this vast net, each diamond contains every other diamond. This is one thing, all things, moving among and intermingling without distinction. The diamond net is "the unfailing source of life." Indeed, it is life itself, your life itself. We separate ourselves from this unfailing source of life with our mind, our thoughts, our ideas. But the only way you can separate yourself is mentally, because "one thing, all things, / move among and intermingle" is the way it is, whether we realize it or not. Regardless of whether we live our lives according to this understanding or not, the fact remains that it is the way things are. With our minds we separate ourselves and immediately create all the dualities of life. On one side we create pain, greed, anger—fundamental ignorance. We also create the other side—joy, compassion, wisdom, and enlightenment.

"When love and hate are both absent, / Everything becomes clear and undisguised." When duality is absent, everything becomes clear. But we shouldn't cling to this "clarity" either. The other side of clarity is confusion; both are diseases of the mind. All of the dualities are mutually arising; they are all codependent. You can't have one without the other: good and bad, heads and tails, heaven and earth. That is why it is said, "Make the smallest distinction . . . And heaven and earth are set infinitely apart." They are not set apart until we separate them in our minds (and by "we" I do not mean only Westerners—the same thing holds true for people in China, Japan, India, and everyplace else). Civilization itself is founded on the dualistic use of the mind. The Buddha went beyond dualism, beyond the distinction between this and that, to show that there is no self, that what we call the "self" is a creation of our own consciousness, which separates us from everything else.

Picking and choosing, coming and going, love and hate, inside and outside, having and not having, accepting and rejecting, asserting and denying, form and emptiness, right and wrong—they all begin with making the smallest distinction. They all begin with the idea of a separate self, a boundary between the self and the rest of reality, an inside and an outside. Coming and going is such a difficult and painful process. Our lives are filled with the pains of coming and going: coming into a relationship, a marriage, a new job, a new place; leaving a relationship, a marriage, a job, the place where you live. We do not seem to understand how to execute these life functions without creating pain, anger, or confusion. We are tearing ourselves away from some imaginary thing that we stick to—that by its very nature cannot be stuck to or torn away from. Coming is always right here and right now. Going is always right here and right now. It is because there is no coming and no going that we can speak of coming and going.

Because of that illusion of separateness, we find it hard to come and go. We find it difficult to come together, difficult to part. I know many people who have had wonderful relationships, but because of the time, the circumstances, or various changes in their lives, they have had to go their separate ways. To be able to do that, somehow the creation of anger is usually necessary. There is that need to feel justified, to have a reason to separate. Since love is what brings us together—that is our rationale—then hate must be what will drive us apart. So we create anger. It is unnecessary and so poisonous. Coming and going is a function of life, like waves rising and falling. We can learn to come and go without coming and going. We can learn to avoid picking and choosing. So how can we avoid picking and choosing, coming and going? Just to open our mouths to speak is picking and choosing. Just to say, "Avoid picking and choosing," is picking and choosing. What kind of practice avoids picking and choosing? Avoids coming and going?

This suffering, this picking and choosing, this painful coming and going is related to ignorance. Master Sengcan says, "[I]t is due to our choosing to accept or reject / That we do not see the true nature of things." Later in the sutra, he tells us, "The changes that appear to occur in the empty world we call real only because of our ignorance." Ignorance means not knowing what is real. It is very easy to get totally lost in the confusion between the apparent and real. In a way, our lives are based on that confusion, on our fundamental assumption of a separate self, an assumption that is simply false. The consequence of this basic premise and all the delusive thoughts that arise from it is suffering in its multitude of forms. The practice that avoids picking and choosing, coming and going is the practice that avoids dualism, that brings us back to the ground of our being.

The great master Zhaozhou [Joshu] very often used this *Faith Mind Sutra* of Master Sozan to teach his monks. One day a monk asked him, "It is said that the Great Way is not difficult; it only avoids picking and choosing. Now what is not picking and choosing?" Zhaozhou said, "I alone am holy throughout heaven and earth." The monk responded, "That is still picking and choosing." And Zhaozhou said, "Asshole! Where's the picking and choosing?" The monk was speechless.

Zhaozhou answered him with the words of the Buddha: "I alone am the Honored One between heaven and earth." He is saying there is nothing outside of me; I am the Diamond Net of Indra. In a sense, that is picking and choosing, but only when you are coming from a position other than the position Zhaozhou was standing in. The monk was standing outside of that, and from his point of view, he was justified in saying, "That is still picking and choosing." Position is everything. Everything changes, even when the circumstances remain identical, when you shift your position. Try it sometime with someone who is an adversary. Shift your position. Be that person, and the adversary disappears. Shift positions with whatever barrier you are facing in zazen, in your life. Be the barrier, and it is no longer there. It is only there because we pull back, separate ourselves from it. The more we pull back, the bigger and more overwhelming it gets, and the angrier or the more frightened we become. If we really look at the anger that makes us crazy or the fear that stops us cold, we see that it develops step by step from our thought process. And the starting point of that thought process is separation. Is the cause of the fear something that might be lurking in a dark alley? The possibility of falling down and breaking your neck? Losing your job? No, it is yourself. When you really acknowledge that it is nothing but yourself, when you realize this fact, you cannot live your life in the old way. You've suddenly taken responsibility for it. Before, the problem was outside—your bad luck, what others did to you, the circumstances you could do nothing about.

When you realize that the cause is you, you empower yourself.

You suddenly become a ten thousand–foot–high buddha—you fill the universe. There is no picking and choosing, coming or going—no place to go, no place to come from. Zhaozhou was trying to show the monk that ten thousand–foot–high buddha. But the monk was standing in a different position. So Zhaozhou yelled, "Asshole!" Actually the Chinese word is usually translated as "country bumpkin" or "stupid oaf," but this sounds too tame for our ears. It was meant to shock, to stun the monk into experiencing the reality of what the Buddha said: "I alone am the Honored One between heaven and earth!" Nothing is outside of you.

Zhaozhou was coming from the position of the absolute, which would become a kind of blindness if he stuck there. But when the monk said, "That is still picking and choosing," Zhaozhou shouted, "Asshole! Where's the picking and choosing?" immediately shifting positions, slamming right into that monk from the relativistic standpoint. He was showing him "You and I are the same thing, but I am not you and you are not me. We should not stick anywhere—not in the relative, not in the absolute."

To deny the reality of things
Is to miss their reality;
To assert the emptiness of things
Is to miss their reality.

Sticking to clarity, to enlightenment, is the worst kind of delusion. In Zen there is going beyond clarity. As Zen master Dogen says, "No trace of enlightenment remains, and this traceless enlightenment continues endlessly." Going beyond clarity, not abiding in it, is very ordinary. There is no stink of Zen about it, no holiness to hold on to.

In the vast Diamond Net of Indra, each thing contains everything, and each thing is separate and distinct from everything else. Thinking, talking, and doing are the ways we create our lives, the ways we create our karma. We can see how our actions create causes, and we can see that every cause has consequences. The same is true

for our thought. It is because of our interconnectedness, our intermingling and moving among this one thing, that it works in that
way. Because of that, talking and thinking and doing can create
karma. We can use karma to poison or to nourish, depending upon
how we manifest it. How do we manifest it so that it nourishes, so
that it heals? By nontalking, nonthinking, nondoing. How do you do
nonthinking and nondoing? How can you possibly avoid picking
and choosing?

> The more you talk and think about it,
> The further astray you wander from the truth.
> Stop talking and thinking
> And there is nothing that you will not be able to know.

Stop knowing and not-knowing. Knowing is another kind of
holding on, of separation; not-knowing is blank consciousness,
emptiness. How do we avoid these extremes of form and emptiness,
enlightenment and delusion? By learning to be ourselves, but not
self-consciously, not passively. "Be serene in the oneness of things"
does not mean "Watch the world go by" or "Do not do anything."
That is not what Sozan is talking about, and it is not what our practice is. Being yourself means giving yourself permission to be who
and what you are. That is "faith mind," having faith in your true self,
trusting yourself. Until that happens, you cannot really trust anything or anybody. When you have that trust, your defensiveness disappears. You don't need to be arrogant or to put yourself down, to
hide, or to withdraw. These two extremes are the same thing, different ways of protecting that idea of a separate self. Being yourself,
being intimate with yourself, is the beginning of intimacy with all
things. Being yourself is "no separation."

> The Great Way is not difficult:
> Direct word, direct speech.
> In one, there are many phrases:

In two, there is one.
Difficult, difficult,
Picking and choosing, coming and going.
Be still, watch,
See for yourself.

Why I Have to Write

Norman Fischer

Buddhist masters have long used poetry to express the inexpressible. Chinese, Japanese, and Tibetan Buddhism all have important poetic traditions, and the connection between Buddhism and poetry has been avidly picked up in the West, beginning with the Beats and continuing to this day. Norman Fischer is a Zen teacher and poet and one of the most elegant essayists in Western Buddhism. Here he contemplates the apparent contradiction between his Zen vocation and his need to write, and concludes that all language is a form of prayer.

Though I know writing is a bad habit for a Zen priest, I can't help it. I seem to be writing all the time. I write poems of several varieties in several voices, journal entries, dharma talks, essays, books, notes, lists, stories, e-mails, blogs. In doing all this, I have no special purpose I can discern or explain. Though I hope it does somebody some good, I am not at all sure. It may even do some harm. More likely, it may just be a waste of time. What am I doing when I write? I am not documenting my life for my friends or posterity, nor am I telling anybody something they don't already know or need to hear from me. Why go on? I am compelled to, delighted to. There seems to be something crucial about working with language, something that wakes me up or brings a quality of density or significance to my life, even though I can't say what that significance is more than that it is a feeling or a texture. Besides, writing is a deep pleasure. And besides that, I have always written, seem to be a writer by temperament and impulse, and what writers do is write; they just can't help themselves.

Maybe I should get over this. Maybe there's an adhesive patch I can put on that will block the neural pathways that lead me down to the arteries of language. But if there were, I wouldn't wear it. Whether writing is good or bad, I affirm it like an athlete affirms her sport, a mother her child, or a believer his religion. I have noticed over the years in my conversations with writers that for a writer, writing is a sort of absolute bottom line. "Are you writing?" If the answer is yes, then no matter what else is going on, your life—and all of life—is basically OK. You are who you are supposed to be, and your existence makes sense. If the answer is no, then you are not doing well, your relationships and basic well-being are in jeopardy, and the rest of the world is dark and problematic.

Where does this need to splash around in language come from? Is it a disease? I'm not sure, but if so, I don't think (William Burroughs notwithstanding) we will find the virus. I suppose the need to write comes from the connection between human consciousness and language-making. Language-making isn't incidental or ornamental to human consciousness; it is its center, its essence. No language, no person. And no language, no concept of life, of death, of sorrow or joy. No relationships, no tools. We are what we tell ourselves we are. Meditation practice brings the mind to a profound quiet that comes very close to the bottom of consciousness, and right there is the wellspring where language bubbles up. So does meditation get us beyond language? Is it true, as the old Zen teachers seem to be saying, that language is our whole human problem, the basic mistake we make, the mechanism of our suffering? Is this why it's such a big no-no to write?

Yes. Language is our big problem. Language ruins us and makes us suffer. Language is certainly my big problem. All my dissatisfactions would instantly disappear if I couldn't identify them or talk about them. But so would I. Without language I'd have no experience, no life in the world. To say that language is the problem is to say that life is the problem: it's true, but what are you going to do about it?

Well, you live. And if you are a writer, you write. But here's the strange part: you write for the writing, you write alone and in silence, and you don't know if it does anyone any good—yet somehow you need a reader. This shouldn't be the case, but it is. Until there is a reader, some reader, any reader, the writing is incomplete. This is not true, for instance, with meditation practice or, say, with working out. You can run or bike or sit watching the breath without anyone ever witnessing it. It makes no difference whether someone witnesses or not. Because nothing comes of your running or sitting; there's nothing to share. But when you write, you produce something that can be shared and somehow must be. You can't write without being read. This doesn't have to do with ambition or desire; it is built into the nature of writing.

I have been thinking about this for a thousand years. In the 1980s I sponsored a symposium in New York called Meditation and Poetry, in which I brought together a number of serious poets who meditated. My idea was to try to discover what these two activities have in common. I remember Jackson MacLow, the great avant-garde poet, saying, "I am chary (I particularly remember his use of this word) about mentioning these two in the same breath. They exist in different worlds. Writing is effective and public; meditation is private." Something like that.

But, one could argue, MacLow's writing was utterly private. He worked with chance operations and cut-up words, so that there was no intention or conventional communication in his work. He was never trying to say or describe anything. Still, he published copiously. Why?

A decade later I was involved in a similar symposium at Stanford. On the panel with me were the poets Leslie Scalapino and Michael McClure, both of whom practice meditation. We were asked by someone in the audience, "Whom do you write for?" and we all answered, in different ways, "No one." I remember that one of the professors in attendance (who, as it happened, was a Zen scholar) took serious issue with this. Writing must always be social, he argued. What we meant was not that we were uninterested in readership—we all publish a fair amount—but that in the *act* of writing we did not consider who the reader is or what he or she is going to make of what we are writing. We write to someone, but that person is essentially Nobody, without a name or social circumstances—we write for God. The Beyond. The Empty Nature of All Phenomena. Buddha Nature. The Mystery. We speak, and however little or much our words communicate, they touch something Out There. And somehow within the mind and within the words, that Out There is already implied. Don't ask me to explain.

Years ago I went to the Wailing Wall in Jerusalem and did what all tourists there do: wrote some words on a scrap of paper that I tucked into a crevice in the wall. When I closed my eyes and touched my head to the warm stone, it came to me: "All language is prayer." This must be so. Who is it we are speaking to when we speak to anyone? To that person, and also past him or her to Out There. If there is language, it means there is the possibility of being heard, being met, being loved. And reaching out to be heard, met, or loved is a holy act. Language is holy.

And so, dear reader, know that at this moment of your reading this text, you are also touching the Mystery, the Nobody, at the center of your language-charged silence. I, the supposed author, about whom you may have formed some impression entirely of your own making, am not now talking to you. At the moment of your reading, amazingly enough, although I seem to be present, I am elsewhere, doing something else. I am unaware of who you are, and I don't know that you are reading these words now. And yet, at this moment, the moment when I am composing these words—a moment long past for you but immediate to me now—I am as close to myself, and to you, as it is humanly possible to be.

The Sutras of Abu Ghraib

Aidan Delgado

There was a lot about Aidan Delgado that set him apart from other GIs in Iraq. The son of a U.S. diplomat, he had lived abroad as a child and spoke some Arabic. And he was a Buddhist. The empathy he felt for the Iraqi people put him at odds with his fellow soldiers, many of whom expressed racism and hostility toward the very people they were supposed to be liberating. These selections from Delgado's memoir trace his difficult journey toward conscientious objection.

April 13, 2003. Assigned to the prison camp again, I settle in as usual, but something is different tonight. I'm different; my mood is darker. The faces of the prisoners shuffle past me into the central holding area, drained of vitality, led by young guards whose faces seem equally grim and lifeless. A bitter taste rises in the back of my throat. It all seems so pedestrian and unheroic, nothing at all like Army commercials or those brilliantly colored war movies. This is just bureaucracy. The world around me seems to have no color at all: gray walls blending seamlessly into gray dust, populated with the ashen figures of prisoners squatting amid razor wire. This is not at all the way it's supposed to be. But what was I expecting? I wrap the radio around my neck and begin a letter to Amy.

I'm writing to you from one of the destroyed and abandoned offices that the military has claimed for its own use. . . . I'm sitting here, terribly bored and suddenly very lonely. Maybe it's the sight of all these prisoners: ragged, dirty, half-starved, with looks of utter bewilderment and confusion on their faces. I watch them being herded into barbed-wire cages, and I can't help but feel terribly sorry for them, no matter who they are or were, no matter how black their hearts have been. Something stirs in me when I see them. They're not being abused or beaten or anything, but I just feel this deep, abiding sorrow for them. They seem so utterly wasted and defeated.

I set my pen down for a moment. My handwriting has become erratic as I scribble the words as fast as I can, trying to match the volume and forcefulness of my thought. The words flow out in a torrent, unplanned:

The other day, I was told, a seventeen-year-old boy came in [to the prison camp] and cried from the moment he was led in till the time they released him. He was a civilian whose parents and entire family were killed in the war, and he had been walking along with his donkey when I guess he wandered into the wrong place and time. He was arrested and taken to our prison camp. He wept so bitterly because he thought he was being taken to a death camp. One of our chaplains, a Christian who spoke no Arabic, sat down with the boy and comforted him, even cried with him . . .

It occurs to me that I'm no longer writing to Amy at all, I'm writing to myself. On the window next to me there are thousands of dead insects crammed into every cavity. Dried-out husks of moths and beetles litter the windowsill and the floor, and ants cart these forms away to cannibalize them. Just over my head, tilting lazily under the ceiling fan, is a strip of putrid yellow paper coated in glue, on which a dozen insects are held fast in varying degrees of slow death. Some still struggle, and their feeble attempts to free themselves make the flypaper ripple like a spider's web. I fixate on their tiny, delicate legs, the armored shells twinkling like shards of reflective glass. The moths look as soft as feathers, covered in pale down, stuck fast to the brittle yellow paper. They fight impossibly hard, ripping their bodies to pieces and tearing holes in their soft paper wings to be free. They want so badly to live.

> I'm too soft for this business, the sight of defeated enemies depresses me and fills me with pity and loathing. . . . Even in this room, there's a strip of flypaper hanging from a window and on it a moth is helplessly stuck, its antennae waving feebly. When I look at it, I want to cry. A trapped and dying insect moves me almost to tears and here I am in this great and victorious war. I'm supposed to be a soldier, some kind of tough guy, and here I am writing about a poor moth. I hate it. I hate seeing any living thing suffer. I can't stand it, it's like needles in me, and the worst thing of all is to be surrounded by pain and unable to do anything. I feel wretched and hypocritical. I can honestly say that I am the worst Buddhist in the world . . .

> Here, writing atop one of the empty crates in a dusty corner of the old sports stadium, I am hopeless. I despair. The Way seems so impossibly distant, an unreachable dream. Reading the sutras makes me feel almost physically ill, so far am I from the ideal. I feel like there is nothing Buddhist about me, except that word, hovering over me like a badge of hypocrisy. Compassion . . . Loving-kindness . . . Although I call myself a Buddhist, I know that I am no follower of the Way, soldier and jailer that I am. How did I ever come to be here? A Buddhist—can I even call myself that? I have come so far from what I wanted to be.

> My [Buddhist] practice is weak and irregular, my will is deficient and lazy, and I have gotten myself into a situation

where, far from preventing suffering, I am actually adding to it. I had not realized how important to my identity it was to think of myself as a Buddhist, and now I feel I cannot honestly claim that. I am a dissolute and irreligious man. I know what I want to do and be, but I can't muster my strength enough to do it. I am irrelevant as a human being and as a Buddhist. I can't even master my body enough to sit upright and meditate for a few minutes. Without the truth that Buddhism represents for me, my entire life is meaningless and sinful, and my every pretense at Buddhism that much more laughable and deceptive. I can't even bear to read a word out of the Buddhist bible [Dwight Goddard's *A Buddhist Bible*, originally published in 1932] I brought because it only drives home to me how far I am from sincere, how Buddhism is still so intellectual for me and not natural or spiritual. What a waste my life has been. . . . I can't see how my frail, undisciplined self will ever advance along that path into the kind of man I want to be. I can keep the Precepts, but the actions have no value without the mind-set that goes with them.

This letter has gone on too long already. What will she think when she reads it? It will be weeks before my next letter arrives, and she'll be worried about me. I shake out my hand, which is burning from the fatigue of nonstop writing, and draw in a long, slow breath. Breathe in, breathe out. You're okay, you're in control. I pick up the pen again and close the letter with words of affection and longing.

The act of writing the letter leaves me drained. I know what I believe. What am I going to *do* about it? In the days to come I will spend countless hours sitting on my bed, working underneath trucks, or staring out into the sunset thinking about this question. I will agonize over it and burn for it, night after night. I will speak with my sergeants, my friends, and my superiors about it; it will not go away. In Zen, the koan is a puzzle, a paradox; "like a ball of red-hot iron in your throat," you can neither swallow it nor disgorge it. My question is like that, a koan: I live with it. I cannot push it out of my mind. *What are you going to do about it?* It dangles like the sword of Damocles over every night I spend in Iraq, every page I thumb through in my Buddhist texts. This question, and my answer to it, will become the defining spirit of my deployment, of my Iraq war . . . and like all great questions, it begins with something small, as tiny and inconsequential as a strip of flypaper.

My longest night at the prison camp ends, and I believe it is my last. By fate, I'm never reassigned there again. The other mechanics will soon arrive from Camp Arifjan, and I will be needed full-time as a mechanic. I bid farewell to the prison camp without regret. The next morning I feel better, as mornings always allow me to do. The world seems brighter and more manageable, with Sergeant Toro groaning his way out of bed as Stevens mixes and pours his predawn coffee. I breathe in, and the world seems more manageable. I breathe out, and I can get out of bed and begin the day. Last night's crisis recedes in my brain as I set my two bare feet down on the tile. As always, at the end of each crisis, I find some reservoir of balance that I didn't know I had, a base of calm that I always return to.

I am still new to the Way, but this sensibility has been with me all my life, it seems.

Spring 2003. I'm in the back of a Humvee, my SAW unloaded across my lap, my translation books tucked into my vest pockets. More often than not, I hold the pocket-size Arabic-English dictionary in my hand close to my smudged glasses so I can read through the glare. I'm reviewing the vocabulary I'll need for this mission, specific words that might come up: *air conditioner, medic, roast chicken, resistance fighter, dry cleaning,* and most importantly, *ice,* although I already know the word for that. I've reviewed the same words before every mission, I should know them by now, but each time we go out I'm fraught with nerves. When the pinch comes, every member of the team expects fluency and I have to try to fake it. These missions aren't exactly "combat operations"; once the command learns that most of the locals are friendly to the Coalition, our forays revolve around purchasing luxuries for the company: food, fans, and ice, always ice. The first couple of times out, I manage to hem and haw my way through a few simple Arabic exchanges with Iraqis, and the company is dazzled. I develop a reputation for being very useful on an "ice run," and thereafter I am included in just about every trip.

Nasiriyah is what you would expect: buildings caked with soot and sand, open sewers and piles of garbage, the occasional donkey cart blending in among the traffic of old junker cars from the late 1980s. Nature pokes through here and there: stands of tall water rushes beside a slow-moving stream, date palms with pictures of local clerics nailed to them, undeveloped lots of open sand. Dogs are everywhere. It's not very different from Cairo, not very different from the dozens of third-world cities I have lived in and visited. Wherever you go outside of the United States, poverty and want look the same. Combining the memories of my childhood and adulthood, I could piece together patches of urban sprawl from Bangkok to Nasiriyah to Dakar, and nothing would change except pale skin to brown to black, Thai to Arabic to French. One long slum across two continents. The only thing that stands out about Nasiriyah is that every so often along the road you see a pile of rubble where a building once stood, and you *know* what destroyed it. The city is dotted with these ruins. Sometimes whole streets have been leveled; in other neighborhoods, individual buildings have been picked out and flattened with almost surgical precision. Almost. Most of the buildings show pockmarks of bullets or pieces of wall torn away by the bigger, high-velocity rounds. Ours or theirs? You really can't tell.

In spite of the residue of war, the city of Nasiriyah seems almost to have returned to life. People are out on the street, the bazaars are crowded, there's fresh fruit in the stalls, and vehicles zip up and down narrow lanes, blaring their horns in lieu of signaling or stopping. White flags still flutter on every car antenna and rooftop, but the people of Nasiriyah seem to be carrying on with their lives. Iraqi men working in shops look up at us and wave, or regard us sternly until our convoy passes by them. Hordes of children crowd the sides of the street as we pass and every time that we stop, calling out in chorus, "Mister, mister, give me water. Give me food. Give me money." We hear this "Mister, mister" so often, some of the MPs start referring to Iraqi children as "mistah-mistahs." We have our guns up, the brims of our helmets down, looking for trouble, but we never find any. Once or twice far in the distance, we hear a pistol shot and everyone goes ramrod stiff, but nothing ever befalls us. This isn't really enemy territory; the Coalition units passing through left only a token presence, and it seems to me that the war has mostly passed Nasiriyah by.

One day I'm sleepwalking though a trip to Nasiriyah: chicken, sodas, ice, the same old deal. We're stopped at a large roundabout near the city center, pulled off to the side of the road while I ask for directions. There's a crowd, as usual; people curious to see all the guns and helmets and armor up close. Nothing to worry about, just spectators. But there's something unusual about today, something ominous. The usual conversation has died down, and when people speak, it's in short, clipped phrases. Traffic and crowd noises reverberate off the densely packed buildings, rising to a dull roar. The MPs seem on edge, continually scanning the rooftops and blind alleys, uncharacteristically vigilant. There's a tension in the air that hasn't been there before; a buzzing in the crowd and the stiff, contorted movements of the soldiers. The MPs are scowling, cross, irritable. It's hot as hell today, and the sun is bearing down directly overhead. The mission's taking longer than expected. Tempers are bound to flare.

"Get the fuck away from me, you fucking hajjis!"

I know the voice—a good guy, a friend of mine, Nick Sollugob. We met back at the unit because we enlisted together. Funny guy. I turn and see the barrel of his rifle pointing at the face of an Iraqi.

"I swear to God, one of these days I'm going to shoot one of you fuckers."

Something seizes up inside me. I've heard things before, little flashes of aggression toward the Iraqis, but this is the first time it's boiled over. I'm hot and I'm angry. Why does he have to act this way? The Iraqis weren't doing anything. My own weapon is slung across my back. I walk up and get in his face. I raise my voice. "Chill out, man. They weren't doing anything. Why do you have to be so god-damn aggressive to them all the time?"

It was a mistake to confront him like this, in front of everyone. His face is flushed. He shoves me back a step.

"Why you always gotta be such a bitch, Delgado?"

"Fuck you, you don't have to threaten them. You don't have to put your gun in their faces," I say as we inch closer together.

"All right, all right. Break it up you two. Get back in the convoy, we're rolling."

A sergeant interposes himself between us. Sollugob turns away in disgust. As I climb back into the Humvee, I look around at the other MPs in the convoy and see suspicion and disdain on their faces. *They agree with him.* They think I'm a coward or a sympa-thizer. Five minutes ago I looked around and saw friends; now I see strangers. In an instant, a huge chasm opens between the lower-enlisted MPs and myself.

I never feel comfortable on missions in town again, unless I'm working directly under one of the older sergeants. Where was all this sentiment before? I heard the idle talk, the posturing, the usual stereotyping of Arabs, Muslims, the "bad guys," but I never thought it was this personal. Back in Florida when I told people I spoke Ara-bic, they had gotten these wary looks on their faces, as if I were someone not to be trusted. I didn't pay much attention then. Now I remember their sideways glances, the sudden distance. After the in-cident with Sollugob, it all comes back into focus. Rumors filter back to me that people don't want to go on missions with me anymore; they don't trust me because I took a stand against one of our guys, I stood up for "them." They whisper that I'm a Muslim, that they should keep an eye on me. The revelation of these sentiments is intensely painful to me.

The Army's just like high school in a lot of ways, everyone wants to be popular. And in one afternoon, I'm out of the clubhouse.

After that trip to Nasiriyah, I begin noticing all sorts of things I had overlooked before: a whispered remark, a scowl, a casual comment about "those people." Seemingly random words and actions are coming together into a pattern; the character of the company is changing. Maybe the stress of the deployment and the growing homesickness is wearing everyone down. We're all sick of this desert, sick of the barracks, sick of being here. An ugly kind of mood is arising, or perhaps it was there all along and just bubbled to the surface now. Prejudice. You can dance around it all you like: talk about war stress, call it "dehumanization of the enemy," quote dozens of books on the history of warfare, but that doesn't change the simple truth of it—hatred. I see it in stark relief now, an undercurrent of anti-Arab and anti-Muslim sentiment.

I'm no paragon. My mind is as full of violence and prejudice as everyone else's, yet because of my background overseas, anti-Arab sentiment doesn't happen to be one of my problems. Yet ever since basic training, it's been a steady diet of hatred for "the enemy." At Fort Knox, drill sergeants would often try to motivate us by reminding us of the attack on the World Trade Center and, during the war in Afghanistan, how we might someday get a chance to go over there and "kill us some towelheads." A few of our marching and running cadences had been "updated" to mention the new enemy of the United States in less than enlightened terms. It's a little shocking at first to have three hundred people chanting racist tunes, but gradually it fades into the background and you just do it because that's what everyone else is doing. You start participating automatically, singing along, forgetting what you're actually saying. I've certainly done it, and I can say with confidence that probably every soldier since September 11 has done the same in one form or another. It's part of the training.

In our unit, the bigotry seems even more pronounced. Just before we left Fort Stewart for the Middle East, our commander had given us a little "pep talk." He warned us that there would be news-papers and TV cameras at the department site, so we should watch what we say.

"Now, there's going to be media over there, so I don't want you to go telling them how you're going to go over there and kill some ragheads and burn some turbans."

He laughed knowingly, and half the unit laughed along with him. It had shocked me when the commander said those words, only because he admitted so openly what everyone already thought: Mus-lims were the enemy, Arabs were the enemy, terrorists and suicide bombers all. I had stood there, stunned by the casual bigotry. Now in the middle of Iraq, looking around at my unit, I wonder how I could have been so dense for so long.

Here in Iraq, it's gone way beyond the occasional "raghead" and "terrorist" slur. In reference to Iraqis, every other word is "hajji," the current anti-Arab, anti-Muslim epithet of choice. In Arabic, a *hajji* is one who has gone on the Hajj, the pilgrimage to Mecca that is one of the five pillars of Islam. It is often used as a mild honorific, espe-cially to describe an older man. In Army usage, it means "gook" or "Charlie" or "nigger." Within a few months, I don't hear the word *Iraqi* anymore, it's always *hajji*. The word becomes so deeply embed-ded in the Army dialect that it becomes the norm, and the words *Iraqi* and *local* and *host-country national* sound stilted and awkward. Once I start listening for it, I hear it everywhere, even in casual con-versations that don't have any hostile overtones. It takes the ultimate form of subtle racism, becoming so ubiquitous that people forget it's a slur.

"Oh, it's just what we call them. They call each other that. I didn't think it meant anything racist." Really? They call *each other* that? It's a lame attempt at justification.

It's odd to find myself in this position, feeling betrayed and iso-lated by my company's growing hypernationalism. When I lived in Egypt, I went out of my way to assert my Americanness and by ex-tension America's superiority, because when you live overseas, your Americanness becomes magnified in your mind. America becomes the ideal, the place where all good things are. Now that I'm in the U.S. Army, listening to the trash talk of the 320th, I feel more and more like a foreigner. By the time I came to America, I had lived for eighteen years in other countries: seven years in Thailand, four years in Senegal, and the last seven years in Egypt. When members of my company told me that Muslim and Islam were two different religions or that Osama bin Laden was the "head" of Islam, I saw that I was dealing with an ignorance that was deep and fundamental. I *knew* better. Most of the guys in the company didn't; they'd never had the chance to learn. For one of the first times in my life, I'm grateful for my unusual childhood, glad to have had all those years overseas. I'm glad I can see what's really happening here.

Summer 2003. The growing hatred in my unit has begun to weigh on me more and more, intruding into my waking thoughts. I can no longer relax in my off-hours. My sleep is growing increasingly brief and fitful. One morning Shoe asks what I was yelling about, and I look at him questioningly. He says I was shouting something in my sleep; woke the whole squad up. He says I do it a lot. Sergeant Wallace reminds me that I used to do the same thing back at Fort Stewart.

Even awake, I find myself consumed with self-doubt, self-loathing, about being where I am. I've started to talk to Sergeant Toro about it, either when we're lifting weights or when we're relaxing in our room. Like a good officer, Sergeant Toro tells me to relax and be patient. He tells me I'm still just adjusting to Army life, that my feelings will change. The trouble is that it's been two years since I enlisted, and my feelings haven't changed. I feel intensely hypocritical, believing in compassion, meditation, and nonviolence while simultaneously carrying a machine gun and serving in an occupation force. The conflict seems irreconcilable. Every day that I stay in the military I feel more a traitor to my beliefs. The Army that I imagined, the mythological Army that captured my imagination as a boy, has proven illusory. I've come to see the Army in its worst form, a distortion of itself: violence, threats, dogma, and hatred. I see the way the soldiers bully each other for dominance and then watch as those who are bullied turn and dominate the Iraqis. I feel my friends and comrades pulling apart from me, diverging from the ideals I believe in. They have changed; something in them has gone black. I have changed too; the man I am now and the boy I was in Sarasota have grown vastly apart. Between me and the other privates, those who hate "ragheads" and long to kill the enemy, there is an unfathomable gulf. Seeing the prisoners, seeing the Iraqi civilians, fills me with profound sadness and loss. I have no bloodlust in me. I do not wish to fight.

I feel literal pain whenever I open one of my books and read the sutras, pain at my hypocrisy and inadequacy. Although Buddhism doesn't teach sin as a concept, I feel sinful all the time. I dread the future as if a terrible judgment were hanging over my head, retribution for all my wrongdoing. Everything about this place seems wrong: what we're doing to the Iraqis, the destruction, the meaningless loss of life. It overwhelms my senses. I coast through my daily tasks as if on autopilot. On missions, I look out at the crowds of desperate people and feel impotent to help them in any way. In the motor pool, I work with dull bitterness, knowing that all my labor accomplishes nothing but to perpetuate the cycle.

One of the few books I packed in my military kit back in Sarasota was a ragged, Scotch-taped paperback of the *Bhaghavad Gita*, a gift from Amy and her parents. I have read it many times, and I find myself reading it again in these dark days, fascinated by its meaning. The *Bhaghavad Gita* is a Hindu religious text—its title roughly translated as *The Song of God*—that forms one section of the much larger epic poem called the *Mahabharata*, which tells the story of the Bharata dynasty's interactions with the Hindu gods. The *Bhaghavad Gita* describes the commencement of a huge battle between two rival factions of a family and tells the story of its protagonist, Arjuna, and his discussion with the god Krishna in human form as his charioteer. The book begins with Arjuna looking out over the ranks of his army and the enemy army and recognizing many familiar faces: friends, relatives, and teachers. Upon seeing these comrades, Arjuna is overcome with grief at the prospect of fighting and killing people he loves and respects. In his despair, he drops his bow and arrows and refuses to fight. The opening passages have always thrilled me with their passion and eloquence. Now, in the depths of a war I do not wish to fight, their stanzas take on a new meaning. I read of Arjuna's despair and the words come alive to me, thousands of years after they were written, the words of a distant soldier who had lost his will to fight.

> Krishna, Krishna!
> Now as I look on,
> These, my kinsmen,
> arrayed for battle,
> My limbs are weakening,
> My mouth is parching,
> My body trembles,
> My hair seems upright,
> My skin seems burning,
> The bow Gandiva
> Slips from my hand,
> My brain is whirling
> Round and round,
> I can see no longer:
> Krishna, I see such
> Omens of evil!

Reading these words in Iraq, my own hair seems to stand on end.

> Though they should slay me
> How could I harm them?
> I cannot wish it:
> Never, never,
> Not though it won me

The throne of three worlds;
How much the less for
Earthly lordship!
. . .
Evil they may be,
Worst of the wicked,
Yet if we kill them
Our sin is greater.
How could we dare spill
The blood that unites us?
. . .
What is this crime
I am planning, O Krishna?
Murder most hateful,
Murder of my brothers!
Am I indeed
So greedy for greatness?
Rather than this
Let the evil children
Of Dhritarashtra
Come with their weapons
Against me in battle;
I shall not struggle,
I shall not strike them.
Now let them kill me,
That will be better.

Having spoken thus, Arjuna threw aside his arrows and his
bow in the midst of the battlefield. He sat down on the seat
of the chariot, and his heart was overcome with sorrow.

The plain truth is that I have no desire to fight anyone, even
those I am supposed to call my enemies. I'm not even sure they are
my enemies, those old men and teenagers trussed up in the prison

yard. How could I ever want to kill them? Were they not conscripted to fight us? Both of us, men on both sides, have been set against each other as pawns. They had no more choice in the matter than I. "Ain't no point in looking pale, go to war or go to jail" is the refrain from an Army marching cadence. We and the Iraqis have no quarrel, and yet no choice but to fight and die. I feel despair at this intractable conflict, sensing at last that we're all trapped in something beyond our control. My heart is overcome with sorrow.

One day I dig into the depths of my B-bag and pull out a battered, cloth-covered binder, something a buddy of mine sent me a long time ago, when I was deployed to Fort Stewart. I had asked him for it in a moment of doubt and introspection but had put it out of my mind in all the chaos of deployment, tucking it away in case I needed it later. Inside the binder is a plain, brown, mailing envelope. I undo the clasp and a packet of papers spills out. At the top of one of the papers, in large, bold letters, are the words "Army Regulation 600-43. Personnel-General. Conscientious Objection." I unclip the packet, set it beside me on the bunk, and begin to read.

Aidan Delgado served his full one-year deployment in Iraq before he was granted conscientious objector status. He was honorably discharged from the U.S. Army in 2004 and is now an active member of Iraq Veterans Against the War and the Buddhist Peace Fellowship.

Hitting the Streets

Lin Jensen

*Whether it's a natural extension of Buddhist values or just a sixties
generation thing, the vast majority of Western Buddhists are politically
liberal. Buddhism is renowned as a religion of peace, so it is not surprising
that many Western Buddhists actively oppose the war in Iraq. Writer and
Zen teacher Lin Jensen felt the best way to work for peace was to sit down
on a city sidewalk every day and be peace.*

More than twenty-five hundred years ago in ancient China, Lao-
tzu wrote a little book of eighty-one verses called *Tao Te Ching* or, in
English, *The Book of the Way*. Without exception, every verse bears
witness to the wisdom of "doing nondoing," what the Chinese call
wei wu wei. Wei wu wei is not a kind, passive inaction, but rather a
movement in concert with circumstance. "Nondoing" ultimately
means trusting the wisdom of the universe to show the way rather
than imposing one's arbitrary will upon it. As Lao-tzu puts it, "The
Tao never does anything, yet through it all things are done."

And yet I've tried to do many things to bring about peace since
America went to war against Iraq. I've written my representatives repeatedly, submitted all the letters to the editor I could get printed,
written whatever articles on peace I could persuade someone to
publish, joined the peace rallies and marches, and given all the talks
on nonviolence I could find an audience for.

And then, in the fall of 2004, with the war in Iraq entering its second year, I began sitting daily peace vigils on the streets of Chico, California, in protest. Wanting to do *something* for peace, I discovered I first had to learn how to do *nothing* for peace—which is harder to learn than it might seem. But I increasingly felt it was essential to give bodily witness to the practice of nonviolence. Peace, as it turned out, was less a matter of something you *do* than one of something you *are*—and I soon learned that the ends I sought required of me more than simply sitting protest on the sidewalks of my hometown.

I learned much about myself that hadn't been so apparent before, things worth noticing if I ever hoped to embody in my own person the sympathetic kindness I'd come to the streets to encourage in the world. For one thing, I underestimated the extent of my own frustration, the urgency I felt over the continuing world violence—and often saw anger well up in me. I would sit an hour's meditation on a downtown street corner in an outward attitude of calm and peacefulness and feel like a perfect hypocrite because I felt so little peace within. What I wanted for others, I first had to find in myself. It was as if I had to have it already in hand in order to even begin to look for it. Like mercy or kindness, peace was a consequence of its own presence and not something of my willful devising.

I took to the streets because I couldn't do otherwise. Almost every day now for nearly two years I've bicycled from the "Avenues" neighborhood where I live and crossed Chico Creek into the downtown area where I pick out a patch of sidewalk on Main or Broadway streets. And there I put down my meditation mat and cushion, and sit an hour's peace vigil. I do this as a public witness for nonviolence in a time of war.

Our world is extraordinarily violent as all of you know, and much of the violence emanates from our own nation. I'm a Zen Buddhist, and I take to heart the Buddhist teaching of noninjury, though that teaching's not something Buddhists have a monopoly on. The wish to do no harm is a human thing. I'm human and I don't want to harm other humans, though I'm often told that doing so is crucial to my "security." I don't want to purchase security at the cost of forfeiting someone else's.

This current war with Iraq began with a display of "shock and awe" that the United States Air Force treated us to in the initial bombings of Baghdad. I have since learned a great deal about the victims of those bombings—the men, women, and children huddled together in their doomed houses, clasping their hands over their ears to shut out the terrifying blast of the explosions, scurrying about in the darkened streets, calling out to neighbors who will never again answer. These images festered in my mind like splintered glass until I couldn't talk about it without my voice rising shrill and taut with anxious urgency.

There are times in my life when I've felt a call that demands an answer. This was one of those times. And so in the absence of knowing what else to do, I began sitting peace vigils, though I wasn't convinced that doing so would make any difference at all.

When I first trained in Soto Zen, Reverend Master Jiyu-Kennett set all of us to facing a wall. We did hours of zazen with our noses pushed up against the plaster. The reverend master taught that there's a person, a mind present in all of us that isn't caught up in the particulars of this exact moment in history. It was a mind, she said, not set to the measure of a clock or calendar, a mind that would give us rest when the clock-and-calendar mind was troubled. Zazen, we were taught, was the place to look for this. And so that's what I did.

The longer I sat facing the zendo wall, the more I realized that the wood and plaster wall had its counterpart in a wall I'd built within my mind. I thought if I could just get beyond the mind-wall, I might find the person Reverend Master had set me to look for. And so I scraped and chipped away at the obstruction for weeks and months, and the deeper I dug, the more I saw that the mind-wall was merely a construct of my own opinions and judgments, my fears and aversions. It was stuffed with all sorts of treasures I'd once wanted and feared to lose but that now appeared as mere impediments, useless to any purpose at hand.

I'm a little embarrassed to admit that at times I literally called out to whoever was hidden from me beyond all this junk I'd stacked up in the way. It was like calling myself out of hiding. And then one day the wall simply fell apart, and there, reflected in my own eyes and face, I saw the person who loved me and had been waiting for me since before I was born.

And so in October 2004, with the war still raging in Iraq, I remembered how walls fall away. I also remembered a story of the Buddha sitting meditation at the border of two kingdoms, putting himself in the path of an advancing army in hopes of preventing the hostilities. One version of the story has it that the generals of the invading army were moved to pity and remorse by the sight of the Buddha's silent witness and so turned the army around and went back home.

I don't know of any other nation that exports more death than my own, and so I thought that anywhere within the continental boundaries of the United States that I might happen to sit myself down in protest would put me at the very border where violence crosses over.

On Saturday, October 16, 2004, I joined the weekly peace vigil that gathers on the corner of Third and Main streets in the northern Sacramento Valley town of Chico, California. I entered that day into a Chico tradition that can trace its roots back to the early 1960s when the U.S. military built Titan missiles with nuclear warheads to be stored in underground bunkers at a base northeast of town. In solitary protest, Chico resident Wilhelmina Taggart began weekly visits to the base to pray. Eventually the missiles were removed, but by then Wilhelmina had been joined by Florence McLane and Helen Kinnee, and the three of them began holding a weekly peace vigil in downtown Chico. Forty-six years later, the vigil Wilhelmina began still takes place, every Saturday from 12:30 to 1:30, winter or summer, wet or dry.

I made a sign that could be propped up next to me as I sat in meditation rather than held high. It was designed in several colors and featured a peace symbol incorporating the words *Peace Vigil,*

Nonviolence, Justice, and *Mercy,* and identifying me as a member of the Buddhist Peace Fellowship. The following Saturday, I went down to Third and Main where a couple dozen others stood on the four corners of the intersection, waving banners and holding aloft messages of protest painted on squares of poster board. I picked a spot on the sidewalk near the curbside where I could prop my new sign against a bike rack with the message facing the oncoming traffic. Then I sat down on my cushion, crossed my legs, formed the "cosmic mudra" with my hands, the mudra of meditation, and began my first formal hour of sidewalk-sitting. I don't know that my presence there changed much of anything, but I felt the urgency within me subside a little and an unexpected peace settled over me. The next day, on Sunday, there was no Chico peace vigil scheduled. But there was my peace sign resting against the closet wall with my cushion and mat stored on the shelf above. I looked at them, and I thought, "Why not? Someone has to do it. It might as well be me." And thus my Saturday peace vigil expanded to a daily affair. If I bicycled to S&S Produce for a head of lettuce or to the Chico Natural Foods co-op for fair-trade coffee or to the bank to make a deposit, I took my peace gear along and sat an hour's vigil while I was there.

To sit on a public sidewalk is an act so exposed to the eyes of others that there's no place to hide. Everyone can see what anguish or fear, what strength or weakness, what tenderness or sadness, I've brought to the street. It's not a circumstance where hypocrisy or pretense is easily disguised. For me, it's a time to call upon the one beyond the walls I keep erecting, the one who's not so angry and who responds to human error and brutality with forgiveness and compassion. After all, if I can't make my own peace, how can I ask it of others?

I love my townspeople, and I love you, my countrymen and fellow humans. I will sit right here on the pavement and offer you the visible presence of my dismay and grief over the brutality our nation is engaged in. I offer my rejection of our country's claim that it is acting on our behalf, yours and mine. And so I've brought my protest to the very place where you come to shop or get a cup of coffee. You may acknowledge me or ignore me as you see fit, but I am here, nevertheless, to remind us both, you and me, that something has gone drastically wrong in our nation, and I'll be back tomorrow to remind us again.

Gratitude

Joanna Macy

If anything can save this world, it is something we might call ecospiritual-ity. Only when we approach our lives on this planet from a spiritual per-spective will we find the tools to make the profound personal and social changes that the environmental crisis demands. Only then will we see ourselves and the natural world as sacred and act accordingly. If there is a founder of ecospirituality, it might be Joanna Macy, who contributed this new chapter to a revised edition of her classic World as Lover, World as Self.

> Just to live is holy,
> To be is a blessing.
> —RABBI ABRAHAM HESCHEL

We have received an inestimable gift. To be alive in this beautiful, self-organizing universe—to participate in the dance of life with senses to perceive it, lungs that breathe it, organs that draw nourish-ment from it—is a wonder beyond words. And it is, moreover, an ex-traordinary privilege to be accorded a human life, with self-reflexive consciousness that brings awareness of our own actions and the ability to make choices. It lets us choose to take part in the healing of our world.

WHERE WE START

Gratitude for the gift of life is the primary wellspring of all religions, the hallmark of the mystic, the source of all true art. Yet we so easily take this gift for granted. That is why so many spiritual traditions begin with thanksgiving, to remind us that for all our woes and worries, our existence itself is an unearned benefaction that we could never of ourselves create.

In the Tibetan Buddhist path we are asked to pause before any period of meditative practice and precede it with reflection on the preciousness of a human life. This is not because we as humans are superior to other beings, but because we can "change the karma." In other words, graced with self-reflexive consciousness, we are endowed with the capacity for choice—to take stock of what we are doing and change directions. We may have endured for eons of lifetimes as other life-forms, under the heavy hand of fate and the blind play of instinct, but now at last we are granted the ability to consider and judge and make decisions. Weaving our ever-complexifying neural circuits into the miracle of self-awareness, life yearned through us for the ability to know and act and speak on behalf of the larger whole. Now the time has come when by our own choice we can consciously enter the dance.

In Buddhist practice, that first reflection is followed by a second, on the brevity of this precious human life: "Death is certain; the time of death is uncertain." That reflection awakens in us the precious gift of the present moment—to seize this chance to be alive right now on Planet Earth.

EVEN IN THE DARK

That our world is in crisis—to the point where survival of conscious life on Earth is in question—in no way diminishes the value of this gift; on the contrary. To us is granted the privilege of being on hand to take part, if we choose, in the Great Turning to a just and sustainable society. We can let life work through us, enlisting all our strength, wisdom, and courage, so that life itself can continue.

There is so much to be done, and the time is so short. We can proceed, of course, out of grim and angry desperation. But the tasks proceed more easily and productively with a measure of thankfulness for life; it links us to our deeper powers and lets us rest in them. Many of us are braced, psychically and physically, against the signals of distress that continually barrage us in the news, on our streets, in our environment. As if to reduce their impact on us, we contract like a turtle into its shell. But we can choose to turn to the breath, the body, the senses—for they help us to relax and open to wider currents of knowing and feeling.

The great open secret of gratitude is that it is not dependent on external circumstances. It's like a setting or channel that we can switch to at any moment, no matter what's going on around us. It helps us connect to our basic right to be here, like the breath does. It's a stance of the soul. In systems theory, each part contains the whole. Gratitude is the kernel that can flower into everything we need to know.

Thankfulness loosens the grip of the industrial growth society by contradicting its predominant message that we are insufficient and inadequate. The forces of late capitalism continually tell us that we need more—more stuff, more money, more approval, more comfort, more entertainment. The dissatisfaction it breeds is profound. It infects people with a compulsion to acquire that delivers them into the cruel, humiliating bondage of debt. So gratitude is liberating. It is subversive. It helps us realize that we are sufficient, and that realization frees us. Elders of indigenous cultures have retained this knowledge, and we can learn from their practices.

LEARNING FROM THE ONONDAGA

Elders of the six-nation confederacy of the Haudenosaunee, also known as the Iroquois, have passed down through the ages the teachings of the Great Peacemaker. A thousand years ago, they had been warring tribes, caught in brutal cycles of attack, revenge, and retaliation, when he came across Lake Ontario in a stone canoe. Gradually his words and actions won them over, and they accepted the Great Law of Peace. They buried their weapons under the Peace Tree by Lake Onondaga, and formed councils for making wise choices together and for self-governance. In the Haudenosaunee, historians recognize the oldest known participatory democracy and point to the inspiration it provided to Benjamin Franklin, James Madison, and others in crafting the constitution of the United States. That did not impede American settlers and soldiers from taking by force most of the Haudenosaunees' land and decimating their populations.

Eventually accorded "sovereign" status, the Haudenosaunee nations—all except for the Onondaga—proceeded in recent decades to sue state and federal governments for their ancestral lands, winning settlements in cash and license for casinos. All waited and wondered what legal action would be brought by the Onondaga Nation, whose name means "keepers of the central fire" and whose ancestral land, vastly larger than the bit they now control, extends in a wide swath from Pennsylvania to Canada. But the Onondaga elders and clan mothers continued to deliberate year after year, seeking consensus on this issue that would shape the fate of their people for generations to come. Finally, in the spring of 2005, they made their legal move. In their land rights action, unlike that of any other indigenous group in America, they did not demand the return of any ancestral land or monetary compensation for it. They asked for one thing only: that it be cleaned up and restored to health for the sake of all who presently live on it and for the sake of their children and children's children.

To state and federal power-holders, this was asking a lot. The land is heavily contaminated by industrial development, including big chemical processing plants and a number of neglected "Superfund" sites. Onondaga Lake, on whose shores stood the sacred Peace Tree, is considered to be more polluted with heavy metals than any in the country. The governor of New York urged the court to dismiss the Onondaga claim as invalid and too late.

On a bleak November afternoon, when the suit was still in process, I visited the Onondaga Nation—a big name for this scrap of land that looks like a postage stamp on maps of central New York. I had come because I was moved by the integrity and vision of their land rights action, and now I saw how few material resources they possess to pursue it. In the community center, native counselors described outreach programs for mental health and self-esteem, bringing young people together from all the Haudenosaunee. To help with the expenses, other tribes had chipped in, but few contributions had been received from the richer ones.

They were eager for me to see the recently built school where young Onondagans who choose not to go off the Nation to U.S.-run schools can receive an education. A teacher named Freida, who was serving for a while as a clan mother, had waited after hours to show me around. The central atrium she led me into was hung about with shields of a dozen clans—turtle clan, bear clan, wolf—and on the floor illumined by the skylight was a large green turtle, beautifully wrought of inlaid wood. "Here is where we gather the students for our daily morning assembly," Freida explained. "We begin, of course, with the thanksgiving. Not the real, traditional form of it, because that takes hours. We do it very short, just twenty minutes." Turning to gaze at her face, I sank down on a bench. She heard my silent request and sat down too. Raising her right hand in a circling gesture that spiraled downward as the fingers closed, she began. "Let us gather our minds as one mind and give thanks to our eldest brother the Sun, who rises each day to bring light so we can see each others' faces and warmth for the seeds to grow . . . "On and on she continued, greeting and thanking the life-giving presences that bless and nourish us all. With each one—moon, waters, trees—that lovely gesture was repeated. "We gather our minds as one mind . . ."

My eyes stayed riveted on her. What I was receiving through her words and gesture felt like an intravenous injection right into my bloodstream. This, I knew, can teach us how to survive, when all possessions and comforts have been lost. When our honored place in the world is taken from us, a practice like this can hold us together in dignity and clear mind.

What Freida gave me is a staple of Haudenosaunee culture. Similar words, in an equally short form, have been written down by the Mohawks, so the rest of us can have it too.

THE MOHAWK THANKSGIVING PRAYER

The People

Today we have gathered and we see that the cycles of life continue. We have been given the duty to live in balance and harmony with each other and all living things. So now, we give greetings and thanks to each other as people. Now our minds are one.

The Earth Mother

We are all thankful to our Mother, the Earth, for she gives us all that we need for life. She supports our feet as we walk about upon her. It gives us joy that she continues to care for us as she has from the beginning of time. To our Mother, we send greetings and thanks. Now our minds are one.

The Waters

We give thanks to all the waters of the world for quenching our thirst and providing us with strength. Water is life. We know its power in many forms—waterfalls and rain, mists and streams, rivers and oceans. We send greetings and thanks to the spirit of Water. Now our minds are one.

The Fish

We turn our minds to all the Fish life in the water. They were instructed to cleanse and purify the water. They also give themselves to us as food. We are grateful that we can still find pure water. So we turn now to the Fish and send our greetings and thanks. Now our minds are one.

The Plants

Now we turn toward the vast fields of Plant life. As far as the eye can see, the Plants grow, working many wonders. They sustain many life-forms. With our minds gathered together, we give thanks and look forward to seeing Plant life for many generations to come. Now our minds are one.

The Food Plants

With one mind, we turn to honor and thank all the Food Plants we harvest from the garden. Since the beginning of time, the grains, vegetables, beans, and berries have helped the people survive. Many other living things draw strength from them too. We gather all the Food Plants together as one and send them a greeting of thanks. Now our minds are one.

The Medicine Herbs

Now we turn to all the Medicine Herbs of the world. From the beginning they were instructed to take away sickness. They are always waiting and ready to heal us. We are happy there are still among us those special few who remember how to use these plants for healing. We send greetings and thanks to the Medicines and to the keepers of the Medicines. Now our minds are one.

The Animals

We gather our minds together to send greetings and thanks to all the Animal life in the world. They have many things to teach us as people. We are honored when they give up their lives so we may use their bodies as food for our people. We see them near our homes and in the deep forests. We are glad they are still here, and we hope that it will always be so. Now our minds are one.

The Trees

We now turn our thoughts to the Trees. The Earth has many families of Trees who have their own instructions and uses. Some provide us with shelter and shade, others with fruit, beauty, and other useful things. Many people of the world use a Tree as a symbol of peace and strength. We greet and thank the Tree life. Now our minds are one.

The Birds

We put our minds together as one and thank all the Birds who move and fly about over our heads. The Creator gave them beautiful songs. Each day they remind us to enjoy and appreciate life. The Eagle was chosen to be their leader. To all the Birds—from the smallest to the largest—we send our joyful greetings and thanks. Now our minds are one.

The Four Winds

We are all thankful to the powers we know as the Four Winds. We hear their voices in the moving air as they refresh us and purify the air we breathe. They help us to bring the change of seasons. From the four directions they come, bringing us messages and giving us strength. We send our greetings and thanks to the Four Winds. Now our minds are one.

Grandfather Thunder

Now we turn to the west where our grandfathers, the Thunder Beings, live. With lightning and thundering voices, they bring with them the water that renews life. We bring our minds together as one to send greetings and thanks to our Grandfathers, the Thunderers. Now our minds are one.

Eldest Brother the Sun

We now send greetings and thanks to our eldest Brother, the Sun. Each day without fail he travels the sky from east to west, bringing the light of a new day. He is the source of all the fires of life. We send greetings and thanks to our Brother, the Sun. Now our minds are one.

Grandmother Moon

We put our minds together to give thanks to our oldest Grandmother, the Moon, who lights the nighttime sky. She is the leader of women all over the world, and she governs the movement of the ocean tides. By her changing face we measure time, and it is the Moon who watches over the arrival of children here on Earth. We send greetings and thanks to our Grandmother, the Moon. Now our minds are one.

The Stars

We give thanks to the Stars who are spread across the sky like jewelry. We see them in the night, helping the Moon to light the darkness and bringing dew to the gardens and growing things. When we travel at night, they guide us home. With our minds gathered together as one, we send greetings and thanks to the Stars. Now our minds are one.

The Enlightened Teachers

We gather our minds to greet and thank the enlightened Teachers who have come to help throughout the ages. When we forget how to live in harmony, they remind us of the way we were instructed to live as people. We send greetings and thanks to these caring teachers. Now our minds are one.

The Creator

Now we turn our thoughts to the Creator, or Great Spirit, and send greetings and thanks for all the gifts of Creation. Everything we need to live a good life is here on this Mother Earth. For all the love that is still around us, we gather our minds together as one and send our choicest words of greetings and thanks to the Creator. Now our minds are one.

Closing Words

We have now arrived at the place where we end our words. Of all the things we have named, it was not our intention to leave anything out. If something was forgotten, we leave it to each individual to send such greetings and thanks in their own way. Now our minds are one.

THE SPIRAL

There are hard things to face in our world today, if we want to be of use. Gratitude, when it's real, offers no blinders. On the contrary, in the face of devastation and tragedy, it can ground us, especially when we're scared. It can hold us steady for the work to be done.

The activist's inner journey appears to me like a spiral, interconnecting four successive stages or movements that feed into each other. These four are (1) opening to gratitude, (2) owning our pain for the world, (3) seeing with new eyes, and (4) going forth. The sequence repeats itself, as the spiral circles round, but ever in new ways. The spiral is fractal in nature: it can characterize a lifetime or a project, and it can also happen in a day or several times a day.

The spiral begins with gratitude, because that quiets the frantic mind and brings us back to source. It reconnects us with basic goodness and our personal power. It helps us to be more fully present to our world. That grounded presence provides the psychic space for acknowledging the pain we carry for our world.

In owning this pain and daring to experience it, we learn that our capacity to "suffer with" is the true meaning of compassion. We begin to know the immensity of our heart-mind and how it helps us to move beyond fear. What had isolated us in private anguish now opens outward and delivers us into wider reaches of our world as lover, world as self.

The truth of our interexistence, made real to us by our pain for the world, helps us see with new eyes. It brings fresh understandings of who we are and how we are related to each other and the universe.

We begin to comprehend our own power to change and heal. We strengthen by growing living connections with past and future generations, and our brother and sister species.

Then, ever again, we go forth into the action that calls us. With others whenever and wherever possible, we set a target, lay a plan, step out. We don't wait for a blueprint or fail-proof scheme; for each step will be our teacher, bringing new perspectives and opportunities. Even when we don't succeed in a given venture, we can be grateful for the chance we took and the lessons we learned. And the spiral begins again.

> Then all the work I put my hand to
> widens from turn to turn.
> —RAINER MARIA RILKE

Learning Forgiveness

Noah Levine

With all the emphasis we put on ideas and concepts, the really important changes in life—and it's as true politically as personally—take place at the emotional level. Here the tattooed "dharma punk" Noah Levine talks about the crucial place of forgiveness. It is the ultimate balm for ourselves, for others, and even for nations.

A huge part of the revolutionary path of awakening is forgiveness. Henri Nouwen, a famous Christian mystic, wrote,

> Forgiveness is the name of love practiced among people who love poorly. The hard truth is that all of us love poorly. We need to forgive and be forgiven every day, every hour—unceasingly. That is the great work of love among the fellowship of the weak that is the human family.

Forgiveness is the journey and practice of intentionally cleaning up the stuff of the past that is sticky, that we have been holding on to, that has caused us emotional suffering. Traditionally this is done through the practice of repeating phrases of forgiveness toward ourselves, toward those who have harmed us, and toward those whom we have harmed. In other words, training the mind to let go, to meet past pains with understanding and acceptance.

I feel that for most it is necessary to take forgiveness a step further. After doing that inner work of letting go, we must also take direct *relational* action. The process of releasing the heart-mind's grasp on past pains and betrayals almost always includes taking responsibility and offering forgiveness, and very often includes communication with those whom we have harmed, as well as those who have harmed us. This direct communication is the relational aspect of forgiveness.

Forgiveness is a process that continues throughout our life. We can't just say the phrases or do the meditation a couple times and be done with it. We can't just decide to forgive and magically let go of all the past pains and resentments. But it has to begin somewhere, and it begins with the understanding that all harm caused comes out of suffering and ignorance. There is no such thing as *wise* abuse or *enlightened* harm. This is the core truth of harm: it always comes from confusion. Anger, violence, and all forms of abuse and betrayal are always motivated by an ignorant or confused intention. When the mind is *un*confused, it cannot intentionally cause harm. The awakened mind acts with only wisdom and compassion.

That understanding of harm has crucial implications for us as we practice forgiveness, in that it forces us to distinguish between the confused, suffering actors and the actions themselves. This is perhaps the most essential perspective in forgiveness: the separation of actor from action. Whether the harm that requires forgiveness was an unskillful act that we carried out, hurting someone else, or an unskillful act on the part of another that we felt victimized by, we must see that the act and the actor are not the same thing. Most of the time the anger and resentment we hold is directed against the actor; in our minds we don't separate the abuser from the abuse. But this is exactly what we must do. We must come to the understanding that confusion comes and goes. An action from a confused and suffering being in the past doesn't represent who that being is forever; it is only an expression of that being's suffering. And if we cling to resentment over past hurts, we simply increase our own suffering. By holding on to our anger and resentments, we make our own lives more difficult than need be.

This in no way means that we should subject ourselves or others to further abuse. Part of the forgiveness and healing process is to create healthy boundaries. We may forgive someone but choose never to interact with that person again. We must not confuse letting go of past injuries with feeling an obligation to let the injurers back into our life. The freedom of forgiveness often includes a firm boundary and loving distance from those who have harmed us. We may likewise need to keep a loving distance from those we have harmed, to prevent them further harm. To that extent, this practice of letting go of the past and making amends for our behavior is more internal work than relational. As my father, the author Stephen Levine, likes to say, "We can let them back into our heart without ever letting them back into our house."

Forgiveness is not a selfish pursuit of personal happiness. It alleviates suffering in the world. As each one of us frees ourselves from clinging to resentments that cause suffering, we relieve our friends, family, and community of the burden of our unhappiness. This is not a philosophical proposal; it is a verified and practical truth. Through our suffering and lack of forgiveness, we tend to do all kinds of unskillful things that hurt others. We close ourselves off from love out of fear of further pains or betrayals.

I have witnessed the power of forgiveness most fully in my work with prisoners. While working at San Quentin State Prison as a counselor and meditation teacher, over and over I have witnessed deep healings of men who had committed violent crimes. As these inmates approached the inner pains of their past and acknowledged that their own suffering had been spilling out onto others, they were able to start a process of internal forgiveness and compassion that eventually led to personal commitments to nonviolence—commitments that in turn made the communities to which they returned a safer place.

Some *actions* may not be forgivable, but all *actors* are. For the actor, the person whose own suffering has spilled onto other people, there is always the possibility of compassion. There is always a potential for mercy toward the suffering and confused person who hurts another.

Early on in my own meditation practice, I clearly saw that I had been in a lot of pain for a long time and that my pain had affected others in incredibly unskillful ways. Then I began to see that the people toward whom I had been holding resentment had also been in pain and that they had spilled their pain upon me.

This allowed me to begin to separate the person from the action and truly see the confused being behind the hurt. This was the hardest part: not associating the people with their actions, but seeing them as confused human beings trying their best and failing miserably, just as I had. I found trying to take that attitude toward everyone in my life incredibly challenging. It took years of trying and failing to come to a real sense of this understanding.

That's a common experience, because forgiveness can't be forced. Having held on to anger and resentment for so long, we have allowed that reaction to become our habit. And habits take time and intentional action to break. In forgiveness we are retraining our mind and heart to respond in a new and more useful way. By separating the actor from the action, we are getting to the root of the suffering, both caused and experienced. This is a counterintuitive process. Our biological instinct is to respond to all forms of pain with aversion, anger, hatred, and resentment. This is the basic survival instinct of the human animal. It works quite well to protect us from external harm, yet it seems to create an even more harmful inner experience. The process of forgiveness is the process of freeing oneself from internal suffering.

At a recent meditation class, a student said that she felt her forgiveness was a gift that some people hadn't earned. This is a common feeling among many of us who have felt injured by others. Yet does our lack of forgiveness really punish them, or does it just make our hearts hard and our lives unpleasant? Is forgiveness a gift to others or to oneself?

When it comes to forgiving *ourselves*, we are more obviously both the giver and the recipient of the gift. We are stuck with ourselves for a lifetime, so we might as well find the best way of understanding and accepting the pains of the past. It is in our best interest, and the most beneficial thing we can do for others as well, to find a way to meet ourselves with compassion rather than resentment. Though this sounds simple and straightforward, forgiving oneself is often the most difficult and most important work of a lifetime.

It helps if we investigate our mind's tendency to judge and criticize ourselves, paying special attention to any feelings of unworthiness or self-hatred. If we can bring a friendly awareness to our mind's fears and resentments, we may discover that our minds are actually just trying to protect us from further harm. The barrage of fears and insecurities may be a psychological defense system, an attempt to avoid future harm—a confused attempt, of course, because resentment and anger toward oneself never lead to happiness. But if we can understand and accept that we have been confused, we may find it easier to begin to meet ourselves with mercy and forgiveness, responding to the judging mind with the kind of gentle patience and understanding that we would show a sick and confused friend.

As I began the long process of forgiveness, I found it much easier to forgive myself as a confused child than to approach my adult pain. Recognizing that, I placed a picture of myself as a child on the altar where I meditate. Every day when practicing meditation, I sent forgiveness to that kid who became the man who had experienced and caused great harm. Gradually, I became friendly with the child in the photograph. I began to care about him and all the confusion he experienced. Eventually, I was able to forgive him—the younger version of me—for allowing his confusion to hurt me and so many others. From that place of understanding and mercy, I was then able to touch myself as an adult with the same forgiveness.

My experience with forgiveness is that it, like everything else, is impermanent. While some resentments seem to vanish forever, others come and go. The most important thing to remember is that we must live in the present, and if in the present moment we are still holding on to old wounds and betrayals, it is in this moment that forgiveness is called for.

There was a time when I thought I was totally done with forgiveness. I had done years of forgiveness meditation, had made amends for the harm I'd caused, and had come to a genuine sense of love and understanding for myself and others. Then, as my mind became quieter and my heart more open, more subtle levels of resentment began to show themselves. In deep meditation experiences, I saw that I was still holding on to some old feelings of betrayal; the core parental issues were still there. So once again forgiveness was called for in that moment.

The experience of forgiveness may be temporary; more may be revealed. If and when that happens we have the tools to forgive again and again. Just as Henri Nouwen reminded us at the beginning of this discussion, *we need to forgive and be forgiven every day, every hour—unceasingly.*

The Practice of Lojong: Cultivating Compassion through Training the Mind

Traleg Kyabgon Rinpoche

Buddhism is sometimes accused of neglecting the emotional and interpersonal side of life, and many Western Buddhists combine psychotherapy with meditation to help them work through their personal issues. Yet Buddhism has a practical, detailed system of practices called the lojong *teachings, precisely for the purpose of working with these problems. As the outstanding contemporary Tibetan teacher Traleg Rinpoche shows us here, the pithy lojong slogans are guidelines for living sanely and compassionately.*

We have been born into an imperfect world, characterized by unpredictability and adversity, as finite human beings who have foibles, make mistakes, get confused, and think irrationally. There is much to contend with, and our ability to prevent or circumvent difficulty is quite limited. We aren't omnipotent beings, and while we try to protect ourselves and maintain order in our lives, we simply don't have the ability to safeguard ourselves from disasters.

It is self-evident that the natural world doesn't behave in a predictable way or do our bidding. We can see this in the examples of the Indian Ocean tsunami and the hurricane that decimated New Orleans. Natural disasters have occurred repeatedly in the past and are likely to continue to do so in the future. Millions of people have lost their lives, are losing their lives, and will lose their lives to disease: the typhoid, cholera, dysentery, and bubonic plagues of the past; the HIV epidemic of the present; and so on. Even at a personal level, many things go awry, and our efforts to complete projects are constantly thwarted and disrupted by sickness, mental distress, and all kinds of deception and mistreatment by others.

Adverse circumstances and situations are an integral part of conditioned existence. They tend to arise as sudden interruptions, so we shouldn't be surprised that natural calamities and upheavals occur in both our private and our public lives. Buddhists do not believe in divine authorship or omnipotent governance of any kind; things just happen when the proper conditions and circumstances come together. As Shantideva tells us in his chapter on patience in the *Bodhicharyavatara,* "Conditions, once assembled, have no thought / That now they will give rise to some result," but our ignorance about this process doesn't change the fact that they are interdependent. The importance of understanding dependent arising cannot be underestimated, because we have to be realistic about what we can and cannot do. As Padma Karpo (1527–1592) writes,

> If you look closely at your normal activities
> You will discover that they do not deserve the trust you
>   accord them.
> You are not the agent in power but the victim of your
>   projections.
> Don't you think you should look closely into that?
> Please turn your mind within and reflect on this.

We can't tailor the world to suit ourselves nor force it to fit into our vision of things. This doesn't mean we shouldn't aspire to make things better. The bodhisattva ideal specifically recommends trying to improve our world to the best of our ability, but that ideal is based on a realistic recognition that the world is imperfect and likely to remain that way. Things may sometimes work a little better, sometimes a little worse, but so long as there is ignorance, hatred, jealousy, pride, and selfishness, we will all be living in a world that is socially and politically imperfect. Shantideva counsels equanimity in the face of life's changing circumstances:

> If there is a remedy when trouble strikes,
> What reason is there for despondency?
> And if there is no help for it,
> What use is there in being sad?

If things are interdependent, as Buddhists say, we can never expect to protect ourselves against unexpected occurrences, because there is no real order to existence apart from the regularity of certain natural processes. The fact that anything and everything can and does happen would then come as no real surprise to us. The question then becomes not so much why these things happen, but what we can do about them once they do. We cannot control the environment in any strict sense, so we must try to change our attitude and see things in a different light. Only then will we be able to take full advantage of our situation, even if it happens to be a bad one. While it often seems there is nothing we can do in the face of insurmountable obstacles, the *lojong*, or mind training, teachings tell us this is not true. The imperfect world can be an opportunity for awakening rather than an obstacle to our goals.

Sometimes things just happen, and there may be nothing we can do to change that, but we can control our responses to events. We don't have to despair in the face of disaster. We can either continue to respond in the way we've always done and get progressively worse, or we can turn things around and use our misfortune to aid our spiritual growth. For example, if we suffer from illness, we should not allow despondency to get the better of us if our recovery is slow. Despite seeing the best doctors and receiving the best medication, we should accept our situation with courage and fortitude and use it to train our minds to be more accommodating and understanding. No matter what situation we encounter, we can strengthen our minds by incorporating it into our spiritual journey. A text on mind training known as *The Wheel-Weapon Mind Training* states that our selfish actions create a sword that returns to cut us. This text advises us to accept adversity as both the repercussions of our own negative actions and the method for removing the self-obsession that caused them. As the text says,

> In short, when calamities befall me, it is the weapon of my own evil deeds turned upon me, like a smith killed by his own sword. From now on I shall be heedful of my own sinful actions.

We grow more quickly if we are open to working with difficulties rather than constantly running away from them. The lojong teachings say that when we harden ourselves to suffering, we only become more susceptible to it. The more harsh or cruel we are toward others, the more vulnerable we become to irritation or anger that is directed at us. Contrary to our instincts, it is by learning to become more open to others and our world that we grow stronger and more resilient. It is our own choice how we respond to others. We can capitulate to the entrenched habits and inner compulsions deeply ingrained in our basic consciousness, or we can recognize the limitations of our situation and apply a considered approach. Our conditioned samsaric minds will always compel us to focus on what we can't control rather than questioning whether we should respond at all. However, once we recognize the mechanical way in which our ego always reacts, it becomes possible to reverse that process.

The great strength of the lojong teachings is the idea that we can train our minds to turn these unfavorable circumstances around and make them work to our advantage. The main criterion is that we never give up in the face of adversity, no matter what kind of world we are confronted with at the personal or political level. When we think there is nothing we can do, we realize there is something we can do, and we see that this "something" is actually quite tremendous.

SLOGAN: When beings and the world are filled with evil, transform unfavorable circumstances into the path of enlightenment.

Mind training enables us to utilize adversity instead of allowing misfortune to drive us into a corner with no answers. This tendency to adopt a defeatist attitude in the face of evil is the biggest obstacle to our everyday lives and the greatest hindrance to the attainment of our spiritual goals. We need to be vigilant about the acquisition of more skillful ways to deal with our difficulties and thereby circumvent the habit of waging war on ourselves. Responding with fortitude, courage, understanding, and openness will yield a stronger sense of self-worth and might even help to mend or ameliorate the situation. This is also how we learn to face unfavorable circumstances and "take them as the path," so that we are working with our problems rather than against them. Because fighting with others and ourselves only exacerbates our problems, we continually need to examine our negative responses, to see whether they serve any real purpose or whether they're capitulations to the unconscious patterns that habitually influence us.

It is not only when things are going our way and people are kind to us that we can benefit from others. We can also benefit from them when they're not treating us well. This is a very delicate point, especially in the West, where people are quite sensitized to the notions of abuse and victimhood. People sometimes misconstrue this slogan to be promoting a form of exploitation, as if the victim were being told to participate willingly in the continuation of his or her abuse, but that is not its intent at all. Its purpose is actually to strengthen our mind, so that we can step outside our solipsistic state and freely enter into the wider world.

If we are skillful and precise about generating love and compassion, it will make us a person of significance—with integrity, dignity, depth, and weight—rather than someone who adds to another's sense of self-inflation or advances his or her own reputation by eliciting a positive response from others.

This slogan is about the development of compassion. In Mahayana Buddhism, compassion is identified with "skill in means" (*upaya*) rather than self-sacrificing or self-serving acts. It is altruistic motivation merged with insight, as John Schroeder, a scholar of early Buddhist studies at Saint Mary's College of Maryland, explains:

> Very generally, upaya refers to the different pedagogical styles, meditation techniques, and religious practices that help people overcome attachments, and to ways in which Buddhism is communicated to others. [It] arises from the idea that wisdom is embodied in how one responds to others rather than an abstract conception of the world, and reflects an ongoing concern with the soteriological effectiveness of the Buddhist teachings.

The cultivation of *bodhichitta*, or an "enlightened heart," has two aspects and two associated sets of skillful means: absolute and relative. You could define absolute bodhichitta as the wisdom mind and define relative bodhichitta as the cultivation of a compassionate heart. While relative and absolute bodhichitta are ultimately inseparable, it's important that we first learn to distinguish them. The lojong teachings are predominantly concerned with the cultivation of relative bodhichitta, but we should never forget that absolute bodhichitta is the main frame of reference and therefore the basis of our training.

The cultivation of compassion is the veritable heart of the lojong teachings. Compassion is not just about alleviating the suffering of others; it is also a powerful tool for effecting our own spiritual transformation. We must learn to be compassionately concerned about others, because that concern is what enables us to go beyond our discursive thoughts, conflicting emotions, and self-obsessions and break down the barriers created by ignorance, prejudice, fear, uncertainty, and doubt.

Absolute bodhichitta, on the other hand, is our authentic and original state of being and therefore relates to the wisdom aspect of enlightenment. Despite the fact that sentient beings experience a multitude of delusions and obscurations, an element of the mind remains uncorrupted. There is an open, empty, clear, spacious, and luminous clarity of mind that is beyond concepts, ideas, or sensations. It does not come and go because it never enters the stream of time and is beyond both experience and intellectualism. Alternative terms for this supreme aspect of bodhichitta are *emptiness, the natural state, buddhanature, the nature of the mind, the ground of being, ultimate reality,* and *the primordial state,* depending on the context. They all refer to an innate wakefulness that is present even when the delusions and obscurations of the mind are at work.

THE SKILLFUL MEANS OF RELATIVE BODHICHITTA

When we suffer from events that are beyond our control, it makes our suffering infinitely worse if we regard ourselves as victims. Since most of our emotional experiences are the direct result of how we interpret and personalize the events in our lives, the real factor in determining how things affect us is the skill with which we handle our own responses. It is easy to see that no two individuals ever respond the same way to a given situation, so we need to ask ourselves how one person can remain largely untouched by an event when someone else is completely devastated by it.

The explanation lies in their respective responses. For example, while it is quite common to experience some envy at first when hearing of another's success in an area where we feel ourselves weak, that experience will affect us even more profoundly if we continue to dwell on it, for it is really our fixation that intensifies any negative impact. That's why it is so important to investigate the real causes of our suffering rather than assume that our initial responses are always undeniably true and correct. As Chandrakirti claims,

Attachment to one's own belief,
Aversion for another's view: all this is thought.

A life without challenges and difficulties would hardly be worth living. While we know this to be true, we all still tend to drift into laziness rather than approach life with a courageous and expansive attitude. However, even when we manage to pamper ourselves, it never seems enough; we continue to rail against our misfortunes and find fault with what we have, focusing on what we don't have. People who have experienced a few knocks and difficulties and have learned to handle them effectively usually survive much better than people who have been spoiled from the beginning. It is only when we tame our egoistic drives that we can disrupt our ingrained behaviors and develop real character.

Handling difficulties and coming out of them a better person are the whole purpose of the lojong teachings, but we can only do that if we aren't constantly defending our egos. Because the ego is unable to face difficult situations, preferring to indulge instead in emotional dramas and negative states of mind, it blames everyone else for its problems. And it is in that sense that the degree to which we experience pain and suffering depends on us rather than on the external circumstances themselves. When we blame others, we are really only giving them power over us and completely disempowering ourselves as a consequence. Taking responsibility for our own lives, on the other hand, empowers us and cures our tendency to victimize ourselves in any given situation. The following two slogans address the way in which we handle adversity by dealing directly with our self-obsession; the first relates to ourselves, while the second relates to others.

SLOGAN: Drive all blames into one.

As ordinary sentient beings, we are governed by our own selfish needs. Our history books are filled with well-known personalities who ended in ruin as a direct result of the lying, cheating, murder,

and theft they engaged in to serve their own perceived needs and desires when their extreme lust, greed, jealousy, and hatred failed to deliver the good fortune they were hoping for. If we examine our own
lives, we'll see that our egoistic drives have actually attracted the
difficulties that beleaguer us, a fair indication of the foolishness of
our behavior. We might stay in an abusive relationship or exhibit a
shameless and reckless disregard for everybody, including ourselves.
Some people even place their own lives at risk in the pursuit of their
selfish desires. The more self-absorbed we become, the more entan-
gled and confused we become. These delusions are actually self-
deceptions, because at a certain level we mislead ourselves into
thinking they are good for us. Shantideva clearly states,

> O my mind, what countless ages
> Have you spent working for yourself?
> And what weariness it was,
> While your reward was only misery!

Even though we don't possess the kind of influence that ultimately makes people change their behavior or attitudes, an awareness of our own egoistic drives can help eliminate the obsessive
fixations that cause us and other people so much harm. Our egoism
endlessly promises satisfaction but never gives us any real return. We
invest, we try hard, we do all the things it directs us to do, but the return is not there.

Many people take this teaching the wrong way at first, thinking,
"Now I have to blame myself for everything!" However, the lojong
teachings condemn only our egoistic, deluded mind, not the totality
of our being. Blaming the ego is not the same as blaming the whole
self. If that were all we were, then once that mind was transcended,
we wouldn't be able to function. But we are also in possession of
unborn awareness, or buddhanature, and we don't annihilate ourselves when we turn away from self-regarding attitudes. Buddhism
acknowledges a structural formation of self-identity, with many
different types of identification based on various levels of con-

sciousness and distinctive levels of being, but it doesn't endorse a separately existing "self." When we blame the egoistic mind for our misery, we are just blaming that particular aspect of our identity. We need to understand that it's possible to think independently of our ego. It is not essential that the ego assume the role of commander-in-chief. As Dharmarakshita says,

> Since that's the way it is, I seize the enemy! I seize the thief who ambushed and deceived me, the hypocrite who deceived me disguised as myself. Aha! It is ego-clinging, without a doubt.

If we regard ourselves as a unity, we might mistakenly feel that it is useless to try to effect any change. When we come to understand the destructiveness of the ego, we sometimes believe that we are simply wretched creatures. However, this is an incorrect view and will only interfere with our mind training and spiritual goals. We are wretched in one way only, and that is in our egoistic self-obsession. When something undesirable happens, rather than blaming somebody or something else, we should look at how we might have contributed to the event. Because our perceptions are not always correct and may not be a genuine reflection of what has taken place, we should always ask ourselves, "Maybe this isn't how things really are. It might just be my own biased, egoistic mind projecting something onto the situation."

If we examine how we constantly personalize everything, we'll see that the real source of our misery is this failure to manage, educate, and transform our mental states. Whenever something goes wrong, we look for someone or something external to blame and become completely outraged by whatever we decide is responsible for our discomfort. That is really no solution to our predicament, for even if we do find someone or something to blame, it only inflames our anxiety, frustration, and resentment. We might think that the act of blaming others releases us from unfair responsibility, but it really only disempowers us. We'll have to spend our entire lives trying to stop other people from causing problems for us, something that realistically can never be done. In order to cure an illness, we need to make the correct diagnosis. The lojong perspective is the correct diagnosis for our samsaric condition and is the exact antidote to the incorrect diagnosis, which is thinking that other people are to blame. As Shantideva points out, dealing with our own reactions to things is a far more practical way to mitigate our suffering:

To cover the earth with sheets of hide—
Where could such amounts of skin be found?
But simply wrap some leather around your feet,
And it's as if the whole earth had been covered!

When the lojong teachings say that we should look at our own egoistic mind and blame everything on that instead of blaming everybody else, it is not denying that other people influence us. In fact, this is why the lojong texts say that we ourselves will become great if we consort with great beings, whereas consorting with evil people will ensure that we are contaminated by evil. The Mahayana teachings use the myth of a gold mountain and a poisonous mountain to make this point. In this myth, the gold mountain turns the surrounding area into gold, while the poisonous mountain turns everything to poison. As Gyalsay Togme Sangpo advises,

When you keep their company your three poisons increase,
Your activities of hearing, thinking, and meditation decline,
And they make you lose your love and compassion.
Give up bad friends—
This is the practice of Bodhisattvas.

We'll never gain insight into the real source of our suffering until we truly understand our existential condition. The ego always adopts some kind of defensive posture; however, this will guarantee a certain level of paranoia by always trying to determine whether a situation is for or against it. In fact, this is another way in which there is a clear link between negative states of mind and our experience of suffering and pain. On so many levels, our habitual way of thinking is very taxing and undermining. This is why we need to train in the mental strengthening of lojong and stop thinking that every time we have a painful experience it is someone else's fault. If we don't critically analyze things, we become lost in a world of make-believe that has very little correspondence with reality. Shantideva compares self-obsession and its attendant conflicting emotions to a demon:

> All the harm with which this world is rife,
> All fear and suffering that there is,
> Clinging to the "I" has caused it!
> What am I to do with this great demon?

The Buddhist definition of a demon is something harmful. In fact, self-obsessive emotions are listed as one of the "four demons" (*maras*) of the Mahayana tradition. Self-obsession is not an isolated experience that only takes place in our own mind; it drives us to do all kinds of very unwise acts. Thus the Mahayana teachings advise us that if somebody completely loses control, "blame the poison, not the person," because the poison is what is driving him or her to that extreme behavior. If we understand this, we can cultivate a different perspective in the way we respond to others. We will cease to be provoked by their actions and stop thinking the worst or expecting the worst from other people, or we can at least give them the benefit of the doubt. Aryadeva states this clearly:

> Just as a physician is not upset with
> Someone who rages while possessed by a demon,
> Subduers see disturbing emotions as
> The enemy, not the person who has them.

Some Western Buddhist authors have presented this slogan with a slight twist: they play down the need to relinquish our fixation on our personal stories, anguish, and resentments, claiming that

Westerners have fragile egos and thus need to build a healthy ego first before they can deconstruct it. That sort of logic is total nonsense. The lojong approach has nothing to do with weakening the part of us that helps us function. Only people with a genuine belief in themselves could work with adverse circumstances and situations in this way. Westerners need to give up overfocusing on their personal desires and problems, because they have a tendency to dwell on their own stuff far too much. It is easy to misunderstand the Buddhist notion of egolessness. Put simply, Buddhism makes the radical observation that there is no fixed, unchanging, singular, separately existing entity, and that applies to all phenomena, including the ego. It is quite true that, in the relative world, we cannot just casually get rid of our ego, for the ego is a vital part of us that has a function. However, we can train ourselves to harness the ego's energy on the spiritual path, and in the process of doing so, we *transform* a problematic aspect of our lives into something transcendent and inspiring.

SLOGAN: Meditate on the great kindness of everyone.

From the cradle to the grave, other people do things for us, even if we think we are neglected and unloved. If they had not helped us, especially when we were babies, we would never have survived. We continue to survive because other people are still helping to maintain our world. Whether we think our upbringing was good or bad, people provided us with some kind of education and made sure we didn't go hungry. Practically all of the pleasure, joy, and happiness that we experience comes to us because of the presence or activities of others. The food we eat is available to us because many thousands of people are involved in producing, packaging, and distributing it. The same applies to the water we drink, the clothes we buy, the electricity and gas we use, and any number of other things. Waiters bring us food in restaurants; hotel receptionists greet us, sometimes even by name; and bus drivers take us to our destination and exchange pleasantries with us. We must rely on others if we are to have any quality of life. It's not only those near and dear to us toward whom we should feel grateful, although the kindness of our loved ones often goes unrecognized the most.

Our habituated responses are disempowering, because they make everything look and feel as if it were working against us. If we can shift our focus from our rigid, narrow, and habituated points of view, we will empower our ability to embrace situations in a new way, so that every situation will start to seem more workable. Because we tend to think other people are taking advantage of us whenever they get the opportunity, we become unceasingly self-protective and suspicious. We need, therefore, to remind ourselves, over and over again, not to take anything for granted and to appreciate the kindness of others.

There will always appear to be circumstances, situations, and people that create difficulties and obstacles for us. This slogan specifically instructs us to think about the kindness of others when we are confronted with negative situations, remembering that we only mature spiritually and psychologically when we are tested. We should endeavor to think good thoughts about people who have, in fact, made our lives quite difficult at times and try to turn these negative situations to our own spiritual advantage, so that we become wiser and stronger. As Shantideva says,

So like a treasure found at home,
Enriching me without fatigue,
All enemies are helpers in my bodhisattva work
And therefore they should be a joy to me.

This is also true in relation to bad situations in general. Every time we overcome an obstacle or an adversity, we become that much more intelligent and resilient, for it's the accumulation of diverse experiences that enriches our lives. Both Christian and Buddhist masters emphasize the importance of dealing with difficulties, instead of allowing them to get the better of us. This may be expressed in different ways and with different recommendations, but they all say that it's through difficulty that we grow. Saint John of the Cross describes what he calls the "dark night of the soul," exhorting people not to give in to the darkness but see it instead as a portent of light. In the same way, our difficulties shouldn't be viewed as something that will automatically destroy us. The metaphor used in the lojong teachings again and again is that the manure of experience becomes fertilizer for the field of *bodhi* ("enlightenment"). Dharmarakshita says in *The Poison-Destroying Peacock Mind Training*,

> If we don't put on the armor of the bodhisattvas who willingly embrace others' ingratitude, happiness will never come to those in cyclic existence. Therefore, willingly accept all that is undesirable.

If we see that it is our response to difficulties that determines what kind of impact they have on our lives, we'll naturally begin to move toward a more meaningful engagement with our lives as they are. For example, blaming ourselves about our negative habits and mistakes often causes more unhappiness than the actual situation. It is also important to learn from the mistakes of others, so that we don't repeat their errors and compound our own confusion. If we think somebody has done something reprehensible, rather than blaming that person, we should pay attention to our own behavior and resolve not to imitate such actions. We may be constantly enraged by other people's behaviors, but if we examine our own responses, we'll often find that we've acted in the same way ourselves, but with a more lenient explanation of our own behavior.

Keeping things in perspective through honest introspection is the way to heed the lojong emphasis on refraining from fixation on others. We'll then view the behavior of others more objectively and open up the possibility of learning something positive from them. Each of us has our own karmic history and has to suffer the karmic consequences of our actions—nobody gets away with anything. It is fruitless to set ourselves up as the arbiters of other people's actions, making judgments about what they do. This doesn't mean that we shouldn't take an interest in social issues, only that we should maintain our spiritual perspective. The only thing we really have any control over is our own experience, and this control is reinforced by learning how to deal with difficult circumstances and situations without anger or bitterness. Chandrakirti states,

> If you respond with anger when another harms you,
> Does your wrath remove the harm inflicted?
> Resentment surely serves no purpose in this life
> And brings adversity in lives to come.

THE SKILLFUL MEANS OF ABSOLUTE BODHICHITTA

Sometimes we generate too much emotion in our lojong practices and run the risk of being overwhelmed. We become so absorbed in our feelings about others that we are swamped by sadness and helplessness and end up thinking, "There's so much suffering out there; I just can't do anything about it." If these negative feelings become too strong, they might become injurious to our lojong practice, so we have to counterbalance that tendency by focusing on the perspective of absolute bodhichitta. This equilibrium between absolute and relative bodhichitta underlies the lojong teachings and is the framework for Mahayana Buddhism in general. As Atisha points out, skillful means and wisdom are the two essential ingredients for overcoming conditioned existence:

> Wisdom without skillful means
> And skillful means, too, without wisdom
> Are referred to as bondage.
> Therefore do not give up either.

In the Buddhist teachings, the notions of both love and compassion are infused with the qualities of detachment and equanimity. If we lose sight of that relationship, we may begin to think that equanimity and compassion are completely different states of mind or that it's impossible to have loving feelings when we are dwelling in a state of detachment. Detachment doesn't equal indifference, and equanimity doesn't mean we don't experience any emotion at all. We are simply trying to combine the two in order to maintain a sense of equilibrium in our emotional responses. The Mahayana masters all say that a blending of the two is far more effective than just generating one without the other. Relating to people only with detachment would not be a genuine Mahayana approach, and relating to people with a love that hasn't been tempered by equanimity would leave us vulnerable to dramatic emotional upheavals.

Compassion doesn't just entail a great outpouring of emotion; it's about skillfully channeling our positive attitudes. In order to express our emotions skillfully, we need to be focused, with our senses intact and our wits about us. While it is important not to suppress our emotions, we have to learn to express them intelligently. That's why it's important to infuse them with detachment and equanimity. This combination is the very definition of compassion. As the *Skill in Means Sutra* makes clear,

> Venerable Lord, Bodhisattva great heroes guard against all attachments. They are like this: Dwelling in skill-in-means that is inconceivable, they course in form, sound, smell, taste, and touch—all of which are occasions for attachment—yet are not attached to them.

When we fixate on other people as autonomous beings, we lose our equanimity in regard to the propelling force of emotion and thereby mentally solidify others' sufferings into seemingly insurmountable obstacles. Meditating on wisdom is the antidote to that problem. We have to remind ourselves that the sentient creatures we care about are also dependently originated, just like us; their real nature is emptiness. Even the confusions that prevent us from perceiving phenomena in a more fluid way are an expression of emptiness, for ultimate reality is not separate from our thoughts and emotions. This approach is about learning to deal with anger and jealousy, as well as other conflicting emotions. We aren't expected to eliminate them completely, but by learning to relinquish them with greater ease, we won't be so predisposed to pursue and perpetuate their habitual tendencies.

This integration of absolute and relative bodhichitta, or emptiness and compassion, is an expression of the Buddhist middle view. Some people argue that our emotions will always lead us astray and that we have to be rational at all times in order to counteract their effect. Others maintain that our capacity to feel is paramount and that an overreliance on abstract thought threatens to impoverish our lives. The Buddhist view lies somewhere between these two views. The Buddha himself constantly emphasized the middle way:

> Katyayana, everyday experience relies on the duality of "it is" and "it is not." But for one who relies on the Dharma and on wisdom, and thereby directly perceives how the things of the world arise and pass away, for him, there is no "it is" and "it is not." "Everything exists" is simply one extreme, Katyayana, and "nothing exists" is the other extreme. The Tathagata relies on neither of these two extremes, Katyayana; he teaches the Dharma as a Middle Way.

Bodhisattva practice is about trying to love and care for all people. All the sentient beings in samsara are suffering in one way or another. As Buddhism says, the mighty and powerful suffer too. The arrogant person is afflicted with arrogance, the disdainful person with disdain, and the rich person with wealth. Shantideva goes to great lengths to describe how painful it is to accumulate, hang on to, and lose wealth, as well as to be obsessed by the constant fear that others are coveting it:

> The trouble guarding what we have, the pain of losing all!
> See the endless hardships brought on us by wealth!
> Those distracted by their love of riches
> Never have a moment's rest from sorrows of existence.

Some people try to shift the emphasis of mind training toward some kind of political or social activism. Mind training's sole concern is to train the mind; it has nothing to do with activism. This doesn't mean we shouldn't engage with the world and support different causes, but when we do, we have to adopt a broader spiritual view. Our view has to be as wide as the sky, but our actions have to be directed precisely to whatever comes to hand.

Grasping ✦

Martine Batchelor

In its detailed analysis of mind, Buddhism identifies one crucial point in the way we create and interact with our world. It is the point where grasping or attachment arises. From our attachment to the objects of our senses comes attraction, revulsion, and all the conflicting emotions that cause suffering. But by applying awareness precisely at the point where grasping appears, we can cut the chain.

No-thought is to see and to know all things with a mind free from grasping. When in use it pervades everywhere, and yet it sticks nowhere.
    —THE SIXTH ZEN PATRIARCH, HUINENG

Grasping is a primordial pattern. We often feel that the world is sticky or that we are somehow *adhesive*—things stick to us. Each time we come into contact with objects through our senses—visual objects, sounds, smells, tastes, sensations, or thoughts—the pattern of grasping has an opportunity to manifest. For example, as soon as we look at something, we identify with it: "*I* am seeing a flower" quickly becomes "*I* like this flower; *I* want this flower for *myself.*" As an experience, it is not impersonal; we do not comment inwardly,

"There is a flower," "The flower exists," or "The flower is perceived." If "I" have a thought, I do not experience or say to myself, "There is a thought." Rather, it is immediately "my" fantastic thought or "my" terrible thought. A problem instantly becomes "my" problem and the only thing that exists in my life at this moment.

When we are not grasping, our experience can become more vast and we can creatively engage with the world in an open manner. In this way, we begin to purify the mind. This kind of purification doesn't have anything to do with becoming perfect and saintly or even getting rid of all *im*purities. This kind of purifying the mind means coming into contact with the world without holding on and encountering events and conditions fully without being attached to or disturbed by them.

By identifying with what we perceive and experience, we solid-ify ourselves and the object of perception. By solidifying ourselves, we reduce ourselves to what we grasp at. By reducing ourselves to what we grasp at, we magnify it and then become truly stuck, and we will feel paralyzed and not free. The thought has me instead of my giving rise to a thought that is ephemeral and rising upon certain conditions. By doing this, we exaggerate a thought's power.

This mechanism can be shown by way of a practical example. I hold something dear, a small Korean golden bowl, for example. Because it is mine and it is precious, I grasp at it. So physically I hold it in the palm of my hand and tighten my fist around it. If I do this for some time, I will get a cramp in my arms. But also I will not be able to use my hand for anything else, which means that I am *stuck to* what I am grasping at. The solution to the grasping pattern upon contact is not, of course, to get rid of the hand that grasps or to get rid of the object being grasped at. That is too dras-tic. The object has not asked to be grasped at, even if advertising and packaging made it incredibly alluring. Meditation can help me open my hand gently and have the object rest lightly upon my palm; in this way, there is the possibility of movement and freedom.

NEGATIVE GRASPING

We grasp in two ways: by wanting and by rejecting. When we reject something, we are grasping at it in reverse, and the same process of identification, solidification, isolation, limitation, and magnification happen. Remember the last time you hated someone. You could not stand to see that person. If you happened to see him, you noticed immediately all his flaws and he was constantly on your mind. When we grasp in rejection, we tighten around an object or a person and expend a lot of energy around that object or person. This could explain some of the tension and exhaustion in our life.

Several years ago, I went on a month-long silent retreat in a new meditation center in North America. As is usual on such a retreat, I had a daily job, which I did for one hour a day. Since I like cutting vegetables, I chose to work at 8:00 A.M. to prepare vegetables for lunch, our main meal of the day. We were thirty retreatants, so there were a lot of vegetables to chop.

I have a weak stomach and cannot eat bell peppers of any kind—yet our cooks seemed to have a certain fondness for that particular vegetable, and every day I was greeted by the sight of a pile of peppers to chop. So I knew there was at least one main dish I would not be able to eat at lunch. Since this was a daily event, I had opportunities to get upset on a regular basis. I could see that I had the choice of grasping at the peppers or not, to identify as them being an obstacle to my meditation or not.

One afternoon I was looking at wispy clouds racing through space. At that moment, I saw that the peppers could be like the clouds passing through the sky. I could let them move through my field of vision, and so encounter their sight in a spacious way, or I could be like a hedgehog—anything that falls on its back would get stuck onto its quills and rot away. In this instance, concentration enabled me to create space when coming into contact with the peppers, and inquiry helped me to see the negative consequences of grasping at them so I could deal with them in a lighter way.

When I returned to Europe from Korea and lived in England I became a housecleaner for ten years. One of my most dreaded moments was cleaning bathrooms, especially the toilets. What would I find in the toilet bowl? I would recoil with great distaste if I found anything and would flush it fast while looking away. Then one day, while doing a community meditation retreat, I went to do my cleaning job as usual. I entered the bathroom very calmly, lifted the toilet seat, and there was something big and brown floating there. I was not upset. I observed it carefully, with interest and impartiality, and saw that it was just matter—nothing more, nothing less. I still flushed it because it was not supposed to be there for very long and it was my job to clear it away. There was no disturbance—just openness and clarity—because in that moment there was no exaggeration. The meditation had created the space to see the thing differently.

The problem is not with any thing itself, but with the *exaggeration* of its badness. This I could clearly see when my grandmother was ill and incontinent. I was taking care of her on my own for a few days, and one morning she had managed to drip feces on the carpet of her bedroom. Coming to get her up, I did not see it and walked in it and trailed it everywhere until I saw what she had done and I had done. For a moment I was paralyzed and I started to feel the habitual tremors of panic, anger, and helplessness when faced with an unexpected and difficult situation. But I realized they were unnecessary. I did not need them, and they would not help me deal better with the situation. On the contrary, they would kill wisdom and compassion.

So I did not exaggerate the sights that faced me and decided to take care of the situation as it was. I saw that even this situation could be accommodated and dealt with skillfully and compassionately. The only thing needed was to clean one spot at a time—first Grandma, then the bedroom, then the dining room, then the kitchen. I was surprised that I could achieve this in an hour without undue hurry. I understood then that if I did not grasp or exaggerate, I could be more efficient and at ease.

Encountering the World of the Senses

Our encounter with the world is multidimensional. We see a flower, we recognize it as a flower, we see its colors, we feel the texture of its petals, and we can smell its perfume. Yet when we see something, can we really see it, encounter it, and respond to it in a nongrasping, nonexaggerating manner? If we *identify* with it in any way, the process of grasping will ensue; solidification will be followed by limitation, magnification, and exaggeration.

If I see a pretty but expensive dress in a shop window, do I see it as the dress of the season that "I" must absolutely have to feel better about myself and impress all my friends? Or do I see a pretty dress with nice colors and shape that possibly I could try on at some point if I have the money and the time to check on it? In the first situation, there will be much aggravation, thoughts, and feelings about getting the dress. In the other, there will be lightness and openness as the object is not encountered in such a tight and obsessive way because my identity does not rest on buying and possessing it.

I used to visit regularly two Zen masters in Korea when I was a Zen nun. What was noticeable about their presence was the absence of tension. They felt very spacious. Often if I had something bothering me, it would evaporate when I visited them. It was as if their spaciousness and openness, their "nongraspingness" was contagious. Sometimes we feel this way ourselves; when we do not grasp at anything and our heart opens, we can creatively encounter and engage fully with that moment.

Seeing

I came back to Korea in 2004 after many years away. Everything had changed; huge apartment blocks had sprouted up everywhere, even at the base of the small temple belonging to a monk friend in the suburbs of Seoul. This temple used to be in the countryside surrounded by hills and pine trees. The green hills are still there at the back, but in front, the only view is of these huge buildings ten times bigger than the temple. I wondered how my friend could live there.

Yet it would be fruitless and painful to hate the apartment blocks because, after all, they will never move away. Instead he just sees them as they are, big and tall with a lot of people who need a place to live and who also have Buddha nature, the potential to awaken. Meditation enables us to look beyond the simple, immediate contact of things to the conditions that gave rise to them. It helps our contact with the world become richer and more multifaceted.

During my retreat in Massachusetts, every day I would go for long meditative walks on the snowy paths. In the forest there were birch trees growing here and there. I loved these trees: they were so tall, straight, and white. I would stare at them standing in the snow. For a while I could commune with their beauty with no agitation in the mind, and then I would start to grasp and proliferate. "Hmm, I really like those trees. It would be nice to have such trees in my back garden. Yes, hmm, the garden should be big enough. Where could I find those trees? What about that garden center near Bordeaux?" By then I was not with the tree anymore, I was in France and in the future. None of this is to say that we cannot appreciate beauty, only that real appreciation will disappear as soon as we grasp and plan, as grasping and planning will remove us from the experience of beauty itself.

Another thing that we do in terms of visual objects is to visually grasp at something that is not there. This is especially pernicious. In 2000 my husband and I moved from England to live in France. Our house was in the process of renovation. We converted the attic into my husband's office and a small meditation room, but we needed a staircase to reach these rooms. I had the vision of a beautiful staircase in hardwood. However, it was difficult to get a good carpenter, and in desperation we asked the only carpenter we could find to make it. We did not get the dreamed-of staircase. Instead, we had to settle for something very functional, in pine with steep steps.

Whenever I used it, there was a feeling of discrepancy and distaste—until I paid close attention. I started to notice that when I
trod on it, I was actually seeing *two* staircases next to each other—
the one that was there and the other imagined one that wasn't. I
did not encounter the staircase as it was, but as it should have been.
The frustration was totally self-created and unnecessary. As soon as
I saw that I was grasping at something that was not there, I let go and
then could use the humble staircase peacefully. After all, it did the
job well enough.

Notice if you grasp in this way at anything that is not there. Do
you go around with a double vision of things—what is and what you
would like to be or what is not there? It's a painful way to live, as it
creates in your life an undercurrent of frustration.

Often one of the things we may grasp at is the way we look. Often
in our mind we have a certain idea of how we look, and we are surprised when we look at ourselves in the mirror and the image in the
mirror does not correspond to the mental image. It can even become
dangerous to grasp at that mental image. One form of anorexia seems
to come from a serious aggravation of this type of double-vision
grasping. The anorexic person has a wrong body perception due to
maladaptation such that what they see in the mirror does not correspond to the mental image of their body created in their brain. To
match the two body images, they have to starve themselves. An extreme example, but it's so easy for many of us to do versions of this.

LISTENING

One of the constant stresses of modern life is noise: ambient noise,
street noises, the noise of other people's lives. When we moved to
France, there was a large concrete foundation in the garden that we
wanted to remove, but it was extremely thick and a man had to come
to break it up with a pneumatic drill. The day the worker came with
the drill was beautiful and I wanted to work in the garden right next

to him. But the sound was very powerful, almost overwhelming—so I decided to experiment with *listening meditation.*

In listening meditation, you listen to sounds without analyzing, naming, grasping, or rejecting any noise that might occur. You do not go following after sounds, but you let them come to you instead. You focus on them as they arise with wide-open awareness.

This is what I proceeded to do in the garden. As I dug the bulbs out, I went into the sounds produced by the pneumatic drill. It was a very powerful and all-encompassing sound, but it wasn't just a single noise. When I really paid attention, listened *intently,* I could also hear that it was fluid and changing. I noticed that when I went away to plant the bulbs, I seemed to have *more* opportunity to be bothered and grasp at the ear-shattering noises. When I came back close to them and went completely into the sound, I was totally fine. The focused attention enabled me to experience the noise in a *spacious* way. But as soon as I created a separation from the sounds and felt myself apart from them, judgment and dislike arose. I could see clearly that I had a choice—to create space within hearing this sound, or fix myself and the sounds as two separate entities not flowing in a continuum of contact and relationship, thereby giving rise to tightness and tension.

Once I was teaching meditation to a group, when a neighbor suddenly started to mow the lawn while listening to loud rock music. I invited people to do listening meditation. At the end of the day, some people told me that the noises had been terribly disturbing, and others said that when they opened to the sounds with direct awareness, they felt very spacious. The sounds were the same for all the participants, but it was their attitude with regard to them that made the difference. Some people, by grasping at the sounds negatively, tightened around them and experienced them as impinging on their space and consciousness. By holding on to the sounds as unpleasant, they held them fixedly, thereby giving them more power of disturbance. Other people, by opening to the sounds, diffused their power of disturbance. The sounds blended into a whole environment in which nothing was rejected.

We must be careful not to equate meditation with sitting in a silent room. I *welcome* any sounds when sitting in meditation as tools of awareness—they help me to come back to the present moment, sitting, standing, walking, hearing, being alive with a great potential. If I listen meditatively, sounds are not intrusive. They become part of the music of life. They remind me of my connection to the world.

On the other hand, we have to be careful of using a noisy ambience as a means to stop us from being aware of and listening to our thoughts, feelings, or sensations. The modern world seems to be full of sounds and music on purpose, to distract us or to soothe us, and silence then can become threatening. How can we find freedom and ease in listening to silence as well as to the sounds of life?

WORDS OF INFLUENCE

Whenever someone speaks to you, notice how much you are influenced by her words. Certain discussion shows on TV can have the same effect. One moment you feel quite fine, and the next moment you feel angry toward somebody who has not done anything to you but about whom, perhaps, another friend has been bending your ears strongly. If someone tells you negative things about someone else, unless you are strong, you will be influenced by their words. If someone criticizes you repeatedly, you would have to be exceptionally stable to not be influenced negatively by these words and feel bad about yourself. This is one of the gifts of meditation: to help you be fully present in a stable, steady manner. It enables you to be as grounded as a mountain but, at the same time, as vast as the ocean. These are the qualities we are trying to cultivate whenever we are listening to someone.

Once at a meeting, someone accused me of being bossy and told me repeatedly to stop organizing everyone. It was rather painful to hear, but I took it on board, striving not to feel bad about myself, but to look at the situations in which it was useful to be organizational and those in which it was better to let go of that tendency. When I investigated that habit of mine, I could see that I was practical and down-to-earth, and this could come in quite handy. But when the pattern was rigid and magnified, it would become bothersome to other people and could make me difficult and tense.

Another time a coworker accused me in strong language of all kinds of things. As he was saying this, it was clear to me that this had nothing to do with anything I might have done or said. So I listened without disturbance because I could not identify with it. At the same time I could see that he was in full flow and nothing I would say would make a difference, so I just waited for him to finish. At the end of his attack, I calmly agreed to disagree and left. Later on he apologized profusely, which I accepted.

What is it that helps you to remain stable and open? In which conditions are you strong and confident, in which others not? To focus in meditation will help you to be calmer in general and so to feel stronger and more stable. To cultivate inquiry will enable you to encounter situations not one-dimensionally but multidimensionally, so that you are not stuck where you find yourself but can respond creatively.

SMELLING

We can be in the same situation of grasping and holding on with odors and smells. If our olfactory sense works properly, then a cornucopia of smells opens to us. This can be a great gift if we are attentive to it. We can enjoy the heady perfume of flower blossoms, the spicy fragrance of a close friend, or the rich smell of baking bread. With meditation we can be more fully aware of smells in that, by not grasping at them, we can actually be more present to them.

I love to try new things and I also love perfume and fragrant smells, but I am allergic to perfume and cannot wear any. So whenever I am in an airport, I am challenged by these two combined patterns of attraction and experimentation when I walk by the duty-free perfume counters. As I experience the contact of the perfumes through the olfactory sense, the temptation to try them out—just a little bit on the wrist for fun—is great. I can feel the strong movement toward it; it is like a physical pull. But this is my airport meditation practice, to resist the lure of the fragrances while being fully conscious of it. This is the test of encountering and smelling without physical ownership, without wanting to make it mine, without grasping.

We can also practice with unpleasant smells. I have a neighbor who regularly burns plastic rubbish on a little pile in her backyard. We have asked her not to do this, but it seems this is the only thing she is allowed to do by law with that type of small plastic rubbish. So it has become my smelling meditation. When the smell of burning plastic wafts toward me as I'm sitting on the terrace, I just notice it as it comes and goes. I do not exaggerate it or proliferate with it—though, like anyone would be, I am pleased when the small fire has been burnt through and I can breathe fresh, clean air again.

EATING

When we eat, grasping often happens. We eat a slice of chocolate cake, and it will be hard not to have another slice if there is the opportunity. How often do we feel heavy and stuffed and regret taking more than our stomach can handle? This is a difficult one because it meets our patterns of survival. We need to eat. Over time we can develop healthy patterns of eating—knowing what to eat and how much. But we can also develop destructive habits of eating when we eat too much or too little or the wrong things for our body.

It is very easy to eat too much, to eat more than your body needs. Grasping is the mechanism that will make it happen. You see young children do it—eat what they like repeatedly until they get ill. When you are eating too much of something that you like, you are grasping at the good taste that you experience, but you are also grasping at the idea of the happiness that is associated with the taste. If you bring meditation to eating, you become aware of the color, the smell, the texture, and the taste of the food. You are conscious of each mouthful, and you do not eat to fill yourself up, but just to eat *fully.*

Grasping at Newness

Eating can teach us something about grasping at newness too—and how exhausting it can become. You might have a favorite dish, for instance, which you have not eaten in a long time. One day you taste it again, and it is as though you were eating it for the first time. It is a wonderful experience—such a wonderful taste. It feels like new, like you have never experienced that dish in that way before. You make the dish again in exactly the same way or you go to the same restaurant, but the experience is not the same. You cannot recover that ineffable something that dish had that day. What you cannot recover is the newness of the experience. As soon as you have experienced something anew, it will never be new again.

As Thai master Ajahn Chah mentioned, if we ate a delicacy like bamboo shoots or asparagus every day, it would not be a delicacy anymore; we would get used to it, and we would look for something different, something new. It is likely that we keep trying to find exciting new things all the time and then move to the next one and the next one, because one after the other they become old experiences. Whenever we try to repeat them, we do not get the same special experience of that first encounter, of that first moment. Can we move from a pattern of excitation to a response of appreciation? Each moment of life is a mystery; we are able to breathe, to see, to hear, to smell, and to taste. We are complex organisms alive in this moment. Can we recover the beauty of that, the sheer mystery of this life?

Once my five-year-old niece was staying with my mother in the flat below us. One evening she suddenly appeared when we were resting, listening to classical music after working in the garden. She looked at us and said that she would dance. She then danced to the music of Schubert for the next thirty minutes while we watched her. She checked that we were attentively watching her and we enjoyed looking at her dancing, listening to the music while sitting quietly on the sofa. It was a very special moment between her and us, very loving, warm, and appreciative. Then she left to eat and go to bed. The next day she came up again, and she wanted me to put some music on so she could dance. She tried to dance, but it was not right; I had to change the music several times, and still it was not right. The following days she tried again. It was like she was trying to recover the exact beauty of that moment; but that moment was unrepeatable and could not be recreated in the same way.

We have to be careful that we are not trying to create a new experience with old ingredients. Each moment can be a new exciting moment if we open to it afresh. Each loved activity or food can be enjoyed if we do not grasp at it in a fixing way. If we try to open ourselves to the relatively same elements within the flux of time and conditions, we can enjoy what can happen, being open to it being the same or different. This is not a blind, superficial, or abstract acceptance, but a creative acceptance that is interested in interacting fully with the moment in its fluidity and its myriad conditions.

Mind in Comfort and Ease ⟩⟩

His Holiness the Dalai Lama

The First Noble Truth is suffering and the Second Noble Truth is its cause. According to Buddhism, the cause of suffering is ignorance, particularly our false belief in a real and permanent self. Tibetan Buddhists have carried on the analytical tradition of their Indian forebears, and one of the greatest teachers of these analytical meditations is His Holiness the Dalai Lama. Here he shows us why this mythical "self" is really nothing more than a transitory collection of bits and pieces.

The root of all the afflictions and the problems that arise from them is the clinging to an "I" or a self. As Chandrakirti says in *The Introduction to the Middle Way*:

> Seeing that all afflictions and faults
> Arise from the view of the transitory collection,
> And that the self is the object of this view,
> The yogin sets out to disprove the self.

All our faults come about as a result of our clinging to the reality of a self. Let's take a look at the process whereby attachment or aversion develops. In the case of attachment, we focus on something pleasant, and we wish to possess it and never lose it. With aversion, it is a matter of something unpleasant that we wish to be rid of. Now, whenever we feel attachment or aversion, we attribute it to certain properties in the objects themselves, and we never consider the role of our own perception. We think that the objects of our attachment or aversion are inherently good or inherently bad. This fosters a belief that there is no possibility for them to change their status. If, for example, we see someone or something as really bad today but as good the very next day, we can hardly believe it. We think it is impossible. This is because when we had our initial reaction of attachment or aversion, we believed we were reacting to inherent properties existing independently of anything else. A truly autonomous property could never change. If something was good, it would have to remain good and never change. If something was bad, it would always be that way. This is how we tend to view things, and this causes us to feel attachment for what we think of as good and aversion for what we regard as bad.

In addition to this belief that the objects of our attachment and aversion are inherently good or bad, if we also think that something is good because it will benefit *me*, or something is bad because it will harm *me*, then that is even worse. In those cases, the sense of a self who is benefited by what we consider good or harmed by what we consider bad is extremely strong.

So not only do we believe that the object of our attachment or aversion is real and inherently good or bad, but we also believe that the self, the one who feels attachment and aversion and who is either benefited or harmed, is real as well. This leads us to make a separation between "self " and "other," and then to feel attachment toward ourselves and all that we perceive as being on our side, and aversion toward what we perceive as "other," or opposed to us and our interests.

Therefore, in order to reduce our attachment and aversion, we can consider the unpleasant features of the objects of our desire or the positive qualities of the objects of our hatred. Or we can consider the drawbacks of anger and aversion and how they actually harm us and use this as an inspiration to cultivate patience and forbearance. These are the kinds of technique we can use in order to lessen our attachment or aversion; but if we think about it, what really underlies this tendency to feel attachment or aversion is the belief that the objects themselves are actually the way we perceive them to be and that there is a real self who is being benefited or harmed by them. It is this strong belief—that both things and the self are real—that is triggering the responses of attachment and aversion.

THE SENSE OF SELF

However, if we think deeply about the objects that provoke our attachment and aversion, we will come to see that they are not real in the way we first thought they were. Similarly, if we think deeply about the one who is supposedly being benefited or harmed by these objects, we will discover that we cannot find any such self. Then, when these two—the objects and the self—no longer seem as real and solid to us, there will no longer be any grounds for our attachment and aversion. What originally seemed such a solid and stable basis will begin to crumble and look insubstantial and false.

This is something we should really take time to reflect on. We should think about what goes through our minds when we feel attachment or aversion. The first thing we will discover is that there is a strong sense of our own self, a sense that "I exist." And not just a sense that "I exist," but that this "I" is independent from anything else.

In the general philosophical tradition of the buddhadharma, we speak of the "four seals that are the hallmark of Buddha's teachings." They are:

All compounded phenomena are impermanent.

All that is contaminated is suffering.

All phenomena are empty and devoid of self.

Nirvana is true peace.

1. As we saw earlier, things are impermanent because they are dependent on causes. The aggregates, like all conditioned phenomena, depend on certain causes, and this means they too are impermanent.

2. Then the main cause of the aggregates is ignorance. The fact that they are caused by ignorance means that they are all, by nature, suffering. Everything that comes about as a result of ignorance is said to be "contaminated" and is, by its very nature, suffering.

3. The third of the four seals is "All phenomena are empty and devoid of self." We just noted that everything that is contaminated is suffering, but it is possible to become free from this suffering. The reason is as follows. It is because we are subject to ignorance that we suffer, but this ignorance that causes us to suffer is basically just a misperception of things. We take things to be real when in fact they are not real. In fact, all phenomena are empty and devoid of self. If we stick to the general presentation that is accepted by all Buddhist schools, then "devoid of self" refers mainly to the absence of any concrete personal identity. The sense of "I" and the sense of "mine" that we impute upon phenomena are actually absent from phenomena themselves. This means that the ignorance that lies at the root of our afflictions can be eliminated.

4. And when we have eliminated it, the peace that will ensue is genuine and lasting happiness. This is what is meant by "nirvana is true peace."

All the various schools of Buddhism accept this notion of selflessness. They agree that the root cause of all our suffering and afflictions is the strong clinging to a sense of "I." To put it simply, they assert that there is no self or individual that exists apart from, and independently of, the aggregates. If we think about this deeply, after a while it can gradually undermine and reduce our strong clinging to such a self, a self that exists independently of the aggregates and controls them. The simple understanding that there is no such independent self can counteract our tendency to believe in it.

When we classify the philosophical schools of ancient India and delineate between Buddhists and non-Buddhists, those who subscribe to a belief in this kind of a self are categorized as non-Buddhists, while those who seek to refute this belief in a self are considered to be Buddhists. In the teachings, in fact, it says, "The assertion or refutation of the basis for the view of self is what separates followers of the Buddha from others."

DESIRE OR ATTACHMENT

Let's take an everyday example to look at desire or attachment. Imagine we go shopping and see something we want to buy. What happens next takes place in two stages. First, as soon as we see the object, we simply perceive it as something good. At that point there is not yet any attachment. There is still the sense that the object is real, but there is no clinging. Then, *in the next moment,* we start to think about the object. We say to ourselves, "Mmm, this is nice. I need something like this. It really suits me too." At that moment, it is as if our mind becomes absorbed into the object. It feels like the mind is almost sucked in. This is what we call attachment. Then, impelled by this desire and attachment, we buy the object. Once we own it, our new possession seems even more attractive. It is the same object, but because we are now treating it as something connected with ourselves, something we own, it seems much more precious and desirable.

But then imagine we go into a shop and see some beautiful object, and somehow, it suddenly falls onto the floor and smashes. We are slightly startled and disappointed, but we are hardly likely to be too upset. On the other hand, if we have actually paid for the item and bought it, and then it drops on the floor and breaks, we feel a sudden jolt, almost like a blow to the heart. It is when we start relating to something as being closely connected with ourselves and with our sense of self that we feel much more tightly attached to it.

If you think about this, it is quite clear. In the beginning the mind evaluates things in terms of good and bad, but as soon as we start relating to them in terms of our sense of self, then attachment and aversion crop up. Once we feel attachment, it is easy to feel aversion or aggression to an identical degree of intensity. Because with desire comes anger. When we feel attached to ourselves and our own self-interests, we will feel the same degree of aversion or hostility as soon as we suspect those interests are in jeopardy or actually being harmed.

The Harm Inflicted by Anger and Hatred

Yet the one who really does us harm is our anger. The real damage, the real violence, is inflicted on us by anger itself. The moment we feel angry, our minds become agitated and completely ill at ease. The discomfort anger causes in our minds even transforms our entire physical appearance. Our face changes and looks ferocious and ugly. Our breathing becomes uneven and wild. Our whole manner of speaking changes, and we bark out harsh and spiteful things. This is the real violence, and it is something that anger is doing to us. Then, at the same time as we feel miserable ourselves, we lash out and cause harm to others. But the perpetrator of all this harm is our anger.

Compared to anger, desire seems quite gentle and pleasant, friendly even, but it is actually desire that causes us to feel anger and aversion.

It goes without saying that desire and aggression are not just problems from a spiritual point of view. They cause all kinds of trouble for us as individuals and for society as a whole. It does not make any difference where people are, whether they live in a tiny village or a huge city, in the West or in the East, or if they are rich or poor. If you take someone who is constantly plagued by attachment and aversion and compare him or her with someone who has less desire and aggression, the one who has less will definitely be happier and more at ease, there is no question. The person who is prey to strong attachment and aversion will never really feel settled and happy. You can see the effects on family life at home. With someone who is more relaxed, the whole family is more serene as well, and there are not so many arguments and disagreements. But with someone who is temperamental and riven by strong feelings of craving and hostility, every other member of the family will be affected, and there will be never-ending problems and quarrels. This is something we can observe for ourselves from our own experience of living in society.

Think about it carefully, and you can see that it is actually impossible to fulfill all the desires that come from our strong feelings of attachment and aversion. They are insatiable. Look at anger. When we fly into a rage, we cannot destroy every single thing and every single person who is irritating us. If some insect is annoying us, we might swat it and make ourselves feel better or give ourselves some tiny sense of triumph, but there are just so many things that feed our irritation and make us angry. We cannot destroy the whole world! In fact, there is nobody in the history of the world who has ever succeeded in satisfying all the impulses excited by attachment and aversion.

As long as you are dominated by inordinate attachment and aversion, it is absolutely impossible to be happy. But apart from joy and well-being, there is another meaning to the word *happiness*, and that is contentment. It is when we are content that we can relax and feel at ease. As long as we are dissatisfied, happiness will elude us. And what prevents us from finding that contentment is attachment and aversion. The more prominently they figure in our lives, the harder it will be for us to find satisfaction. So you can see that on a personal level, it is attachment and aversion that really cause us the most harm. If we look at others too, we can see that it is really desire and hatred that are the source of every conflict and every quarrel; it is not the people themselves. So it is crucial that we distinguish between the individuals and their attachment and aversion.

As we have already observed, the afflictions agitate and disturb our mind, which then has its effect on a physiological level, making us much more susceptible to health problems. The evidence for this is very clear. I often mention the psychological research that showed how people who use the words *I, me,* and *mine* most frequently in their conversation—and who are, in other words, intensely preoccupied with themselves—face a greater risk of heart disease than others do. This is quite a significant finding.

Whenever we are driven by desire and hatred, it really does torment our minds. Imagine, for example, we finish work one day and go back home. When we get there, we simply relax and take a break from it all. This is our chance to refresh ourselves. We can be sitting comfortably at home on our own, with no one else around to bother us, but if our mind is unsettled, we will find it impossible to rest and relax. At night we will toss and turn in bed, and we cannot sleep. If we get desperate, we resort to pills or tranquilizers. Then, as despair sets in, we become self-destructive and turn to alcohol or drugs, even though we know them to be harmful. When the mind is ravaged by attachment and aversion, it can make our life a misery.

There is a story that I tell, half-jokingly but half-seriously. Let us imagine that we have a next-door neighbor who for some reason or other does not like us and who is always trying to pick a quarrel or get the better of us. If we let him goad us into feeling resentment and animosity, those feelings will not have the slightest harmful effect on him. But on us, they will have an immediate effect: they will rob us of our peace of mind. After a while we can think of nothing else. We lose our appetite. Or if we do feel like eating, our food is devoid of any flavor. We have trouble sleeping. If a friend comes over to visit, we cannot shake off our mood, and all we can say to ourselves is, "Why does he have to come and bother me?" Word gets around to our other friends; they are surprised to hear about the change in our character and that we are no longer good company. People stop coming round, one after another, and soon we have no more visitors. Finally, we are left alone to brood over our gloomy thoughts. We cannot even go out and enjoy the flowers in our garden. Stuck indoors by ourselves, seething with angry, resentful thoughts, disheartened and depressed, our hair starts to turn gray, and we begin to grow old before our time.

If this is what happens, our neighbor will be thrilled. This is exactly what he wanted. He wanted to harm us. When he sees how lonely, sad, and depressed we have become, he will applaud and think, "I've done it!"

But what if, when our neighbor does his best to spite us, we remain completely serene and at ease, we eat and sleep well, we go on seeing all our friends, and we enjoy all the pleasures of life? He is going to be exasperated. Not only do we stay in good health, but our neighbor's desire to harm us is thwarted.

The only thing then that anger ever achieves is to disturb our mind, and it can never hurt our adversary.

What is more, it is totally ineffective to get angry. There's an example I have that is quite comical. Imagine you have a stick in your hand. You have lost your temper; you are so worked up, you want to hit someone, and you just lash out indiscriminately in all directions. You might land a blow on anything at all; you even risk whacking yourself on the leg. On the other hand, if you are very composed, with a winning smile on your face and take careful aim, you can be sure to hit the target and not bungle it.

ATTACHMENT AND AVERSION: THE WIDER IMPLICATIONS

Attachment and animosity are definitely *solely* harmful and nothing else. And yet some people believe that these very powerful emotions of desire and hatred are what make life exciting and give it color. Without them, they think, our lives would be bland, colorless, and drained of any vitality. Sometimes we do have the tendency to admire people with a lot of desire and aggression, imagining they are strong and capable individuals who really know how to take care of their loved ones and confront their enemies. But if we really think about this carefully, it is just as Nagarjuna says,

There is some pleasure to be had by scratching an itch,
But it is even more pleasurable to have no itches at all.
Likewise there are pleasures to be had from worldly desires,
But with freedom from desire comes pleasure greater still.

This is really true, and it is not necessarily anything to do with religion. It is just a fact of life. The afflictions, and particularly attachment and aversion, make our lives miserable. They upset us, and they are responsible for all manner of problems.

In modern society we all accept that a lack of knowledge is detrimental, and so we do our best to remedy this by providing education for our children. Everybody agrees that it is vital for children to go to school, and today in the developed countries of the world people who are illiterate find themselves excluded from all kinds of opportunity. To be illiterate or uneducated makes it hard to survive—lack of knowledge and education is a root cause of poverty and destitution. This is why we put effort and resources into education. Yet when attachment and aversion cause us just as many problems in life, why don't we take a stand against them and try to reduce them in the same way that we seek to eradicate ignorance through education? I think this really merits serious thought.

Of course, we might say that desire and hatred are simply natural and that they are just traits we are born with. But then so is ignorance; we are not born educated. So there is no difference. Other species have remained more or less the same for millions of years, but humanity has come to see ignorance as a fault, and we have worked hard to educate ourselves. In some ways, this has made our lives much more complicated and given us much more to think about, so it has been a mixed blessing, but the fact that we all see ignorance as a fault is definitely correct. We do need to eliminate lack of knowledge and poor education. But just as ignorance can cause us many problems in life, these other negative states of mind like attachment and aversion are also responsible for immense suffering, and so as a society, we must find ways of dealing with them.

I am not talking about religion or spirituality here, because this is a concern for society at large.

TRUE PATIENCE AND FORBEARANCE

When we get angry with people, it is usually because of the harm that they have done us. But what really helps in this kind of situation is to make a clear distinction between the actions committed and the person who commits them; this is related to the development of patience or forbearance. Far and away the most important quality that can prevent us getting angry or resentful toward someone who is harming us is patience.

Now patience should not be construed as just passively accepting mistreatment from others without confronting it. We need to understand this properly—as I said earlier, many of us believe that the people who show strong emotions of attachment and aggression are the strong and capable ones because they stand up for themselves. You might mistakenly think that being free from desire and anger, cultivating compassion, and practicing patience mean simply putting up with verbal and physical abuse from others. But this is not the case. We should not accept mistreatment from anyone, but face up to it and take action to stop it. At the same time, however, we should not feel any anger or malice toward the person who is the cause of harm.

There are particular reasons to feel compassion for that person. This is something we may need to reflect on a little. Whenever we ourselves do something wrong, and later on we feel remorse and apologize for what we have done, we distinguish between the mistake and ourselves as the ones who made it. However, when it is others who are harming us, we don't make that separation between the action and the perpetrator quite so readily. We use the harmful action as an excuse to get angry with the person who did it. Instead, we should draw a distinction, just as we do in our own case.

Then again, just as we would see our own wrongdoing as a

mistake, we should understand that, as the victim of disturbing emotions like desire and anger, the other person is also making a mistake. This is why we ought to feel compassion. From our own experience we know just what it is like, just how terrible it feels, to be overwhelmed by compulsive feelings of attachment and animosity. If we remember that this is what the other person is going through, naturally we will feel compassion for this individual who is harming us. That is true patience and forbearance. Meanwhile, if his or her actions are unjust and unwarranted, we should face up to them, tackle them, and try to stop them.

PERSONAL SELFLESSNESS: THE EMPTINESS OF "I" AND "MINE"

In the teaching of Buddha, the way to prevent attachment and aversion is not simply to see their faults and avert them temporarily, but to get to their very root: grasping or clinging to the sense of a self or an "I." There are different types of clinging, but in this case, it means grasping at the notion of some substantially existent self that is somehow autonomous or independent of the psychophysical aggregates and yet in control of them. This is how the self seems to be, and the belief that it actually is the way that it seems is what we call *self-grasping*.

So we start by establishing that this autonomous basis for our self-grasping does not exist. Then we become progressively more used to this fact by reflecting and thinking about it deeply, over and over again. At some stage, even though that notion of the self still arises very stubbornly because of our strong habituation, we reach the point where we can see for ourselves that when we search for this "I" or self, we cannot find it at all, anywhere, from the top of our head down to the soles of our feet. If there really were some autonomous self in control of the aggregates, we should be able to find it somewhere, either in the body or in the mind, somewhere amid the different states of consciousness, coarse and subtle. But it is too difficult for us to find. When we see that there is no such independent self as there appears to be, then this has an impact on our self-grasping, undermining and reducing it.

Among the schools of Buddhist philosophy, the Vaibhashikas and the Sautrantikas understand selflessness only in terms of personal selflessness, or the emptiness of "I" and "mine." They do not speak about the selflessness of all phenomena. As I said earlier, this view of the selflessness of the individual helps to reduce the clinging to the notion of "I," and it also diminishes the attachment and aversion that are connected with the sense of self—the result of viewing things as "mine" and seeing them as good or bad. Yet this does not undermine attachment and aversion by establishing the absence of any inherent identity in the *objects* of attachment and aversion themselves.

SELFLESSNESS OF PHENOMENA: THE MIND ONLY VIEW

In addition to the selflessness of the individual, the higher philosophical views of the Mind Only and Middle Way schools speak of the selflessness of phenomena. They establish that even the phenomena of our experience, such as the aggregates, are not real and solid in the way that they appear to be. There are many stages and layers to this process. The approach of the Mind Only school is to analyze the phenomena of our everyday existence, such as the psychophysical aggregates; break them down into their component parts, down to the smallest particle; and show that, in all of it, there is nothing to be found. This makes us question our everyday assumption that things are real, solid, and substantial. In other words, we begin to challenge the assumption that external things and events have an intrinsic reality of their own, from their own side, independent of our subjective projections. This process leads us to the conclusion that these phenomena are of the same nature, the same substance, as the mind that perceives them.

How this helps us overcome attachment and aversion is by

undermining the assumption that things have their own real, intrinsic qualities of good or bad, somehow independent of the projecting mind. Then the question arises, if these phenomena are not real intrinsically and from their own side, in what way do they exist? The answer is that they arise as a result of habitual tendencies implanted in our consciousness. This is a little difficult to understand.

There are said to be four types of habitual tendencies: those of expression, similar type, the view of self, and the links of conditioned existence.

Let us relate these four to our perception of this flower here in front of me. When we analyze the flower, we find that there is nothing intrinsic to it. So then we may wonder what it actually is. According to this presentation, the mind that perceives the flower and the flower that the mind perceives both arise from habitual tendencies planted in the all-ground consciousness. We have had the perception of similar flowers in the past, and when those perceptions ceased, they became habitual tendencies planted within the all-ground consciousness. When they meet the right conditions, these habitual tendencies are activated—they arise partly as the aspect of the perceived object and partly as the aspect of the perceiving mind. Both the perceived object and the perceiving mind are of the same substance. They both arise from the same perpetuating cause or seed. It is because the subjective and objective aspects of the perception both come from the same seed that we say they are of the same identity. That is how the perception comes about through the awakening of *the habitual tendency of similar type.*

Then the basis for labeling it as a flower is the imprint of *the habitual tendency of expression.* It becomes slightly complicated here, because that basis for labeling is said to exist according to its own characteristics; in any case, there is some basis for the labeling yet not something that exists from its own side, which is how it seems to us. Our clinging to it as being the way it appears is *the habitual tendency of the view of self,* and also *the habitual tendency of the branches of conditioned existence,* but mainly the habitual tendency of the view of self. This is how it is explained, so that even a single cognition involves various different imprints from different types of habitual tendencies.

For example, the fact that this flower appears as a flower is based on the habitual tendency of similar type. Our labeling of this flower as a flower is based on the habitual tendency of expression. The impression that this basis to which we apply the label "flower" exists from its own side comes from the habitual tendency of the view of self. This impression is false; it is what is being negated—in other words, what we need to disprove.

In any case, if we refute the existence of outer objects, we need to come up with an alternative explanation for all the phenomena of samsara and nirvana. So according to the explanation offered by the Mind Only school, these appearances are aspects of consciousness that arise due to the activation of habitual tendencies. It gets complicated when we explain the process in detail, but the point is that these appearances are simply the self-perceiving mind and its perceptions. This is how they explain the selflessness of phenomena. And this explanation is helpful, because when we see that these objects that cause us to feel attachment and aversion do not exist independently of our perception, that will help to reduce our attachment and aversion. Still, as proponents of true existence, the followers of Mind Only make a distinction between the outer objects that do not truly exist and the inner perceiving mind that does really exist inherently from its own side.

SELFLESSNESS OF PHENOMENA: THE MIDDLE WAY VIEW

To look at this more profoundly, according to the texts of the Middle Way, there is not this separation of knowable phenomena into the categories of outer and inner, and both perceived outer objects and perceiving mind are found to lack any true or inherent existence. Attachment and aversion are states of mind, and all states of mind are shown to be lacking in true reality.

So through the meditation on the selflessness of the individual, the clinging to "I" is reduced, and then through meditating on the selflessness of phenomena and realizing that all the phenomena of our experience are not truly existent, we begin to see things as more like illusions. We begin to lose our habitual impression that things are so solid and fixed and, along with it, the idea that what is good is only ever good and what is bad is only ever bad. That is how the realization of selflessness cuts through the clinging to self at its root.

Why Bother with Meditation?

Steve Hagen

This is a surprisingly difficult question, because any reason or purpose we come up with will be wrong by definition. In fact, doing it with no purpose in mind is the very definition of meditation.

Why bother taking up the practice of meditation when, even in its simplicity, it is so difficult?

As soon as we hear this question, we come up with a list of reasons to justify meditation. We think that we're going to get something from it—that it will lower our blood pressure, reduce our stress, calm us down, or enhance our concentration. And, we tell ourselves, if we meditate long enough and in just the right way, it might even bring us to enlightenment.

All of this is delusion.

As long as we insist that meditation must have some use or purpose or meaning, or fulfill us in certain ways, we fail to understand it. As my teacher (and many other teachers before him) used to say, "Meditation is useless."

One of the obstacles we face when we first begin to practice meditation is our desire to know and reap its benefits. "How can meditation help me?" This approach assumes we are fundamentally sick and in need of spiritual medicine to make us whole. So when we hear that meditation is useless, that it's not about generating some benefit, we wonder, "What's the point?"

But if we are to understand meditation (or anything at all), we must drop our preconceived notions, biases, prejudices, and expectations at the door. Instead, let's look at the mind we bring to this practice. If it's a mind of getting somewhere, a mind that seeks peace, calm, enlightenment, or freedom, then it's not the mind of enlightenment. It's a mind that seeks gain and keeps coming up short, a mind of strain and frustration.

Here is why meditation is useless: meditation is, finally, just to be *here*. Not over there, in some other place called peace or freedom or enlightenment. Not longing for something else. Not trying to be or to acquire something new or different. Not seeking benefit.

We need to understand that the wanting mind is the antithesis of the mind of meditation. The mind of meditation is a mind not driven by desires and fears and longings. Indeed, a mind that seeks to rid itself of these painful mental qualities is *already* the dissatisfied and confused mind from which we seek to free ourselves.

When we desire the desirelessness, we remain trapped in desire. When we want the wantlessness, we bind ourselves with yet another chain.

We can't do meditation for any reason other than to be aware. We have to learn to see all of our desires and expectations as the forms of immediate dissatisfaction that they are and then forget them.

If you're sitting in meditation to get something—whether it's tranquility, lower blood pressure, concentration, psychic powers, meaningfulness, enlightenment, or freedom from the desire for en-lightenment—you're not *here*. You're off in a world of distraction, daydreaming, confusion, and preoccupation.

Meditation doesn't mean anything but itself—full engagement in whatever is going on. It's not about looking for something.

To look for meaning or value is to look for a model, a represen-tation, an explanation, a justification for something other than *this*, what's immediately at hand. In meditation, we release whatever reasons and justifications we might have and take up *this moment* with no thought that *this* can or should be something other than *just this.*

Meditation is not our mental and emotional business as usual. It's about deeply *seeing* what's going on within our own mind.

If we wish to free ourselves from a mind that's tormented by greed, fear, obsession, and distraction, we must first clearly recognize that it's the same tormented mind we are using to blindly pursue meditation. Since we can't throw away this tormented mind, we can instead begin to look at it honestly, with all expectations, fears, and desires.

In meditation, we do not try to forcefully detach ourselves from the feelings, thoughts, and expectations that arise in the mind. We don't try to force anything into or out of the mind. Rather, we let things arise and fall, come and go, simply be.

In meditation, the things you come up with pass, then come up again. The same goes for things you fear or dislike. In meditation, we simply see this clearly, without trying to grip or control any of it.

There will be times in meditation when we're relaxed, and times when our minds are agitated. We let both of these states be what they are. We do not seek to attain a relaxed state or to drive out our agitated and distracted mind. That is just more agitation.

When we allow the mind to function and just be *here,* with whatever comes up, without grasping, the mind settles on its own.

If we stay with meditation and continually keep our eyes open, gradually the unhealthy aspects of the mind, including ideas we have about what we're going to get out of meditation, will drop away on their own.

The Mindful Leader

Michael Carroll

Here's a paradox, one of Buddhism's many—that purposeless meditation serves many purposes. That's because wisdom automatically creates skillfulness, and leaders of all kinds are finding that the openness of the meditative approach works a lot better than the traditional imposition of the boss's will. Business consultant Michael Carroll calls this "leading from the inside out."

The kinds of leaders we encounter at work are generally what we call "top-down" leaders. We are all pretty familiar with this approach. There is the boss who has the "top" job and tries to get others "down" in the organization to do things. Small organizations such as medical teams and big organizations such as governments all have a leader at the top and others down below who are expected to follow. All of us at times are the leader and at other times the follower, and when it's our turn to lead, we work hard to get results. Surprisingly, becoming the boss at the top is usually more distressing than we expect, but nonetheless, we do our best to get the job done. While overly simplistic, this is the kind of leadership we normally encounter at work, and we tend to take such an approach pretty much for granted.

This kind of top-down leadership can be quite effective for

managing organizations. Setting priorities, allocating resources, directing strategy—these and much more can best be done when we, as leaders, have a wide view from atop an organization. And when top-down leadership works, we all feel pretty good. We know what's expected of us, we have a clear sense of purpose, and we all pull in the same direction. But things don't always go so smoothly at work, and instead of pulling in the same direction, we can sometimes feel as if we have lost our way; we can feel "misled" and a bit discouraged, as if a burdensome and limiting "lid" were placed on top of us and our workplace.

Lids are common at work: unreasonable deadlines, rude colleagues, careless managers, onerous bureaucracy, frivolous demands—unfortunately, the list is long and familiar. Such lids are permitted to cover organizations when we, as leaders, lose our perspective and become out of touch with the realities of getting the job done. Instead of taking a wide, realistic view of work, we mistakenly hurry through our circumstances, overlooking advice, chasing deadlines, ignoring business facts, and frantically pursuing success. And despite all our good intentions, such a narrow, determined view drives us to put lids of pointless pressure on ourselves and others— demanding results rather than inspiring them, chasing opportunities rather than inviting them, insisting on respect rather than earning it. In the end, when lids are placed on organizations, we can find ourselves losing patience with our lives and in turn trying to conquer or dominate our work rather than accomplish it.

A doctor who manages a thirty-five-person dermatological medical center had come to one of my recent mindfulness meditation seminars in order to "unwind and get some perspective." She was physically fit and gracious, with a quick and winning smile— a doctor/surgeon of some fifteen years and decidedly *burned out.* As she told her story, she had begun her career as a dermatologist with great enthusiasm, inspired to build a medical practice dedicated to helping people. And she and her two partners, working hard for more than ten years, had achieved just that: a medical center equipped with the best technology, employing dozens of professionals, serving hundreds of patients daily. But despite her success, she wanted to quit. Her partners squabbled, employees gossiped, and vendors cut corners. Overhead was more than twenty-five thousand dollars weekly, and malpractice insurance made it difficult to earn a profit. But most disturbing was how she felt she had changed from an inspired doctor to a short-tempered taskmaster. Work had become a burden, and she was part of the problem, inflicting her frustration, frenzy, and disappointment on others. Despite all the business challenges, this doctor knew that she had lost perspective and was placing a lid on others, stifling the team's natural enthusiasm and focus. She was "fed up with the whole mess" and was considering a new line of business—leading hikes in the Colorado Rockies.

Throughout the weekend, many seminar participants recognized themselves in the doctor's story: the pressure to meet unreasonable demands, the stress of managing overly complex processes, the challenge of assembling a successful partnership. Some found themselves leading with an air of frenzy; others found themselves relying on data rather than insight and spreadsheets rather than hands-on experience. Such pressure and stress had pushed some of them to feel, like the doctor, under siege, increasingly rushed, tense, and unfocused, while putting on a game face.

Now we didn't solve the doctor's problem during this weekend seminar—no weekend seminar could. But we did recognize in no uncertain terms how top-down leadership can lose its way and exhaust an organization, placing lids of senseless pressure on colleagues, organizations, and ourselves.

While such lids may be familiar to many of us, they are also a most bedeviling, pervasive, and unintended feature of our modern workplace. Hundreds of studies have documented the effects: 18 percent of full-time American workers are considered "workaholics," working more than fifty hours a week—up from 13 percent in 1999; panic attacks, chronic worrying, and depression have increased by 45 percent in the United States over the past thirty years; one million American workers are absent from work each day due to stress.

Many organizations work quite hard trying to remove these lids in order to encourage trust, candor, and mutual respect—often with limited results. There is no blame here, of course. We all create the lid to some degree—boss and subordinates together. Most leaders I have met throughout my career are often dumbfounded at how people in their organization feel pressured to keep their mouths shut and avoid risks. And most employees are equally dumbfounded at the fact that their leaders seem to be in the dark about the pressures to conform and not rock the boat. Everyone to some degree is well meaning; everyone to some degree is out of touch. And all of us to some degree create the lid.

From a Buddhist point of view, however, removing the lid of pointless pressure and regaining a realistic view of work is a vital spiritual challenge if we intend to lead a confident and inspired life. As workplace leaders, our intention is not to create pressure cookers for our colleagues, and none of us wants to stew in our own juices. While top-down leadership has many benefits, Buddhism does not permit us to view livelihood simply from the top down, nor can we wait for someone else to take the lead in contributing to our world. In fact, for Buddhists, learning to become a leader who can inspire and build a decent world without lids is at the very heart of living a spiritual life, and traditionally, to become such a leader requires us to travel what is called the bodhisattva-warrior path, or the way of the mindful leader.

Leading from the "Inside Out"

As a college student in the 1970s, I befriended a young man who made his living as a Pennsylvania Turnpike toll collector. At the time, I considered his job fascinating: sitting in a small box for hours on end, making change for people as they paid their taxes, struck me as poetic—kind of like witnessing an endless stream of human dramas framed by car windows. Of course, he clued me in to the facts: car exhaust, heat and cold, frustrated commuters, and cramped work

environments made for some difficult times. But what truly fascinated me—and apparently fascinated the *New Yorker* enough for it
to publish an article about my friend—was that he was tremendously cheerful when doing his job, and many of his customers
brought this to the attention of the turnpike authority. He had a
most peculiar workplace habit that seemed to get everyone's attention: he gave a piece of candy to each customer he encountered,
accompanied by a big smile and a heartfelt "Have a good day."
Apparently, this had some impact on the thousands of commuters
who traveled past his window week in and week out. Truckers got
a chuckle, families waved good-bye, frustrated businesspeople
breathed a brief sigh of relief—and in gratitude, some even took the
time to thank his employer for his generosity. And I remember my
friend's enthusiasm and pride when his picture appeared in the *New
Yorker*—his head peering out from his toll booth with a goofy grin
on his face and a piece of candy in his hand. He felt he had made a
substantial contribution to his world, and I, for one, agreed and
could feel his inspiration quite viscerally.

Now on the surface, such a gesture as offering a piece of candy
to people while they pay their taxes may seem uneventful—perhaps
a bit sweet and well intentioned, but not particularly pertinent to the
topic of business leadership. Handing out candy has little to do with
growing market share, striving for commercial excellence, or creating global opportunities. For the mindful leader, however, what is at
play in this simple story is the very seed we seek to nourish—the
essence of leadership itself.

Over the centuries, thousands of instructions have been offered
by many skillful Buddhist teachers on how to cultivate the heart
of a leader. Mastering such instructions is quite demanding and
can take an entire lifetime—actually, many lifetimes, according to
past teachers. But despite these demands, cultivating such leadership within ourselves and within organizations is very doable and
straightforward—maybe even as simple as giving someone a piece
of candy. In fact, mindful leadership is tremendously practical

because it rests on a simple yet profound insight that expands the entire notion of leadership altogether: *all human beings instinctively want to offer their best to others and in turn inspire others to do the same, and this can be done by anyone, anywhere, anytime—even in a highway tollbooth.*

Mindful leadership teaches that this instinct to inspire the best in others is completely natural—utterly human—and is at the very heart of being a leader. A child charming a smile from a parent, a neighbor hosting a spring outdoor barbecue, a world leader planning for the future, or a smiling toll collector offering a piece of candy—all are leaders in their own way, offering a part of themselves in order to inspire others.

From the standpoint of a top-down approach to leading, the fact that a toll collector could inspire others or that a barbecue could unfold as a leadership event may seem trivial or completely off the mark. But for the mindful leader, such simple human gestures hold the very secret of successful leadership. For here, in offering a smile or a piece of candy or a plan for curing cancer, this kind of leadership is the foundation—the core—the vital impulse that drives authentic leadership, which is less about leading from the top down and more about leading from the inside out: offering to others a part of ourselves that inspires. From this perspective, top-down leadership need not lose its way and become a lid when it understands and embraces this simple fact: each and every one of us, by the very fact of our humanity, is capable of leadership and responsible for leading—*from the inside out.*

THE PATH OF OPENING

Typically, when we think of leading, we think of guiding and instructing others, pointing the way, setting direction. And surely these activities are what leaders do. Yet for the mindful leader, leading from the inside out requires a primary act—a fundamental human gesture that must take place first and foremost, before any leader can guide or direct or point the way. According to the tradition of the mindful leader, a leader must first *open*—step beyond the boundaries of what is familiar and routine and directly touch the very people and environment he or she intends to inspire. Leading others requires that we first open to the world around us.

Many business leaders may find such an approach a bit peculiar. It's hard to imagine overhearing leaders in the boardroom saying to one another, "Hey, why don't we all open up to one another? You know, lead from the inside out." Such a view of leadership may appear a bit soft. Flowers and windows open, not leaders. Leaders make stuff happen; they accomplish goals. For mindful leaders, however, opening is not merely "a nice thing to do"—behavior that can be practiced at an off-site management session or during a game of Twister. Opening is how we become available to what is actually going on—how we become realistic about our circumstances, abandoning our version of reality for experiencing reality itself. Opening introduces us to how things are instead of how we want them to be. Consequently, opening is the primary and indispensable act of leaders because it requires that we fully understand and appreciate our circumstances *first* before we act.

I recall once waiting for an appointment in an executive reception area of a Fortune 100 company, and on the wall was an impressive photograph of the Atlantic Ocean. A lighthouse in the photo shed its guiding beam across the waves and shoreline, and the caption read, "Vision is not seeing things as they are but as they will be." I couldn't help running the first part of the saying over and over in my mind: "Vision is not seeing things as they are. . . . Vision is not seeing things as they are. . . ." For the mindful leader, such "vision" is blindness, and focusing on the future without facing reality as it exists is choosing to be lost. I remember thinking to myself as I left the appointment, "I wonder how that picture and trite phrase even got up there on the wall." And I could not help but think, "Maybe no one has even noticed it's there!"

Of course, we understand what the phrase is trying to get at. As

leaders, we naturally want to improve our world, creating clever devices and beautiful spaces that are helpful and inspiring to others.
We want to make the world a better place, so to speak. But seeking to
make the world a better place without first appreciating the world as
it is produces all kinds of problems. Rather than permitting the facts
of life and the melody of circumstances to guide and educate us, we
end up putting a lid on the experience, stifling the world with *our*
views, *our* priorities, *our* vision—*our* hopes and *our* fears.

I recall a story shared with me by a publishing colleague about a
New York CEO who was leading a team in acquiring a portfolio of
medical magazines. The financial characteristics of the properties
were quite attractive, with 25 percent profit margins and solid positive cash flow, and the executive was keen on making them part of
his growing publishing business. After some research and preliminary due diligence, it came time for the CEO and his acquisition
team to meet with the magazines' owner, and the meeting was
arranged in the acquiring company's fancy boardroom.

As planned, the owner of the medical magazines and his lawyer
arrived on time and, after a few cordial introductions, took their
seats across the table from the CEO and his eight-person acquisition
team to discuss the possibilities of joining forces. Before any business began, the CEO set a rather strange stage for discussion:

"Before we get into the details of this deal, let me ask you a very
basic question," he remarked, looking directly at the owner. "Before
this meeting, I asked my business development guy here to go downstairs and purchase your magazines at our magazine kiosk, and I'll
remind you that it just so happens that our magazine store is one of
the best stocked in the world, offering a wider array of magazines
than 97 percent of all magazine kiosks." He paused for effect.

"And do you know what he found? Not one of your magazines
is available for sale. Not one. So let me ask you a basic question: why
would I want to spend millions of dollars to acquire your magazines
when you can't even get them onto the magazine rack for purchase?"
And the CEO sat back with a smug grin on his face.

The owner was a bit taken aback, not so much by the question as by the display.

"Well, it's a good thing that you didn't find my magazines in your kiosk downstairs," he calmly remarked. "My magazines are purchased by neurologists, brain surgeons, oncologists, and osteopathic physicians—and the likelihood that they would be wandering around in your building is pretty slim." The owner paused as quiet discomfort filled the room.

"My properties are what are called trade publications—they are highly focused and technically driven for specialized physicians and nurses. My magazines are not consumer publications, which is what you'll find downstairs. I sell subscriptions, not circulation, which is why my business is so profitable and its cash flow so rich."

Needless to say, the CEO was embarrassed—but not because he didn't know what he was talking about, which would have been perfectly appropriate. The CEO embarrassed himself because he was not open—open to meeting a potential new partner, open to learning new views of publishing, open to "not knowing"—open to just about anything that might happen. Instead, the CEO crudely put a lid on his world and ambushed his potential partner with *his* vision, *his* concerns, *his* opinions. Rather than be genuinely open, he chose one-upmanship; rather than curiosity, he chose arrogance; rather than extending a hand, he chose pretense. Being open in this circumstance would have been tremendously practical, but the CEO chose to hide beneath a lid.

Such clumsy attempts at leading are not unusual in business, and too often, leaders are actually expected to behave with such aggression, placing lids on circumstances. But as we can see from our embarrassed CEO, when we lead from the top down without openness, we can get out of touch, ignore the facts, and misunderstand our circumstances. We try to build our version of reality because we are not dealing with reality itself. When we try to influence our world without first appreciating it, we end up in a lighthouse on the edge of the Atlantic Ocean "not seeing things as they are" but as we want them to be—trying to manipulate our world into an artificial experience tinged with aggression.

JINPA: THE WISDOM OF VULNERABILITY

The primary act of mindful leadership, then, is to open—to fully appreciate our circumstances *before* we seek to influence or act upon them. When we are willing to open to our world before we act, we not only learn what we need to know, but equally important, we express a vital, innate intelligence that is sharp, flexible, and unassuming. At such moments, we view our workplace without any lenses, undistracted by *our* priorities, *our* preferences, *our* vision of the future. Instead, we grasp directly the full measure of our present circumstances, recognizing opportunities, appreciating others' views, acknowledging difficulties, and even delighting in the natural grace and flow of the moment. Such open intelligence, however, demands that we drop any pretense or strategy. Who we are and how we want to be perceived, what we want to accomplish and how we want to get there, become unimportant. In short, we become irrelevant.

By dropping our point of view—indeed, our identity altogether—we discover that to lead from a place of openness is to be vulnerable: undefended, engaged, and raw. At times, such vulnerability can be freeing because we stop wrestling with our personal schemes and anxiety and simply expose ourselves to our world. Yet conversely, such vulnerability can also be terrifying, since there are no familiar emotions or clichés on which we can rely for comfort or reassurance.

The Tibetan word for this vulnerable openness is *jinpa*, which means "complete generosity," and traditionally, cultivating jinpa is considered the basic practice of the mindful leader. It is how we learn to generously offer ourselves to others without making ridiculous demands or placing lids on situations. When we express jinpa—when we are intelligently open and vulnerable—we create the opportunity to genuinely lead and inspire others.

The suggestion that we lead by being vulnerable may seem absurd. Typically, we think that leaders should be equipped with all kinds of armor—invincible and potent, able to withstand the slings and arrows of workplace competition and hostility—and that being vulnerable at work means being weak, inadequate, shamefully flawed. For the mindful leader, however, the vulnerability of jinpa is not an inadequacy, but a wisdom that is poised, skillful, and astute. The Olympic figure skater who flawlessly executes a double open axel understands the wisdom of vulnerability. The classroom teacher who pauses to soak in a child's anxious resistance before reacting understands this wisdom. The manager who genuinely listens to the disgruntled employee, the attorney who drops an adversarial mind-set, the martial artist at her ease, the orchestra conductor fully engaged—each understands the wisdom of jinpa's vulnerability.

On one of my consulting assignments, I was asked by a lead scientist to help her understand why members of her R & D staff were so intimidated, so unwilling to speak their minds and discuss vital issues openly. I spent time listening to many medicinal chemists and biologists, computer scientists and lab experts, and discovered a culture in which candor was clearly lacking. There were many reasons why people were reluctant to speak their minds, of course. But one most intriguing discovery truly defined the dilemma.

Essentially, these R & D scientists, like all scientists, wanted their experiments to succeed. Wedded to highly demanding processes and insisting on exacting rigor, they were trained to seek certainty, but *emotionally* they desired the satisfaction of success with all its recognition and acclaim. By their very nature, however, these particular R & D efforts involved frequent failure—and there was the rub. Intellectually, the scientists could accept failure if their research showed that a particular compound did not perform according to plan. Emotionally, however, to admit such a thing required the courage to be *vulnerable*—vulnerable to the emotions associated with failure; vulnerable to likely criticism, second-guessing, and even doubt. And since frequent failure was a given, such emotional vulnerability was, in fact, an essential and necessary part of the territory.

Unfortunately and somewhat understandably, the scientists were distinctly uncomfortable feeling vulnerable. On the surface, they behaved as if they were open to the facts of failure, but underneath, they were closed to the emotional realities of disappointment, discouragement, and doubt. During R & D meetings, dialogue was more about protecting oneself, proving a point, or defeating an argument than listening, considering options, or speaking candidly. People were more worried about covering their bases than engaging in productive dialogue. And, of course, being wary and defensive in such a way only provoked the very conflicts and tensions everyone wished to avoid. The emotional openness required for candid discussion and vital learning was absent, and the resultant culture was hesitant, lacking resilience and nerve. The lead scientist's challenge, therefore, was to model jinpa—the "wisdom of vulnerability"—encouraging the members of her team to set aside their resistance and hesitation and express themselves openly.

Over many months, she met with team members individually and in small groups, inviting candor and welcoming all remarks—praise, criticism, and suggestions. She gradually dropped much of her own resistance to irritating insults and second-guessing—embracing conflicts rather than treating them as nuisances. R & D review meetings were no longer intellectual wrestling matches but gradually started being managed more openly, with opinions being invited more widely and everyone encouraged to listen fully before probing for weak points. And while work continues to this day on strengthening the openness within the organization, much progress has been made, and in the lead scientist's own words, "The fear level in my organization has clearly been reduced, both by my actions and by stabilizing R & D as a whole."

What was required in this R & D business was for each scientist to open from the inside out and emerge unguarded to discuss his or her research candidly—both successes and failures, certainties and hunches. The challenge was to engage the seeming emotional threats from a standpoint of vulnerability rather than defensiveness, which required courage and daring—total exposure.

Whether we are a lead scientist, a CEO, or an Olympic figure skater, when we lead from a place of total exposure, we discover that we are being authentic. We are not trying to win anyone over or guard our point of view. We are not sugarcoating our experience with trite pleasantries or arming ourselves with rusty emotional knives. Instead, we are simply open to whatever occurs, which inspires others to express such openness as well. Such vulnerability can have a powerful and lasting impact on organizations, promoting a common sense of collegiality, respect, and decency. Yet this wisdom of vulnerability is nothing particularly extraordinary or fantastic; such openness is not the stuff of PowerPoint presentations or management seminar exercises. The wisdom of vulnerability arises as an utterly human moment that can inspire a simple smile or rousing applause or even have such momentous consequences as saving a nation from disaster.

Few Americans know that in 1782, in the midst of the American Revolution, the Continental army mutinied. For all intents and purposes, the Continental Congress in Philadelphia had abandoned its army to suffer in miserable conditions. Soldiers were left unfed, ill-clothed, underequipped, and unpaid, and the officers of the Continental army repaid such lack of loyalty with an ultimatum spelled out in the Newburgh Address, which essentially said to Congress, "Either care for your army properly or we shall take things into our own hands and march on Philadelphia."

No one appreciated the dangers of a potential military coup more than the army's commander, General George Washington, and he moved swiftly to deal with it. And not surprisingly, it was a simple gesture of vulnerability that turned the tide, preventing the mutiny and saving a nation.

Historical record tells us that on March 15, 1782, in the midst of the crisis, General Washington attended a meeting in a large assembly hall with hundreds of his officers in New Windsor, New York. As circumstances would have it, he arrived unexpectedly and alone, without bodyguards or entourage, which was quite unusual, since the British were working tirelessly to kidnap the general. For many years, through many trials, the troops of the Continental army remained fiercely loyal to General Washington and deeply respected him as a leader and patriot, but on that day, as he walked to the podium, the general faced hundreds of angry, frustrated, and hostile men. A bit unnerved, he read from a carefully prepared speech appealing to their patriotism, their military bearing, and even their pocketbook. But George Washington was an ineffective public speaker, and his pleas fell on deaf ears. The officers had not been moved and remained angry and mutinous.

As a last resort, the general had brought along with him a letter from a congressman that pledged to address their grievances, and he pulled out the handwritten note and began to read it aloud. The letter was hard to see in the darkened meeting room, however, and after stumbling through the first paragraph, the general paused and clumsily put on a pair of reading glasses. As the story has been told, many in the crowd began to mumble, taken aback because no one had ever before seen their tough, distinguished general wear frail, ill-suited eyeglasses. What happened next was witnessed by Lieutenant Samuel Shaw and recorded in his journal.

According to Lieutenant Shaw, the general fumbled with his glasses, trying awkwardly to position the reading spectacles on the bridge of his nose while holding the letter, and said, "Gentlemen, you must pardon me; I have grown gray in your service and now find myself going blind as well."

This brief, spontaneous remark—a simple gesture of vulnerability from a loyal soldier—touched the heart of each man in the room. "There was something so natural, so unaffected, in his appeal that it rendered it superior to the most studied oratory; it forced its way to the heart," wrote Shaw in his journal. General Washington's simple gesture was jinpa—total openness—and it instantly reminded all his assembled officers that they shared a profound dignity as patriots and soldiers. They had glimpsed in a flash the noble, authentic fiber of their general—a man who had given up everything to lead them—and just as suddenly, they were inspired to drop their anger and fear and express their own nobleness as well.

According to Shaw, some men trembled visibly, and many broke down, crying uncontrollably. Several comrades consoled one another, hugging like brothers. Apparently, General Washington was startled by the reaction as well and later wrote his officers, thanking them for the "affectionate sentiments expressed" toward him during that difficult moment in history. After he left, the meeting ended calmly with little discussion, and the threat of a coup d'état ceased. History records that General Washington and his army remained united and not only received the much-needed support from Congress but went on to win the Revolution and establish the United States as a free democracy.

As a leader, George Washington had many outstanding traits: administrative brilliance, political savvy, patriotic passion, military vigor, and commercial astuteness. Yet what galvanized a nation to fiercely admire and trust him and truly distinguished him as a great leader was his openness—his willingness to be vulnerable and express his humanity in simple, authentic ways. Such openness—time and again—had a profound impact on his troops, his fellow American patriots, and the Continental Congress, repeatedly inspiring them to act on their most noble impulses. His officers trusted him on that fateful day in 1782 because he was open and vulnerable first and foremost.

In the tradition of the mindful leader, being open and vulnerable—whether we are a highway toll collector, a research scientist, or a noted general—is how we break the habit of placing a lid on ourselves and others. By opening, we discover the possibility of inspiring the very best in others and living a dignified life.

Natural Abundance

Frances Moore Lappé

Undoubtedly the world faces great environmental challenges, yet to what extent is our own sense of outer and inner impoverishment—what Chögyam Trungpa called "poverty mentality"—the problem? Here Frances Moore Lappé, author of Diet for a Small Planet, *traces how Buddhism has helped her see that we and our world are richer and more complete than we think.*

My first exposure to Buddhism was in the form of a gift, R. H. Blyth's 1942 *Zen in English Literature and Oriental Classics.* It was 1968, and I was an intense young woman who'd just left a graduate program at the University of California at Berkeley to find my path. I had a lot of reading time as I sat, directionless and frightened, looking out on San Francisco Bay. I guess my husband, the late science ethicist Marc Lappé, thought Blyth might help me.

I had no idea, of course, how Buddhist insights would come to shape my life. All I knew was that I couldn't see how the community organizing I had been doing addressed the root of suffering. So I made a private vow, and that vow launched a lifelong journey. I promised never to do anything else to try to "save the world" until I could explain to myself how what I was doing was related to the underlying causes of the world's deprivation. Then, as I started asking why deprivation and suffering existed, my youthful intuition immediately took a practical turn: food, that's it! If I could just grasp why people go hungry, I could unlock the seemingly impenetrable mysteries of the economic and political order. Then I'd know what to do. So I began my studies.

During many long hours in the Berkeley agricultural library, I read books, reports, and newspaper coverage all warning us of imminent famine. Paul Ehrlich's *Population Bomb* exploded at that time, and soon Garrett Hardin would be telling us that lifeboat earth just couldn't feed us all. Some might have to be left to drown. But in my own modest, follow-my-nose research, I was uncovering something very different: that there was more than enough food in the world to make our entire species chubby. And that's still true today. We humans cannot blame nature for rampant hunger.

Buddhist teachings emphasize the value of "beginner's mind," and only gradually did I become aware that in a very practical way I was living this insight. At first I didn't get it—all the data I gathered and analyzed was there, waiting in agricultural libraries for *anyone* to put together. So, I puzzled, why hadn't they? My self-doubts were huge. How could I, a twenty-six-year-old kid with no graduate degree, be correct, and all the global development PhDs wrong? Why weren't they seeing what I saw?

In 1971 my ruminations and calculations were published as *Diet for a Small Planet,* and my misgivings began to fade. I slowly realized that, no, I hadn't misplaced a critical decimal point. No, I hadn't made some other massive mistake. What I had uncovered was correct: humans had created an economic system that was actually shrinking the earth's capacity to feed us now and in the future. I called it a protein-factory in reverse.

What was the piece of evidence that had been my first clue? I calculated that we in the United States feed sixteen pounds of grain and soy to cattle to get just one pound of beef back on our dinner plates. Plus, a fear of inadequate protein leads Americans on average to eat twice as much as our bodies can use. So half the protein we eat is wasted.

It dawned on me: humans are actually *creating* the very scarcity we say we fear. I probably saw this while the PhDs didn't, because training in a discipline can teach us to jump over "square-one" questions. A student comes to assume that the foundational questions have all been settled and that to advance knowledge—and get ahead in your chosen field—you have to break ground at the frontier, not go "backward" to fundamentals. The discipline itself becomes the frame through which we see—or fail to see. I recall Jane Goodall saying that archaeologist Louis Leakey chose her to observe chimps precisely because she had *not* been trained. Leakey's hunch was that Goodall would see what professional anthropologists had missed. He was right.

Since starting *Diet for a Small Planet,* beginner's mind has held a fascination for me. Later, I came to think of it as the mind trained for pure, unfiltered experience. Yet at twenty-six, my mind was not trained at all. It was just curious. It was *really* curious. "What?" I thought. "We, the brainiest species, haven't figured out how to make sure all of us could meet the most primal, elemental need of all—feeding ourselves and our offspring? Wow. That's curious."

Curiosity, I keep learning and relearning, if it's fierce enough, goes a long way in keeping our minds open. Over the decades curiosity has propelled me to pursue ever-bigger mysteries—from why hunger exists to why we humans keep creating a world that as individuals we abhor. It *is* hard to understand, for, of course, not even the most callous among us gets up in the morning determined that another child should die of hunger or that another species should be wiped out. Yet every day fourteen thousand youngsters die needlessly and a hundred species are gone forever.

This is the puzzle that has kept pushing me on. And as I have probed for answers, I have come to appreciate how hard it is for humans to keep a beginner's open-minded curiosity alive. I have begun to sense how our mental frames—big, largely unconscious ideas—put blinders on us. Neuroscientists now tell us that for the most part we see what we expect to see, unaware of mental frames that filter, organize, and give meaning to our world. There is, therefore, no task more important for survival—our own and that of other species— than to understand the frames through which we see the world, to investigate whether they are, in fact, life-serving, and then to make needed adjustments.

In my case, I started with challenging the premise of scarcity as it relates to food. But soon I realized that the scarcity scare permeates our culture—that most of us believe there is a scarcity of everything, from energy sources to parking spots to caring hearts.

For his 2002 book, *A Buddhist History of the West*, David R. Loy chose for his subtitle "Studies in Lack." Our sense of self is a construct, he writes, and to be "self-conscious is to experience our ungroundedness as a sense of lack." Loy then artfully explores the resulting sense of scarcity, as it drives the unfolding of Western culture. "The objectification of our lack into impersonal 'secular' institutions," he writes, "means that basic questions about the meaning of our lives . . . have become alienated into a 'not yet enough' that can never be enough."

From a presumption of scarcity—a presumption of a lack of goods and of goodness—it follows that we distrust ourselves to engage in honest deliberation about what's best for all, the sine qua non of genuine democracy. Seeing ourselves as essentially selfish and competitive, we believe we must turn our fate over to automatic, impersonal forces, especially the so-called free market. John D. Rockefeller argued that business must follow what was a "law of nature and a law of God." The law of the market, however, has simply become the highest return to existing wealth, that is, to shareholders and CEOs. As a result, wealth, power, and goods have become concentrated in a few hands, and scarcity has become a reality for most people. The theology of the market is one means by which humanity has created the scarcity it claims to fear.

Breaking free of the myth of scarcity, I have come to believe, can allow us to discover our own capacities to heal our world. But are we up to this heavy lifting? Are we able to bring to consciousness the frames defining our choices and then to remake them? Yes, I believe we are. With fresh eyes we can look, for example, at how our culture presents the environmental crisis to us.

Buddhism teaches that the illusion of lack flows inevitably from the illusion of a separate self. Through believing in separateness, we come to see nature as apart from us, filled with "limited resources" that we're fast "using up." We remain in a constant battle with the earth, struggling either to exploit or to conserve her.

When we shift our frame to one of nonseparation, we realize that in a sense the word *consumer* is a falsehood. Nothing can ever actually be consumed, as in "used up," but only transformed. The challenge then shifts. We are no longer "powering down," as some environmentalists put it, because finite fossil fuel is half-gone. Rather, we are coming to align human societies with nature—with the ongoing transformations within nature's endless energy flows. This shift of frame might offer an example of what Loy calls "a here-and-now liberation from our lack" derived from a "nondual inter-dependence of a no longer alienated subject with a no longer objectified world."

Easing fear can help the shift. We might take a deep sigh of relief in learning, for example, that though fossil fuel is running out, there is a huge surplus of solar energy. In fact, the sun's daily energy dose is fifteen thousand times greater than humans now use for all pur-poses. We might also take a deep sigh of relief in learning that there are other resources that we are still not really making use of. Accord-ing to the authors of *Natural Capitalism,* for instance, in the U.S. economy "only six percent of its vast flows of materials actually end up in products." Fully understanding the magnitude of our waste might help us let go of the compulsive production that clearly isn't making us happy. It might make us realize that there is an enormous scope of possibility as we move to new, more satisfying ways of being on earth in relationships that are not driven by scarcity.

And what about the possibility of remaking our presumption that there is a lack of goodness within us? While the West's culture of lack teaches us that humans are, if we peel away the fluff, essentially selfish, competitive accumulators, scientists now confirm the complexity of our capacities and needs. Simulation studies reveal that our brains experience the pleasure of cooperation and the pleasure of chocolate in similar ways, which suggests we are hardwired for empathy and that we enjoy cooperation. We're probably hardwired to desire basic fairness as well. Even Capuchin monkeys demonstrate an innate sense of justice! Scientists thus confirm that a sense of connectedness flows from our biology.

Consciously surfacing our frames and asking ourselves what is useful and what isn't sometimes requires a kick in the pants. Maybe our wake-up call will be the looming environmental consequences of our scarcity-creating frame.

We know that moving beyond any comfortable mental map, as Buddhists of all stripes remind us, is scary. But there are antidotes to fear—the greatest being curiosity itself, writes Oxford historian Theodore Zeldin. Personally, my life continues teaching me just how on target his insight is.

So here I am, four decades away from the "aha" about food's abundance and the myth of scarcity that shook me awake, and I've just created a time capsule for my first grandbaby, Josephine. It's to be opened on her sixteenth birthday, and among the little treasures she'll find in it is *Zen in English Literature*.

"The end of our exploring," T. S. Eliot famously wrote, "will be to arrive at where we started, and to know the place for the first time." I hope that I've *not* come to the end of my exploring—that I am still able, at least from time to time, to let go of my learned frames and to peer again through my beginner's eyes.

Above the Fray

R. J. Eskow

Many people bemoan the decline of civility and respect in American political discourse, and nowhere is it worse than in the high-volume, no-holds-barred world of partisan punditry. Huffington Post *blogger R. J. Eskow wonders how he can practice right speech and cultivate equanimity and still keep his edge as a political advocate.*

> There is no way out of a spiritual battle
> There is no way you can avoid taking sides

In the years since Diane di Prima wrote those words in a poem called "Rant," the United States has become a rantocracy of screaming politicians, pundits, and talk-radio hosts. They shout even when they whisper. Some of us try to make ourselves heard above the shouting, and that raises Buddhist questions: Can a person maintain equanimity and stay in the political debate? And what about the precept of right speech? It forbids lying, of course. But it also means no harsh words, rumormongering, or frivolous talk.

In today's political dialogue, what's left?

I started writing about politics on my own blog in November 2004. The election results had thrown millions of Americans into deep depression. I told myself my only goal was to help, to cheer up the discouraged and persuade the undecided. If nothing else, the act of trying to serve others might bring some longed-for serenity into my life.

In the United States of 2004, even this small act felt important. News outlets had begun the Bush presidency by refusing to broadcast images of massive demonstrations against his inauguration. Now the country found itself in the grip of an unprecedented media blackout of opposing voices and unpopular facts. After the invasion of Iraq, war opponents were rarely seen on the mainstream media. When they were, they were routinely derided as "un-American" or "objectively proterrorist."

A few bloggers began to offer different perspectives. They were punchy, aggressive, colorful, informative. Eventually, blogs began drawing millions of readers hungry for dissenting voices. They began to show their political power. A well-known blogger asked, "Is blogging the new punk?" I felt right at home. My prose was sometimes awkward at first—blogs have their own style—but I slowly began to find an audience and was asked to write for Arianna Huffington's *Huffington Post*, one of the Internet's best-known sites. Within a year of adopting my new vocation, I was appearing on television and radio, being called a slanderer and a hack and throwing my share of punches in return. Peace of mind was more elusive than ever.

The hate mail became more common. Surprisingly, some of the most vehement and personal insults came from atheists. Although I don't believe in an anthropomorphic deity, I was critical of Sam Harris and other New Atheists for what I took as hostility toward Muslims, for unproven assumptions about the power of atheism to prevent social ills, and—in Harris's case—for endorsement of the practice of government torture. This elicited more than one suggestion that I enjoyed engaging in sexual practices with Jesus Christ.

But it wasn't the hate mail that assaulted my serenity the most. The ongoing cycle of poverty, global warming, and endless violence in Iraq weighed heavily. "The only war that matters is the war against the imagination," wrote Diane di Prima. "All other wars are subsumed in it." Political leaders of both parties seemed to lack the imagination to effect real change. And the War Against the Imagination, relentless and one-sided, raged in the media.

I stuck to my principles at first. I tried raising people's morale with humor. I compiled statistics showing that antiwar sentiment had more support than most journalists acknowledged. Maybe it was Buddhism that reminded me in those days: everything passes in time, even defeat itself. I tried to remind others that the tides of history always turn, and turn again.

But the onslaught continued. Joe Klein was a typical example. Although he was billed as *Time* magazine's "liberal" columnist, he routinely made sweeping derogatory comments about progressive Americans. When he said that that there is a "hate America" wing of the Democratic Party, I lost my temper. Klein hadn't always been this way. He had been a decent guy and had written some good books. We had mutual friends. But when I wrote about him, I threatened to respond physically to his insults. I was joking, but the feeling was real. A friend of his laughed and said, "You could take him in a fight, easy."

My Klein piece was meant to defend those he unfairly maligned, but I didn't like the emotions I was feeling. Could the Buddhist practice I'd abandoned years before help me? I sought out the advice of Dharmavidya David Brazier, a Buddhist teacher in the Pure Land Amida Order. He is no stranger to controversy, political and otherwise. Dharmavidya remarked that "in any set of ethical principles there are conflicts. You have to balance priorities. Putting 'right speech' at the head of your priorities renders you politically impotent."

He added, "There are many occasions when honesty is a much higher priority than niceness."

One night a black car came and took me to a small television studio on the second floor of a shuttered office building. Once the makeup person was finished with her work, I was led into a tiny room with a camera and a television monitor, and left there without direction or instructions. Conservative television pundit Tucker Carlson spoke to me over an intercom during a commercial break. "We're going live in two minutes," he said. "So tell me, why did you decide to write about Vice President Cheney's hunting accident, and to call it 'Cheney's Chappaquiddick'?"

Carlson knew that the vice president had accidentally shot a hunting companion, avoided the authorities overnight, then given misleading statements to the authorities. So my answer was brief. "I disagreed with you conservatives about the impeachment of President Clinton," I said, "but you were right about one thing: character matters."

Once we went live, he tried to surprise me with some new "facts" (unproven to this day) about the case. Still, it seemed to go well and I enjoyed it. The high-pressure sparring was an exercise in mental clarity, and I was able to fix my attention on the glow of the red On the Air light. But the next day Carlson used his MSNBC blog—together with an unflattering image of me—to distort my comments about the hunting accident. That was my introduction to the mainstream media.

While I don't claim to be an investigative journalist, I did manage to break two or three news stories that year that got me some more national attention. One involved a new presidential directive that said the United States could act unilaterally to protect its military interests in space. I thought this might lead to war, and I said so. The *Washington Post*, whose media critic had once found fault with my coverage of another newspaper, ran the story a week later, and it began receiving international attention. Soon Al Gore and others were condemning the administration's policy. Russian president Vladimir Putin issued an angry denunciation condemning what he called "unilateral, illegitimate actions." Putin said U.S. leaders were "seeking to untie their hands in order to take weapons to outer space, including nuclear weapons." And he threatened to retaliate.

An MSNBC analyst said that the story was "overblown." He argued that previous space directives under President Clinton weren't very different, and that reports like mine—rather than the administration's actions—could trigger a new Cold War. Was he right? In some small way, could I have helped to *increase* the likelihood of war? It doesn't get worse than that for karma or conscience, but I felt certain he was wrong and wrote a detailed rebuttal. Even right-wing commentators (including the leader of a think tank funded by Boeing) agreed that there was a new administration effort to militarize space.

"Me, help start World War III?" I wrote jokingly. "I *hate* when that happens."

Still, it made me pause. I saw that I carried more responsibility than I had realized. Buddhism teaches that our actions reverberate in unknown ways, but this was more than I had bargained for.

Not long afterward, I took a break from politics to explore the story of JonBenet Ramsey's "beauty pageant" career and her murder at age five. The first comment attached to the piece was short and sharp: "Who cares? Write about Darfur!"

I was furious. I hadn't written a gossip piece. My point was that we—and our children—were being used to fuel an economic engine. We were turning young girls into commodities, encouraging the greed and yearning of adults, and passing our soul-killing cravings to new generations. Now this sanctimonious commenter was calling me—me!—*trivial*? I wrote a scathing response. "I *have* written about Darfur," it began. "Many times, in fact. What have *you* done?"

But I took a deep breath before I posted it. "Guard against mental irritation," say the sutras. "Be restrained in mind." I erased my words, but the unexpressed sentiments turned into a world-class headache. Why was I suddenly so sensitive to criticism? In the *Dhammapada*, the Buddha quotes a saying: "They disparage one who remains silent, they disparage one who talks a lot, they disparage one who talks in moderation."

Criticism is inevitable. It's how we handle it that counts. Perhaps I needed to practice a little harder.

In September 2006, I appeared on Sean Hannity's Fox Radio show with Christian right leader Gary Bauer to argue against anti-Islamic bigotry. Phoning in to the studio from my home, I began by saying that extremists exist among all people and that anti-Islamic fervor was being used by the right for political purposes. They asked me about a recent threat on the Pope's life, where he had been told to convert to Islam or be murdered.

"We all abhor violence and terrorism in the name of religion," I began, "whether it's Muslims exhorting the Pope to convert to Islam, or Ann Coulter saying that we should kill their leaders and convert them to Christianity. That's hateful speech, and all decent people oppose—"

In classic Fox style, Hannity cut me off. "Kind of like Howard Dean saying all Republicans are dark, evil . . . "

"I'm sorry," I answered, "you probably didn't realize I wasn't done yet."

"I *did* realize you weren't done," he snapped. "I just wanted to know if you're just a liberal hack who just likes to go after Republicans."

I tried to remember the Buddha's words: *Let us remain free from hatred in the midst of people who hate.* But my blood was boiling.

"See, this is what you guys do. You don't let people finish—"

"I'll let you finish when I *want* to let you finish."

Do not say anything harsh, or what you have said will be said back to you. "Stop," I said. "Let's do something a little different. Let's see if we can't all agree."

Pause.

"Maybe we can all agree that there is a very hateful, dangerous movement within Islam that needs to be stopped. Can we agree on that?"

Longer pause.

"The most effective way to do that . . . is to support moderate Muslims like the five hundred imams in Britain who signed a fatwa condemning terrorism—"

"Whoa, whoa, whoa. Stop right there." Hannity, an experienced radio performer, cut in to let his equally polished guest make an un-related point. Soon Bauer was concluding, "People like your other guests are more interested in scoring cheap shots against the president than they are in facing the evil that confronts all of us." I was given no chance to respond before the show suddenly ended. The audience of millions was gone in an instant. Standing in my kitchen, I became aware of a humming sound that seemed to come from a long way off. It was the dial tone from the phone in my hand.

I was left feeling angry and frustrated. It was two against one. I had been interrupted, silenced. Friends questioned why I appeared on Fox Radio in the first place, but I had thought I could say something meaningful. Vanity played a part too. A lot of people listen to Sean Hannity.

When I told the story to Dharmavidya, he said, "A crucial point is to try not to lose your cool." How? "Take a time-out. And also recognize that this is the sort of creature we are. Picture the Buddha watching and smiling to himself, saying, 'This is how these humans behave.'

"I think Western Buddhists need to recognize that we are imperfect beings," he said. "In an awful lot of Buddhist groups everybody is pretending to be two millimeters off enlightened, but we're not. Even Thich Nhat Hanh talks in one of his books about how somebody stood up and called him a coward when he was giving one of his talks in the United States during the Vietnam War. He said he was livid and had to leave the hall."

"Hey, big fella!" the e-mail read. "You need to do some more basic research! Ah, no, you don't. Just break more wind and put it up as information."

The *New York Times* reporter was enraged. I had slammed his latest article. His e-mail said I had overlooked some basic points in his story, but I hadn't. It was obvious that he had never read past my first paragraph.

The e-mail was a major blunder for him, and potentially a major win for me. I was ethically free to print it, since he hadn't asked that it be kept off the record. It would make him—and his newspaper—look both rude and careless with the facts. It would bring a lot of readers too. But I hesitated. There was an ongoing debate about carelessness and bias in the *Times*'s foreign policy reporting. This could have an impact. Still . . .

I didn't publish it. The next day I responded, telling him what he had overlooked and explaining why his article appeared to have a progovernment tilt. Here's what came back: "Thank you for replying, and for the thoughtful content of your remarks. . . . You're right, it would have been good if [I had addressed your points] . . . and I concede that I lapsed into vulgarity—but not until I read one of your [commenters'] remarks about my 'castrated journalism.' . . . I look forward to your further comments, and feel free to write." In return, I apologized for the tone of my piece. It felt good, but had I done the right thing? Was an influential reporter now going to be more open-minded? Was I growing spiritually? Or was I just *losing my edge?*

I was certainly finding it difficult to maintain an aggressive, ironic tone, so I asked Dharmavidya about irony and satire. "The Buddha was *attracted* to irony," he said. "He was a prophet with a sense of humor. Once when he was debating the idea that bathing in the holy river is purifying, he said, 'There must be a lot of holy fish.' And when he talked about Jain asceticism, he pointed out that it was designed to end suffering by inflicting even more suffering—on its followers."

So irony, or even its evil twin, sarcasm, isn't necessarily un-Buddhist? "Not necessarily," said Dharmavidya. "The Buddha judged these things based on the likely outcome and how wholesome the speaker's intent is."

"First, do no harm." The physician's precept should also be mine. In an ideal world, everything I write would come with a disclaimer that says, "No animals or humans were harmed in the production of these words." No one. Not Tucker Carlson, or Sean Hannity, or Joe Klein. Not even Dick Cheney. I'm not there yet, but I'm trying.

And equanimity? In the end, it seemed to be like dignity: only you can provide it for yourself, and only you can take it away. Yes, anger still appears sometimes. I'm told to accept it and move on. When I feel I've met my original goal—to be of service—it's been deeply satisfying. But the attention itself can be addictive. It seduces. It has brought moments of excitement and ego gratification, but the pleasure has been ephemeral and unsatisfying. Each such moment was like a brief human life, born of craving and vanishing like lightning. The yearning for attention ultimately proved hollow, like all addictions.

Still, the War For the Imagination is everyone's war, a struggle on behalf of all life. Di Prima, herself a Buddhist, says that "you can't be a conscientious objector" in this war. "No one can fight it but you," she writes, "and no one can fight it for you."

A high government official gave misleading testimony today. There may be more needless suffering unless somebody corrects the record. If not us, then who?

And so, in an unquiet world, the battle rages on.

Choosing Peace

Pema Chödrön

There is always a key moment when we have to choose between peace and conflict. It's true for nations; it's true for each of us. Every time we face conflict with another person, there's a moment when we decide which road to go down. The genius of Pema Chödrön is her ability to pinpoint that moment precisely, analyze why we habitually prefer conflict, and teach us how to choose peace instead.

If we want to make peace, with ourselves and with the world at large, we have to look closely at the source of all of our wars. So often, it seems, we want to "settle the score," which means getting our revenge, our payback. We want others to feel what we have felt. It means getting even, but it really doesn't have anything to do with evenness at all. It is, in fact, a highly charged emotional reaction.

Underlying all of these thoughts and emotions is our basic intelligence, our basic wisdom. We all have it and we can all uncover it. It can grow and expand and become more accessible to us as a tool of peacemaking and a tool of happiness for ourselves and for others. But this intelligence is obscured by emotional reactivity when our experience becomes more about us than about them, more about self than about other. That is war.

I have often spoken of *shenpa,* the Tibetan term for the hook in our mind that snags us and prevents us from being open and receptive. When we try to settle the score, we cover over our innate wisdom, our innate intelligence, with rapidly escalating, highly charged, shenpa-oozing emotionality. We produce one hook after another.

What are we to do about that? We could say that this emotionality is bad and we have to get rid of it. But that brings problems, because it's really the same approach as getting even with other people. In this case, we're basically saying that we have to settle the score with ourselves, get even with ourselves, as it were, by ridding ourselves of our emotionality.

Since this approach will not work, what we need to do is to neither reject nor indulge in our own emotional energy, but instead come to know it. Then, as Chögyam Trungpa Rinpoche taught, we can transmute the confusion of emotions into wisdom. In simple terms, we must gain the capacity to slowly, over time, become one with our own energy instead of splitting off. We must learn to use the tools we have available to transform this moment of splitting in two. Splitting in two is the moment when peace turns into war, and it is a very common experience.

Let's say we're having a conversation with someone. We're one with the whole situation. We're open and receptive and there and interested. Then there is a little shenpa pulling-away, a kind of uneasy feeling in the stomach—which we usually don't notice—and then comes our big thought. We are suddenly verbalizing to ourselves, "How am I looking here? Did I just say something stupid? Am I too fat? That was a stupid thing to say, wasn't it? And I am too fat. . . ."

Some thought or other causes us to split off, and before we know it we're completely self-absorbed. We're probably not even hearing the words of the person we're conversing with, because we have retreated into a bubble of self-absorption. That's splitting off. That's dividing in two.

The Buddha taught about this basic split as the birth of dualism, the birth of self versus other, of me versus you. It happens moment after moment. When we start out, we are "one-with." We have a sense of our interconnectedness, though we might not use that fancy word. We're simply listening and there. And then, split! We pull back into our own worry or concern or even our own elation. Somehow we're no longer together. Now it's more about me and self, rather than them and other. By contrast, being one-with is neither about other nor about self. It's just totally open, present, there.

SETTLING THE SCORE

If the path of the peacemaker, of happiness, is being open and receptive and one with your experience, then settling the score is the path of making war, whereby aggression gives birth to aggression and violence gives birth to violence. Nothing is settled. Nothing is made even. But the mind of settling the score does not take that into consideration. When you are caught by that mind, because of the highly charged and ever-expanding emotionality you're going through, you do not see what settling the score is really doing. You probably don't even see yourself trying to settle the score.

If we started to think about and talk about and make an in-depth exploration of the various wars around the world, we would probably get very churned up. Thinking about wars can indeed get us really worked up. If we did that, we would have plenty of emotional reactivity to work with, because despite all the teachings we may have heard and all the practice we may have done, our knee-jerk reaction is to get highly activated. Before long, we start focusing on those people who caused the whole thing. We get ourselves going and then at some irrational level, we start wanting to settle the score, to get the bad guy and make him pay. But what if we could think of all of those wars and do something that would really cause peace to be the result? Where communication from the heart would be the result? Where the outcome would be more together rather than more split apart?

In a way, that would really be settling the score. That would really be getting even. But settling the score doesn't usually mean that. It means I want my side to win and the other side to lose. They deserve to lose because of what they've done. The side that I want to lose can be an individual in my life or a government. It can be a type or group of people. It can be anything or anyone I point the finger at. I get quite enraged thinking about how they're responsible for everything, so of course I want to settle the score. It's only natural.

We all do this. But in so doing we become mired in what the Buddhist teachings refer to as samsara. We use a method to relate to our pain. We use a method to relate to the underlying groundlessness and feelings of insecurity. We feel that things are out of control, that they are definitely not going the way we want them to go. But our method to heal the anguish of things not going the way we want them to is what Dzigar Kongtrul Rinpoche calls pouring kerosene on the fire to put it out.

We bite the hook and escalate the emotional reactivity. We speak out and we act out. The terrorists blow up the bus, and then the army comes in to settle the score. It might be better to pause and reflect on how the terrorists got to the place where they were so full of hatred that they wanted to blow up a bus of innocent people. Is the score really settled? Or is the very thing that caused the bus to be blown up in the first place now escalating? Look at this cycle in your own life and in your own experience. See if it is happening: are you trying to settle the score?

His Holiness the Dalai Lama has said that he promotes the non-violent, nonaggressive approach to the Chinese occupation of Tibet, despite the fact that things are getting much worse. He takes this approach because he sees that violence is bound to create long-term resentment in others. This is basic intelligence shining through. Basic intelligence recognizes that the resentment caused by a violent response, by a score-settling action, will be the source of future conflict.

We can use our intelligence to exploit other people's capacity to get hooked. Look at advertisements. The advertisers have figured us out a bit. They know how to get us hooked so that we buy something. If you wanted to be really smart and conniving, you could exploit your adversaries' propensity to settle the score. You could encourage them to start retaliating all over the place, so that they will have more and more enemies. You could cause people to hate them more and more. Human beings can be this clever, learning to exploit our propensity to settle the score in order to try to settle the score. There are people doing this, but where does it get us?

We could use that same intelligence to figure out for ourselves that retaliation or aggression gives birth to aggression and that if we really want peace, happiness, and harmony to be the result, there has to be some other way of settling the score than retaliation. That's what Martin Luther King, Jr., said in his acceptance speech for the Nobel Peace Prize. We have to find a way to overcome oppression and violence without resorting to oppression and violence. As you know, he was passionate about this idea and charismatic enough to get a lot of people on board with it. Gandhi, of course, is an example of the same idea of settling the score at a more fundamental level. I use famous examples, but there are women and men, unsung heroines and heroes, all over the world who are working this way to help alleviate suffering. These are people I love and respect, and they are my role models for the Buddhist version of settling the score.

Repaying Our Karmic Debt

Buddhist score-settling doesn't really have to be Buddhist per se, but since the notion of karma figures in, it sounds pretty Buddhist. I offer it to you not because I feel you need to buy it as the best and only way. I offer it to you as an alternative that some have tried with some success. The Buddha's approach to settling the score actually settles the score, because both sides are closer to each other rather than more split apart. They are closer to their true nature, their interdependence.

When something happens to us that we find really painful—an insult, a physical ailment, the loss of someone we love dearly—the Buddhist teachings train us to understand that we have just been given an opportunity to repay a karmic debt. It's a way of talking about settling the score. This is the perspective that the Dalai Lama comes from, and I would say that it is also the perspective that

Martin Luther King, Jr., came from. Many other people who don't call themselves Buddhist but who believe in nonviolent communication and finding a solution to oppression that doesn't itself oppress also see things this way.

A very painful turn of events gives us an opportunity to pay a karmic debt. Of course, there is a belief system involved in this understanding, and I acknowledge that belief systems usually cause lots of problems. They polarize people. The belief system of karma could indeed polarize as well, if we used it to get into battles with people who didn't believe in it. The point of this system, though, is that it works.

The karmic understanding need not be religious nor an occasion for guilt. In fact, it can allow us to act without being guilt-ridden. Anything I cause someone else to feel, either pleasant or unpleasant, resulting from my words, actions, and activities, I myself will feel sooner or later. What goes around comes around. It doesn't necessarily mean that it comes back in the same form, but somehow anything I've caused someone to feel, I will feel at some point in the future. This system applies to good feelings as well, but my focus here is on the karmic repercussions that cause us to try to settle the score.

Therefore, when something unpleasant happens to me, I know it is a debt coming back. I have no idea what I did, so it's not something I have to feel guilty about. I don't have to know the origin of my toothache or of someone slandering me or injuring me. I have no need to go into the history of how I got here. I just say, "I am feeling this." At this point, I have a chance for the buck to stop here. This stimulus does not need to be the cause of evening the score in the usual pain-causing way.

Instead, at this point, you could apply a meditation method that would circumvent the habitual score settling. Whatever practice you use, the point is to stay with the underlying uneasiness and lean into it. Connect with the natural openness of your mind. You can feel at that point that "this debt has just been paid." At that point, there isn't going to be any further debt to somebody else or to yourself, no further repercussions from this exchange except further awakening, further connecting with the natural openness and intelligence of mind, further connecting with warmth and loving-kindness toward yourself, further connecting with compassion and love for other beings. Those are the kind of results that our uncomfortable situations could give birth to. That's a notion of settling the score that is much different from the habitual approach that gives birth to terror and war.

I offer an example from my own life of karmic debt, not because it is in any way special, but because it helps to illustrate how intimate our experience of pain is and how it becomes our teacher. After all, it is our own pain, the many gifts of shenpa that our lives offer, that give us the opportunity to settle the score in the way the Buddha understood. I left my first husband in a very unkind way. I left with the children and went off with another man. It was really sudden and shocking for him, pretty brutal. I was about twenty-five years old and really unconscious about the effect this was having on him, my family, my children, and an array of other people. Ultimately, it was the right decision, but the way I went about it was pretty childish.

Then, guess what? Eight years later my second husband left me suddenly, in a scenario that was eerily, awesomely similar. At that point, I knew I was experiencing what I put my first husband through. The first thing I did was to get together with him and say, "I've said I'm sorry before, but now I really am sorry, because I am now feeling what you felt."

Many people have stories like this. They put someone through something and then they experience it themselves, and somehow they know that they are paying back a debt. It has nothing whatsoever to do with punishment. It's more like a law of physics. There's no one punishing you. There is no master planner making sure you get it. There is no vengeance. It is just a principle that you sooner or later start to feel in your bones.

ALWAYS AT A CROSSROAD

This approach to settling the score is that whenever something bad comes your way, it is always an opportunity for further healing. When things happen to you that you don't like, you can either open the wound further or you can heal the wound. Instead of getting strongly hooked into thoughts like "I don't like," "I don't want," "It isn't fair," "How could they do this to me?" "I don't deserve this," or "They should know better," it's possible that you could train yourself so that the natural intelligence becomes stronger than your reactivity.

For most of us most of the time, our emotional reactivity obscures our natural intelligence. But if we become motivated to start contemplating the approach of seeing pain and discomfort as opportunities for healing—for becoming one-with and bringing people closer rather than splitting—our intelligence actually will get stronger than our emotional reactivity. If we take those opportunities for healing, the momentum of the intelligence will gradually start to outweigh the momentum of the reactivity.

In my experience, the emotional reactivity does not stop. We're not talking about getting rid of the experience of getting hooked. We're talking about when you get hooked, what do you do next? There's a choice. The Buddha teaches us that we are always at a crossroad, moment by moment. We have the intelligence to make a choice, so let's educate ourselves about what the implications of our choices are. Let's break it down. We could choose to open the wound further, creating more suffering for ourselves and others, or we could choose to heal the wound.

The question we usually ask ourselves at this crossroad is, "What will soothe me in this moment?" The habitual response is that what will soothe me is to get what I want, to have my needs met, to get even, to straighten this all out so I come out with what I need. But we have seen what this choice leads to. We need to cultivate that other choice.

The choice I have been talking about doesn't preclude resolving conflicts where parties have been in the wrong. If someone breaks a contract with you, for example, that all have entered into consciously and in good faith, I'm not saying you wouldn't address that breach. Leaving it unaddressed would not be soothing the waters. The precedent would be set, and the irritation would just grow and grow. So there are things that definitely have to be addressed, which is where nonviolent communication comes in. You don't just bite the hook. You don't just fly off the handle. You somehow interrupt the momentum.

There is something you can do before you speak and act. Sometimes that "before" might have to take a long time. I've given the advice many times to students, advice I use myself, that if you're really outraged, type out the e-mail or write the letter, then don't send it. Fold it up, put it in a certain place, then look at it a day or two later. Chances are you won't send that letter. Nobody ever sends that letter. You could rewrite it, but even then you might not send the second letter either, and if you wait long enough the natural intelligence will come in. The knee-jerk reaction is not based on intelligence. It's based on obscured intelligence. The results of this reaction are all too obvious.

As you're acting, you could ask, "Have I ever responded in this way before?" If the answer is, "Yes, I always respond this way. This movie is a rerun," then you're acting unconsciously. You aren't even acknowledging that you're doing it again and getting the same result. It's so strange, really, when you think about it. I don't think we needed the Buddha to come along and point this out to us, but somehow twenty-five hundred years later, here we are. It's crazy.

Nowadays we have instant access to news and sounds and images of all the wars and violence happening all over the world. We can see all around us vivid public demonstrations of how biting the hook and getting swept away does not yield good results. It is not adding up to happiness or peace. If you need an example of how the usual approach to settling the score doesn't work, just look around.

Unfortunately, when we see all this suffering, we want fast results. Once again we might act on impulse and out of emotional reactivity, but if we look at the many examples of people trying to heal and settle the score in the intelligent way, we see that it takes time. The results are slow in coming, but from the larger perspective of natural intelligence and openness and warmth, the process is as important as the result. You are creating the future of the planet by how you work with injustice. You may not see it before your eyes immediately, but you are repaying a debt.

Settling the score in the Buddhist sense is letting the buck stop here, because the pain you are feeling allows you to pay back some karmic debt. For what? You don't know, and it doesn't really matter. All you need to know is that the future is wide open and you are about to create it by what you do. You are either going to create more debt or get out of debt. You could start to pay off the cosmic credit card.

Retreat at Plum Village ◑⟩⟩

Cameron Barnett

*Here is what Cameron Barnett learned from one of the era's greatest voices
of peace. Cameron was thirteen years old when he went with his parents to
Plum Village in France to attend a retreat with Thich Nhat Hanh. This is
not a stylish piece of writing; it is simple, direct, and sincere. To me, that
makes his story of taking the lessons of peace back to his school the best kind
of Buddhist writing, because it's about really putting peace into practice.*

Over the summer I went to retreat in Plum Village, France. Plum
Village is a community of Buddhist monks and nuns located about
an hour and a half from Bordeaux. The head of this community is a
man named Thich Nhat Hanh. He is a Vietnamese monk who was
forced to leave Vietnam during the Vietnam War.

He was forced to leave because he was opposed to the war and
both sides wanted him to join them. He left Vietnam to come to the
United States to speak out against the war, and when he tried to return to Vietnam, the government refused to let him back in. He then
moved to France where he remains today.

Plum Village is made up of four communities where the monks
and nuns live during the year. At different times during the year,

Thich Nhat Hanh offers retreats where people can come and stay for one or two weeks. The community where I stayed was very peaceful with a meditation hall, dining room, and ceremonial bell located in the very center. I lived in a farmhouse that was about a ten-minute walk from the center. It was an eight-room house that held about twenty people. Altogether at the retreat there were about seven hundred people coming from fifty countries.

Hearing Thich Nhat Hanh and visiting Plum Village were so important to me because they showed me the importance of being in the moment and taking things step by step. Thay, as his students call him, taught me to feel sympathy for those who are mean to others or who pick on me because their souls were not better off for what they were doing. He is an extraordinary person. In his presence I felt that somehow anything that I had ever done wrong was OK, and I was happy.

When I returned home, I was much more relaxed and helped some new kids in the school dorm move in. One particular individual, who before had picked on me, came up to me the next day after I got back and made fun of me for going on this retreat. Although it was an extremely offensive remark, I thought back to what Thich Nhat Hanh had told me and simply replied, "How are you today?" He yelled at me again and I said, "I had a great break, how was yours?" It took about a week, but by the next Monday, he no longer picked on me.

My teachers also noticed a change in me. From the second I got back to school I was much more relaxed, calm, and patient. I was also happier. Before when someone had done something I did not agree with, I put up a shell and refused to talk to that person. Thich Nhat Hanh taught me that shutting out the person was no better than picking on him and that if I shut someone out once, it would become a habit. With this in mind I worked hard on becoming friendly to everyone and listening to what they were saying. It was a truly amazing experience, and it has changed my life forever.

Grandmother Mind

Susan Moon

Parents must worry about all the nuts and bolts of their children's care,
but grandmothers, says Susan Moon, can reflect on everything in the
background—the water, air, stories, and love. It seems to me that this
"grandmother mind" is exactly what the world needs more of.

> You can understand all of Buddhism, but you cannot go beyond
> your abilities and your intelligence unless you have robai-shin,
> grandmother mind, the mind of great compassion.
> —EIHEI DOGEN

My son, Noah, told me he wasn't going to have children when he
was about four and I was a harried single mother. It was time for me
to take him to nursery school, and he refused to wear anything but
his fringed cowboy shirt, which was in the washing machine, clean
but wet. I exploded in irritation and he announced, "I'm *never* going
to have kids. It's too much trouble!"

I was chastened. "It's worth it, sweetie," I said. "It's definitely
worth it!"

As he grew up, I watched him cuddle pets and babies, but well
into adulthood he held to his plan of not having children, and I
began to think I might never become a grandmother. A person
can take certain actions to make it more likely that she'll become a

parent, but there's not much she can do to produce grandchildren. So even when Noah got married, I tried to keep my mouth shut. I reminded myself that he didn't come into the world for the express purpose of giving me grandchildren. It was his and Arcelia's business. They had their careers, the economic challenge of parenting, and the imperiled planet to consider. Still, I did mention that I would be glad to babysit.

As a child, I was well loved by both of my grandmothers in their different ways. "Grandma" took me to Quaker meetings, wrote out her favorite prayers for me in a little notebook, and took me down the lane to her sculpture studio, where she gave me clay to play with while she sculpted. I was her first grandchild, and when I climbed into bed with her in the morning, she'd take off her strange, black sleep mask and reach out to me so that I felt the cool, soft flesh that hung from her upper arm, and she'd say, "Good morning, my number-one grandchild!"

My other grandmother, known as "Ma," kept lemon drops in a white glass chicken on her dresser, and if you wanted one, all you had to do was cough a little fake cough and she'd say, "My dear, you must have something for your throat." Whenever we children visited, there were freshly baked chocolate cupcakes with vanilla frosting on a blue tin plate in the kitchen, and you were allowed to help yourself whenever you wanted. She always smelled delicious, of a certain perfume unlike anyone else's, and she wore a gold chain bracelet with a tiny gold airplane dangling from it. I asked her why, and she told me it was a replica of the air force plane her youngest son, my uncle Morton, was piloting when he was shot down over Japan, and she wore it so she would never forget his courage. So small you couldn't even read it, the serial number of Uncle Morton's plane was engraved on the replica's wing.

I learned from my grandmothers the amazing truth that my own parents had been children long ago. I was stunned to learn, for example, that my father had been shy and that my mother had been mischievous. They weren't that way with me! I learned that sad

things happen in people's lives and yet they keep going. I learned of
the turning of the generations: children turn into parents, and parents grow old and turn into grandparents.

I was at home in Berkeley when Noah called me on a Sunday afternoon from San Antonio, Texas, to tell me that Paloma had arrived.
His voice was like a bowl of water he was trying not to spill. She was
twenty minutes old at the time, and they were still in the delivery
room. Everybody was doing well. "Are you happy to be a grandma?"
he asked eagerly, even though he knew the answer.

"Are you kidding? Nothing could make me happier!" Then I
heard Paloma crying in the background. She wasn't exactly crying
for joy as I was. She was crying, Noah said, because they were sticking a needle in her heel to get some blood for a bilirubin test and she
didn't like it.

Driving around Berkeley that afternoon, doing errands, alone in
the car, I kept shouting out, "Paloma! Paloma!"

I thought of all of the other babies born that day, all over the
world, so many of them born into war or crushing poverty. There
are about 353,000 human births a day on planet earth, and I felt like
all of the babies that were born the day I became a grandmother
were my grandchildren.

On that day, the front page of the *New York Times* told of civilian casualties in Beirut resulting from Israel's bombing of Hezbol-
lah, and I found myself wanting to propitiate the gods, God, the
Universe, whatever—to thank them for Paloma's safe arrival and to
ask them to keep her and all babies safe from such violence. What offering could I make and to whom? Checking my e-mail that afternoon, I found a request for help from the Middle East Children's
Alliance, and I made a donation in Paloma's name—my first small
effort, as a grandmother, to protect Paloma and all the others.

When I arrived in San Antonio, Paloma was two weeks old. She was
asleep on her back the first time I saw her, so I could see her whole
face. (Nowadays they tell parents always to put babies down to sleep

on their backs because of SIDS. This was new to me.) Right away I saw how much Paloma looked like Noah when he was a baby—defined, not blobby, her whole self already present in her face. And I saw that she had her mother's huge eyes. Soon she woke and Arcelia nursed her, and then I held her against my chest.

I stayed for a week, in the hot Texas summer, leaving the house only twice to go to the grocery store. I did a lot of cooking while the family napped. I danced around the living room with Paloma, trying to soothe her when she was fussy by swinging her in my arms and singing to her. The more vigorously I jiggled her, the better she liked it, and she didn't care if I couldn't remember all the words to the songs I dragged up from the basement of my mind—Christmas carols and old Beatles tunes. When she fell asleep in my arms, I lay down on my back on the couch, holding her carefully against my chest, and I let her sleep on top of my heart for as long as she cared to. In that time out of time, in that air-conditioned suburban living room, I smelled her sweet head and watched the oak leaves shifting in the hot breeze outside the window.

I learned other new things about taking care of babies—new to me, but based on ancient wisdom. I learned about the five S's for soothing fussy babies: swaddling, swinging, letting them suck, holding them sideways, and making shushing noises. Noah was particularly good at the swaddling and he would coo to Paloma in a deep voice—"There, there, Pumpkin Head, now you're all cozy"—as he tucked the blanket corners around her arms and wrapped her into a snug little package. During the course of my visit, I also heard her addressed by both parents as Petunia, Little Miss Piglet, Florecita, Sweet Pea, Calabacita, and even Bunion Cake.

As for me, to my great delight, Arcelia called me Abuelita ("little grandmother").

Sometimes, though it was 102 degrees, I carried Paloma out into the backyard and she instantly quieted. She looked up at the leaves in the trees and the big space of sky, and I could see her feeling the unair-conditioned air on her cheeks. I could see she knew things were different here in the big outdoors. Noah, too, had loved to look at leaves when he was a baby. He still does.

Zen master Eihei Dogen, founder of the Soto School of Zen in thirteenth-century Japan, told his monks they should all develop "grandmother mind." He said, "You can understand all of Buddhism, but you cannot go beyond your abilities and your intelligence unless you have *robai-shin*, "grandmother mind," the mind of great compassion. This compassion must help all of humanity. You should not think only of yourself."

Parents have to have a different kind of mind than grandparents. Parents have to attend to the nuts and bolts of their children's needs—feeding them, sheltering them, keeping them warm. They have to protect them from cars, from sugar, from kidnapping. Parents take care of the foreground. But grandmothers—both literal and metaphorical—can pay attention to the background, to the water and the air. We can tell the babies stories about the stars.

But sometimes grandmothers have to take the place of parents. Sometimes the parents are in prison or are children themselves or have died of AIDS. Sometimes their ability to take care of their children has been destroyed by warfare, homelessness, or addiction. More and more grandmothers are heads of households, heroically raising their grandchildren in circumstances that don't leave them much time to waltz the babies around the house singing "Norwegian Wood." I want to keep all of those other grandmothers in mind.

One day in San Antonio, I rose, made tea, and brought the *New York Times* in from the doorstep while the rest of the family were having their morning nap. A front-page story about the bombing of Beirut was continued inside. I turned the page and suddenly there was a photograph of an infant half-buried in rubble, her face coated with dust, a small hand showing between broken boards. I folded the paper and put it back on the table.

Later, when Noah sat down with his bowl of granola, I saw him open the paper to the same photo. I saw his eyes looking at that dead baby in the broken concrete, and I heard him make a low groan in the back of his throat as he closed the paper even faster than I had done. It was harder for me to see him see the picture than it had been to look at it myself. I am a grandmother, but I am still Noah's mother. We didn't speak of it.

Looking at Noah looking at Paloma, however, was quite another matter. Arcelia told me the experts say you're supposed to gaze into a newborn's eyes in order to promote its healthy emotional development, but when Paloma's parents gazed into her eyes, they weren't just following directions from a book.

To see your child happy to be a parent affirms the whole spiraling process—our ancestors coming down from the trees so long ago, and our babies staring back up into the branches. Noah, the "too-much-trouble-to-have-kids" boy, is a dad. It *is* a lot of trouble; he's right about that. He's tired out from lack of sleep, though he's not as tired as Arcelia. It's trouble getting up in the middle of the night; it's trouble doing all that laundry; it's trouble working to make the planet a safe place for children. It's trouble, but not too much.

It was hard to tear myself away at the end of the week. Noah put my bag in the trunk and we got in the car, and Arcelia stood in the garage doorway with Paloma in her arms. As Noah backed the car out into the blazing Texas sun, Arcelia picked up Paloma's hand and waved it for her. "Good-bye, Abuelita!" Arcelia called.

"Good-bye, Calabacita, Little Pumpkin," I answered.

Yoga Body, Buddha Mind ⤵

Cyndi Lee and David Nichtern

Mind and body completely interpenetrate, so a spiritual practice—or just a healthy, satisfying life—requires working with both. Many people are finding that doing both Buddhist meditation and yoga is the perfect mind-body combination. Cyndi Lee of OM yoga and her husband, David Nichtern, a Buddhist teacher in the Shambhala tradition, explain how the two traditions work together.

Sitting on our veranda at Strawberry Hill, a mountaintop retreat in Jamaica where we are teaching a workshop, it's easy to feel spacious and alive, vast and open, connected to sky and earth. This feeling comes naturally here but just as easily dissolves when we're confronted with the "too many people, too little time, too much to do" syndrome of everyday life back in Manhattan. Maybe if we lived here all the time we'd always feel boundless and accessible—ah, that's a trap. All of us tend to look outside of ourselves for the source of contentment, and that's exactly how we create our own discomfort. We forget that what we need to find this kind of well-being is completely available to us all the time. It's our own body and mind.

Strength, stability, and clarity of mind are said to be the fruits of mindfulness meditation. That sounds good, but if your back is sore, your digestion is sluggish, and your nerves are fried, it's tough to stabilize any kind of mental wakefulness or confidence. Yoga is a path to these same fruits, but when your mind is jumpy, sleepy, or full of angry thoughts, your body will reflect that with a tight jaw, saggy shoulders, or a knot in your belly.

The body and mind need to work together in order to fully experience clarity of mind and radiant health. That's the recipe for experiencing confidence, interest, and friendliness in our lives. Yoga Body, Buddha Mind is a workshop that we have been teaching around the world for the last six years. It began organically as a synthesis of Cyndi's Tibetan Buddhist practice with the hatha yoga tradition that she has studied and taught for more than twenty-five years. Then we synced it up with David's training in the Shambhala and Buddhist teachings of Chögyam Trungpa Rinpoche.

One of the wonderful aspects of Buddhism is that there is a whole range of meaning to the most basic teachings. The most profound instructions are often concealed in the introductory teachings. Our program on Yoga Body, Buddha Mind breaks the practice into four main sections:

- Making friends with yourself (an introduction to mindfulness practice)

- Dynamic equilibrium (cultivating balance in mind and body)

- Obstacles as path (working with obstacles and resistance)

- Opening your heart (developing kindness and compassion)

In our workshops, David presents the basic theme of each section, as well as how it applies to formal and in-the-field meditation practices. Cyndi follows this with a yoga session, weaving these ideas into how we work with our body and elaborating on how to explore these principles in the movements and relationships of our daily lives. We will follow that structure in this article.

MAKING FRIENDS WITH OURSELVES:
MINDFULNESS MEDITATION

We start with our mind, because doesn't everything really start there? It seems strange, but many of us don't know our own mind. Often without even realizing it, we avoid getting to know ourselves because we think we might not like what we find. Mindfulness provides a way to take a gentle and friendly look at ourselves.

Meditation practice teaches us to recognize when our mind and body are dis-integrated; the body is right here, but the mind may be far away. We practice bringing mind and body together to develop a more harmonious, efficient, and creative relationship with ourselves and our world.

Since this process involves uncovering layers of discursive thoughts and habitual patterns, an important ingredient is to take an open and nonjudgmental attitude toward whatever we discover. Then that approach can be extended into our yoga practice, where the yogi is encouraged to work with her or his present situation without adding stress and ambition. Whatever body we have, whatever mind we have, we look at it with an open heart and a spirit of exploration.

DAVID: Taking a look at our mind begins with our body—taking a strong and stable seat on our meditation cushion. Generally we take a cross-legged posture, but this can be done in a variety of ways, based on our flexibility and comfort level. We can also take a kneeling posture or even sit upright in a chair, with feet flat on the floor and the spine upright and unsupported by the back of the chair. We can simply rest our hands palm-down on our knees or on our thighs just above the knees.

Now we can pay attention to the position of our spine, stacking the vertebrae one on top of the other so that we have a good, upright posture without straining. Our back is strong and stable, and our front is soft and open. We can feel uplifted and dignified by sitting this way.

Our chin is tucked in slightly. There is a sense of containment and relaxation at the same time. The jaw is relaxed. Our eyes remain open in a soft, downward gaze, focusing three to four feet in front of us. There is a feeling of relaxed awareness; we are seeing without looking too hard. We are awake and alert, but in a very peaceful and open way.

Having established our posture, we simply continue to breathe normally. There is no attempt made to manipulate the breath. Then we place our attention on our breathing in a very light and uncomplicated way. When our attention wanders, we simply bring it back to the breathing, time and time again. It's like taking a fresh start over and over again.

Rather than creating an idealized or dreamy state of mind, we start with what we actually have, working with our thoughts and emotions as they arise and accepting the situation as it is. This is why we talk about making friends with ourselves. We start by accepting ourselves as we are and gradually and peacefully bring our attention and breath together. This practice naturally creates more focus, clarity, and stability in our state of mind.

CYNDI: Yoga is an ideal bridge practice between formal meditation sessions and the rest of our life, when we move through the world, interacting with others. So much of what we fear, love, crave, push away, and ignore is stored in our physical body. Practicing yoga with a sense of alertness and curiosity can offer a complete program for getting familiar with our habits, creating space between stimuli and responses, cultivating skillful means such as patience, and doing all of this in an environment that includes other people.

But my observation is that this process does not automatically unfold through yoga practice. Without infusing friendly mindfulness into yoga practice, it is typical for overachievers to bring their aggression to the mat, while chronic underachievers wither from the required exertion. Both extremes are framed by a goal-oriented mentality focused on endpoints such as toe-touching. But once these postures are achieved, then what?

The Sanskrit word for posture is *asana,* which can be translated as "seat" or "to sit with what comes up." When yogis are invited to relax their agenda and open to the vibrancy of their immediate experience—lively sensations in hamstrings, inhalations massaging the lower back, shifting textures of the mind—they are finally practicing asana.

Getting curious about our personal experience (and practice isn't really practice unless it's personal), we begin to notice aspects of our process. "Am I holding my breath and grasping? Or through full breathing, open eyes, and patient heart, could I slow down and wake up enough to create the conditions for fingers to touch toes?" Whatever we notice is fodder for further exploration, both on the mat and after class.

This exploration offers us a nonjudgmental method of communication within our most primary relationship—that of our own mind and our own body. Just as we place our attention on our breath in meditation practice, we can do the same thing in yoga. Of course, when we're turning upside down and inside out, our breath shifts, but it shifts in life too, whenever we are challenged, excited, bored, or sad. This is how yoga practice becomes fertile ground for cultivating a friendly attitude as we move through our day.

DYNAMIC EQUILIBRIUM: NOT TOO TIGHT, NOT TOO LOOSE

"It seems so easy—just sit and watch my breath. So why am I still having so many thoughts?" "I've been doing yoga for six months, and even though I'm trying so hard, I still can't do a full backbend!" "I had a really good meditation—my mind was finally clear!" "I can't do that pose. Never. No way!"

These are all examples of how we can overexert or underapply ourselves in these practices. In order to have a balanced approach toward our effort, we need to recognize that equilibrium is dynamic and fluid, not at all a static process.

As we go deeper with our practice, we can begin to let go of what we think we are supposed to experience. Many students can do a full backbend after six months, but others—perfectly happy people—never do a backbend. Every meditation session is going to be different. The key is to cultivate discipline and exertion, and at the same time relax our agenda.

DAVID: Once we have started on the path of meditation, there are further refinements to the practice as we go along. In general, the teachings are like a road map or guidebook to a journey we have to undertake ourselves.

Beyond making friends with ourselves, we can develop greater stability and equilibrium in our state of being. In many cases, our tendency is to think that we can achieve a particular state of mind (or body, for that matter) and hold it. I think this is the most common confusion that many meditators experience—that there is some absolute right way to do it, some ideal state of mind that we can achieve and sustain.

Actually, our situation is changing from moment to moment, and there is really nothing to hold on to at all. Impermanence is a fundamental fact of our existence. Whatever we experience seems to morph constantly, and it seems like every event, every perception, every thought, every situation is slipping away just as soon as we feel we are getting a handle on it. Our meditation practice is really a way to attune ourselves to this ever-changing experience of the present moment. It is training in the art of living as our life unfolds from moment to moment, like developing balance while standing on one leg on a windy cliff.

This approach is summed up by the slogan "Not too tight and not too loose." As we pay attention to our breathing, we use a light touch of awareness rather than a riveted and stiff kind of effort. On the other hand, if our effort is too loose, we simply wander around in a distracted state of mind, without developing any insight or clarity about how our mind works.

Developing equilibrium means that we ride the energy of our mind like a surfer rides the waves. If the surfer holds too tight, she will fall. If she hangs too loose, she will fall. Sometimes she needs to hang ten, sometimes none at all. Likewise, riding the energy of our mind is a dynamic and ongoing process.

CYNDI: Everybody gets too tight or too loose all the time. This is natural and normal. The yogic approach to balance integrates oppositional forces, the most basic elements being active and receptive. This is what distinguishes yoga as more than a mere exercise program and makes it a natural training ground for cultivating mindfulness.

When I begin teaching students how to do a handstand, most can't do it at all. In addition to the fear factor, they simply don't have the strength, coordination, and concentration required. They practice a few inch-high kicks up and leave it at that, a nice balance of reasonable physical effort and mentally letting it go.

But intermediate yogis, who easily do handstands against the wall, start to crave balancing off the wall. They will jump up and fall back so many times they get in a bad mood. Here's what I say to them to help them shift their process: "If you hear a big boom when your feet hit the wall, you are using too much effort. Find out what is too little. Kick up, but don't touch the wall. Get familiar with the feeling of less. When you learn what is too much and what is too little, you can find just enough."

This is a revelation! When they were beginners, they needed to kick hard to get even slightly airborne. With more strength and courage, their balance will come from tighter mental focus and looser physical effort. Things have changed!

Without waking up to what is happening right now, yogis will literally continue to bang themselves against the wall. With the discovery of a middle path the practice really begins, because that sweet spot of stability is elusive—it won't be the same tomorrow.

It is tempting to want to establish a permanent balance point. But a reliable point of stability—or the amount of effort required to hold a handstand, or fairly manage your employees, or consistently discipline your children—will be different every day. In the *Yoga*

Sutra, Patanjali advises us, "The asanas should be practiced with steadiness and ease." Doesn't that sound like a good recipe for life?

Obstacles as Path: Touch and Go

Actually, from one point of view there is no such thing as a path. We may have the feeling we are making some kind of journey and that it has shape and direction. We are going from here to there, with some specific idea of where we have been and where we are going. But this approach is based on an idealized version of our experience. In reality, our journey is unfolding as we go along.

Learning to bring our full attention to that journey could be called "path." So, as many dharma teachers have pointed out, "the path is the goal." That means that what we experience as "obstacles" along the way is usually just a sense of our own expectations falling apart. These same obstacles can be viewed differently, as the basis for reengaging our attention and working through whatever arises, whether it is a sense of purpose and satisfaction, boredom, resistance, or futility. Work with whatever arises.

DAVID: Going further on our path, sometimes we will experience resistance to the practice itself. We may encounter strongly entrenched habitual patterns, and it might feel difficult to move beyond them. Depression, resentment, anxiety, laziness, frivolity—to name a few—can make us feel there is no point in continuing to cultivate mindfulness and awareness.

A revolutionary approach we can take is to see that the obstacles can actually become the stepping-stones of the path. Our irritation, boredom, emotional upheavals, and wandering mind are the basis of the meditation practice itself. Without them, there is no meditation practice, just some kind of gooey, vague, and highly suspicious sense of well-being that lacks any real strength or foundation. We are just trying to pacify our mind in a superficial way, without working with ourselves as we really are—emotional, speedy, tired, anxious, spaced out, or whatever arises.

By touching on these difficult aspects of our experience—really tasting them and then allowing them to exist without judgment or manipulation—we are tuning into a new kind of spaciousness that is refreshing and creative.

Here we can think of another slogan: "Touch and go." When we are trying to pay attention to our breathing and notice we are off in a daydream, nightmare, or drama of some kind, we simply label that "thinking" and come back to the breath.

There is no need to judge or evaluate the thoughts further. We simply let go, which is actually very profound. We do not need to repress or ignore the thought—that is the touch part. We can touch on our thoughts and emotions and become more familiar with the patterns and movements of our mind. This exploration will, of course, include the ripples of "negative" thoughts and emotions that can sometimes grow into a tidal wave of resistance to the practice itself. Whenever our resistance solidifies like this, it can be helpful to remember why we started with the practice in the first place and simply lean again into our effort.

CYNDI: People are always telling me that they don't do yoga because they are too stiff. No problem! Stiff bodies are perfect candidates for yoga, as is every other kind of body. No matter who you are or what yoga class you take, you'll find that some postures come naturally and some are beyond the realm of your current capacity or comprehension.

Typically, when we hit a yoga glitch, we try to identify an external reason: My arms are too long or too short; I'm too fat, too weak, too old, too short, too tall. Yet somehow those same arms are just the right size for that other easier pose. Hm, perhaps these obstacles aren't so solid after all.

I help students explore this through a pose called Utkatasana, nicknamed Awkward Pose. A "perfect" Utkatasana requires quadricep strength; strong, loose shoulders and lower back; long, stretchy Achilles tendons; and cardiovascular stamina. But you don't need all that to work your way into it. You just need an open mind.

The first time in Utkatasana is fine—for a moment. But when I make the yogis stay longer than they expect, the resistance sparks start flying. Some students try an out-of-body experience—anything to ignore the intensity of this challenging pose. I bring them back with "What are you thinking? Where is your breath?"

Finally, I move them into a flowing sequence where Utkatasana becomes a happily forgotten memory, until I take them right back there again. This time I invite them to find their own way to make this pose workable. "What would it take for you to find ease? Perhaps you could widen your arms, bend your legs less, use less effort, observe your feelings changing."

Of course, the third time they come back to the pose they are ready, and somehow it's not so bad. I tell them that *utkata* means "powerful" and ask them to figure out for themselves how they can feel power without being effortful.

This goes on, and with each Utkatasana I can feel their attitude shift. The dreaded feeling of physical struggle transforms from an eye-rolling, "Here we go again" feeling to a sense of possibility, to "I can't believe she's doing this again," to laughing out loud. What would have happened if we'd only done one miserable Utkatasana?

Opening Your Heart: Maitri Practice

Our hearts are always fundamentally open. They're just covered up sometimes by doubt, hesitation, fear, anxiety, and all kinds of self-protective habitual patterns.

The practice of opening the heart is based on exploring and reversing some of these patterns. We cultivate openness while noting and dissolving the habits that obscure our natural sympathy and compassion for others.

At the physical and energetic level, we have an actual heart and surrounding area that can feel shut down and blocked up. So we can work on opening that area, bringing more *prana* and blood flow and breaking through the constriction and tightness that may have become normal for us.

DAVID: Even though we might feel quite alone in our life and our practice, in the bigger picture we live in an interconnected web with others. The measure of success in our meditation practice is not how much we can transcend the pain and confusion of our own existence, but how much we can truly connect with our lives and with the others who share it.

After creating a proper ground by training our mind, it is a natural evolution of our practice to develop care and consideration for others. In fact, there are many meditation practices that are intended to develop kindness and compassion toward others as well as ourselves.

One such practice is called maitri. *Maitri* means loving-kindness or unconditional friendliness. It can be a natural outgrowth of mindfulness and awareness, but it is also a further step into overcoming and transforming our habitual patterns of selfishness and aggression. Maitri is a contemplative practice that encourages us to use our thoughts and imagination creatively. We actually use the thinking mind to help us develop sympathy toward others.

In some sense, we have already trained ourselves to be self-centered, uptight, jealous, and short-tempered. We can also train ourselves to be expansive, open, generous, and patient, because our thoughts are not as solid as we have made them out to be. They actually come and go in a somewhat haphazard fashion, with a tendency to repeat certain patterns that have become comfortable and familiar. It is entirely possible to step out of these patterns altogether and, through contemplation, develop more positive habits that benefit oneself and others.

In maitri practice, we start by tuning into somebody we love and wish well. Then, through the power of directing our thoughts and intentions, we try our best to extend that loving feeling toward our indifferent group, then even to our enemies, and then gradually to all beings everywhere. We recognize that none of these categories of friend, enemy, and don't-care is really solid anyhow. They are all changing year to year, day by day, and even moment to moment.

The traditional form that our good wishes takes is contained in these four slogans:

May you be safe.

May you be happy.

May you be healthy.

May you be at ease.

We bring our loved one to mind, then ourselves, then the neutral person, and then the "enemy" or irritating person. In each case, we simply repeat these slogans or contemplate their meaning. In this way, we can deliberately cultivate and direct our goodwill and positive intentions toward ourselves and others.

CYNDI: There's good news right off the bat here for yogis, because just the fact that you've come to yoga class is an act of kindness toward yourself. Asana practice is an unparalleled method for removing energetic obstructions that make it tough to feel good or to have energy for yourself and others.

In yoga the primary activity of the arms is to support the function of the heart and lungs, the heavenly internal organs associated with feelings, vision, and the primary channels of life force, or prana. When our breath and blood are circulating freely, we feel fully alive and more available to ourselves and others.

Circulate is what we want our emotions to do too. A sunken chest, slumped shoulders, and drooping chin inhibit energy flow and wholesome feelings. They're depressing. The opposite is equally true—if your chest, back, and heart muscles are supported, spacious, and mobile, you will breath better and feel cheerful.

Loving-kindness asana practice focuses on heart-opening poses. We rotate our shoulders, open our ribs, and do backbends that release chest muscles and unlock sensation in the heart center. Some of these poses are challenging, but they can be done with curiosity and gentleness. One way I try to make them fun is by creating community.

Partnering exercises such as supported backbends or holding shoulders in a group tree pose teach us how to support and be supported by others. When everybody falls over, we laugh! It's a clear example that if something doesn't work for everybody, it doesn't work. It's an immediate reminder that our minds and hearts truly extend past the apparent boundary of our body. The sense of "other" starts to dissolve. We can experience interdependence right there on the yoga mat.

Traditional yoga theory emphasizes *ahimsa,* or "nonharming." By applying maitri to how we work with relationships in yoga class, we grow the seed of ahimsa into an active blossoming of seeing others and consciously connecting to them. This shows up in our class etiquette: "Can I move my mat over to make more space for a latecomer?" "Can I pass you a tissue?" Yoga class becomes a safe haven for practicing kindness with like-minded seekers and gives us the skills to handle what we meet when we walk out the door.

The Body and Mind You Have

When we started teaching Yoga Body, Buddha Mind, it appeared to be a somewhat unique offering among both the yoga and Buddhist communities. In general, the yoga community in the West was not familiar with Buddhist practice, and Buddhists were not particularly interested in hatha yoga practice.

But although yoga is a wonderful method for getting a strong and fluid body, it can also be a way to solidify habits of attachment and aversion. And even though you might be able to sit on your meditation cushion for a month, when you try to get up after thirty days—or thirty minutes—it might take just as long for your legs to start working again. That's why we find that the practices of yoga and Buddhism complement each other so well.

Yoga and meditation are not ends in and of themselves. You may not ever put your leg behind your head, but you might find yourself having more patience with your children. You may only have ten minutes a day to practice mindfulness meditation, but you might find that wakeful energy and compassionate outlook creeping into your staff meetings at work.

No matter what your job is, who your family is, what country you live in, or what planet you live on, your body and mind will always be with you. Our identities are all tightly linked with how we feel about our body and our mind—"Am I fat? Am I smart?" Perhaps this integration of meditation and yoga will inspire you to get to know your body and mind better—maybe not the body you had when you were twenty or the mind you had when you got that high score on your SATs, but the good body and mind you have right now.

Emotions: What They Really Are

The Dzogchen Ponlop Rinpoche

What is our most powerful experience as human beings? I think it is our experience of emotion. Emotions create great joy and intense suffering for ourselves and others; they are a powerful source of energy and very difficult to tame. This teaching by The Dzogchen Ponlop Rinpoche offers a step-by-step path for understanding and working with emotions. It exemplifies the practical genius of the Tibetan Buddhist system.

Whatever our condition in life—whether we are young or old, wealthy or impoverished, educated or illiterate, from here or from there—we all are touched by the same emotions that bring happiness one moment and suffering the next. Though we all wish to be happy and pursue that state daily, we may feel that our efforts in that direction are often ineffectual. At the end of the day, instead of feeling content, we may feel that we have missed the boat once again; in fact, we can practically see it sailing off without us.

We might ask ourselves why, when we aim only for happiness, we often end up so far from our target. What is it that interferes with our aspirations and intentions? From the perspective of the Buddhist teachings, four profound truths are taught about suffering.

First, suffering in this life is inevitable. Second, that suffering has specific causes; it is not random. Third, there can genuinely be an end to that suffering; we can go beyond it. Fourth, the transcendence of suffering also has specific causes. Generating those causes is what we call "the path." It is known as the path that leads beyond suffering, the path to liberation, the way to enlightenment, and so forth. In other words, just as suffering has causes, so too does transcendence; it is not random.

In the context of the Buddhist spiritual path, the transcendence of suffering does not just mean that our relative suffering ceases and we achieve a continual state of relative happiness. It means we transcend the causes and conditions that obscure mind's true nature and achieve the state of full awakening. Our goal on this path is the realization of our inherent potential for wisdom and compassion, which is unconditioned, ultimate happiness. Being on this path means that we are willing to work with our minds, and we are willing to be uncomfortable at times in the process. It also means that we have a great curiosity about how things work, and we have a certain degree of passion—for truth and authentic experience.

Since our suffering and pain have causes, if we discover those causes, then we can remedy them. When we are looking for the causes of our suffering, the teachings of the Buddha direct us to look first at the mind as the source of our experience and the means for understanding it. When we look inward, we can see that one of the primary sources of distress in our lives comes from our experience of the emotions: they seem to arise suddenly; they color our world and send us off in different directions; they spawn all kinds of hopes and fears and do not respond well to reason. Under their influence, we may fume with anger, light up with pleasure, or become unresponsive and dull. Therefore, it is essential to see what the emotions are more precisely and completely. We need to get to know our emotions, recognize their various forms, and understand how they work. We also need to uncover any preconceptions we have about them. Do we celebrate them for the richness they bring to our lives or fear their provocative energy? Do we suppress or indulge them? Are we even aware of their presence as we go through the day?

The term that is translated into English as "emotion," is the Sanskrit word *klesha*. While they are generally equivalent, there are also notable differences in their usage. Both refer to mind states in which feeling is predominant, in contrast to cognitive functioning; both describe these mind states as characterized by greater or lesser degrees of agitation, which are accompanied by various physical responses. Therefore, from the Buddhist perspective, emotions are often called "disturbing emotions" or afflicted mind states. The scope of the meaning of the term *klesha* is also broader. It refers not only to our ordinary, confused experience of the emotions, but also to the basic cause of suffering, which is ignorance. It is traditionally taught that there are three primary, or root, kleshas: passion, aggression, and ignorance. From these three, jealousy and pride develop. Together, these five are called the "five poisons." Such afflicted mental states obscure the natural clarity of mind and are the cause of many unskillful actions. Thus, generally speaking, when unattended by mindfulness and awareness, the emotions are regarded as destructive mental states that increase suffering.

A System for Understanding What Emotions Are

As we gain a deeper understanding of our emotions, however, it is possible to see and work with their intense energy in progressively more profound and skillful ways. According to the Buddhist teachings, there are three distinct ways to view emotions, or three different outlooks we can have toward them. The first is to regard emotions as enemies or poisons that are toxic to our well-being and spiritual path. The second is to regard them as friends or as supports for our development. The third is to regard them as enlightened wisdom itself.

Each of these views has a corresponding method or approach to working with emotions. When emotions are viewed as poison, the most effective method for dealing with them is to relinquish or renounce them. When they are viewed as friends or supports, we work with their basic energy to transform negative patterns into positive ones. When they are viewed as enlightened wisdom, the emotions themselves are taken directly as the path. In addition, once we have an understanding of these views and methods, there is a specific, three-step technique that can be applied whenever an emotion arises. These three steps are called: mindful gap, clear seeing, and letting go. Employing this technique is immediately beneficial because it prevents us from being overwhelmed by emotionality, allows us to see the larger context in which an emotion occurs, and brings us closer to an experience of its actual nature.

First, Seeing Emotions as Poison

When we first begin to work with our emotions, we do not know them very well. At this stage, it is necessary for us to approach our emotions carefully, with respect for their destructive power and potential to overwhelm us. Therefore, we initially regard them as enemies, as poisonous states of mind that induce misery and illness. Because of the danger they present, we try to prevent them from developing into full-blown states over which we would have no control. The method we practice at this time is to relinquish, abandon, or reject them on the spot by the application of specific antidotes. When aggression arises, for example, we can apply the antidote of patience.

In this approach, the antidote and the emotion are seen as separate; the antidote is something that must be applied in order to get rid of the emotion. In other words, there is a distinct separation between the antidote and what the antidote is remedying. If we were to contract a bacterial infection, we would go to a doctor who would give us an antibiotic. In this way, we would heal the infection and return to a state of health. In the same way, emotions are regarded as sicknesses and their antidotes are regarded as the medicines that bring about a cure, that return us to a balanced and healthy state of mind.

In general, at this stage, it is important to contemplate the negative effects of our emotions—the many ways they impact us as well as those around us. It is essential to see clearly the full range of destruction they can cause. Furthermore, we must come to see that it is our habitual ways of dealing with emotions that make them so problematic and harmful.

Although the method of relinquishing the emotions is often helpful, there are times when it is not quite enough. No matter how badly you want to cut through an emotion—to stop it or turn it off—it still continues to arise. When that happens, what do you do? If you continue to apply this method alone, telling yourself, "I must get rid of it, I must get rid of it," you will find eradicating that emotion even harder. In that case, it may be more useful to think, "Since I am having this emotion right now, I will look at it in a different way and make the best use of it."

Next, Seeing Emotions as Useful

In the second stage of working with emotions, the view and methods are more profound. At this point, when we look at the emotions, we do not see enemies or danger. Instead, we see friends, helpers, or allies. Viewed as friends, the emotions do not threaten our well-being but are regarded as essential to the development of deeper levels of knowledge and insight; they are therefore seen as containing tremendous potential to liberate us from states of suffering. In fact, it is said that there can be no path without them.

Once we have achieved some degree of familiarity with our emotions, then we can see that they are not inherently negative. Practically speaking, emotions can be either positive or negative; it depends on how we experience them, work with them, and manifest their energy. From this perspective, our disturbing emotions are both the sickness and the cure; they are both the negative factors to be relinquished and the antidote that counteracts their adverse effects. In contrast to the earlier method, the gap between the emotion and the antidote is much narrower—there is not much difference between the two.

How do our emotions transform from enemy to friend, from destroyer to supporter of happiness? At this point, whatever emotion arises, we work with it to transform its negative manifestation into a positive expression. When we see our habitual tendency to become angry manifest, we do not run from it or try to get rid of it. We see it as an opportunity to reprocess or recycle that energy so that it becomes something useful. In this sense, every emotion can be recycled. Nothing needs to be thrown away or treated as garbage, as waste.

Therefore, all our mental afflictions can serve as supports for our path. They can help us to go beyond the cycle of suffering. We should not become discouraged when they arise or irritated with those whom we perceive as provoking them. If there were no one to make us angry, for example, how would we ever perfect our practice patience? The people who make us angry are very helpful. In fact, they are indispensable to attaining enlightenment.

Similarly, the panhandlers on the streets who ask us for spare change are helping us perfect the quality of generosity. An act of generosity depends on there being both someone in need of support and someone who offers it. If we have difficulty with giving, then when we meet with such a situation, it is a great opportunity to see our habitual patterns and transform them. We can practice being more liberal with our resources and more understanding and sympathetic toward those in distressed circumstances. That is why we should not get irritated by being asked for help, but simply give what we can. If we were already perfect, there would be no need to practice because there would be no mental afflictions to overcome. If we were already generous, we would not need to practice generosity, as there would be no miserliness to overcome.

In the same way, we can recycle all our emotions into something positive and useful. We can recycle miserliness into generosity, desire into discipline, aggression into patience, laziness into diligence, distraction into concentration, and ignorance into discriminating awareness. That means that there are no emotions that we need to get rid of, that are useless or a waste of our time. All emotions and adverse conditions we face in our lives have the potential to become valuable supports for our path. That is our view at this stage: once an emotion has arisen, you make the best use of it.

Finally, Realizing Emotions as Wisdom

In the third stage, emotions are viewed as wisdom. That is their true state. They are regarded neither as destructive nor as simply having a positive potential. Rather, the very nature of all our emotions is taught to be wisdom that contains tremendous clarity, insight, and compassion. Therefore, there is no need to change or transform them. From this perspective, we take the emotions themselves as the path.

According to the Buddhist view, the abiding nature of our mind is wisdom and compassion, which are always together, always in union. That nature is perfectly pure; it is luminous awareness that has never been obscured or stained by our confusion, by the occurrence of afflicted mind states. When that wisdom and compassion manifest outwardly, their energy manifests in five aspects, or particular qualities of wisdom. These five aspects are termed the "five buddha wisdoms," or five enlightened qualities of awakened mind. These five wisdom energies are the pure essence of the five poisons.

When the energy of our emotions arises, if we are under the influence of confusion, then we perceive that energy as one the five poisons—passion, aggression, ignorance, jealousy, or pride. If we are free from confusion, then we recognize the emotion's essential nature and perceive it as the display of wisdom.

At this stage, we are looking at a deeper level of experience. We are looking directly, or nakedly, at our emotions and seeing their true state. This is called taking the emotions as the path. The result is that we discover the inherent wisdom of the emotions, and we see that there is no need to change them. When we take this approach, there is no separation between the path and the result. We take the emotions as our path, and there is no other path aside from that.

In contrast, in the earlier stages, the methods are more indirect. We must first either get rid of our emotions or else transform them in order to find our way out of suffering. Even when we have reached the level of appreciating our emotions, there is still a slight sense of dissatisfaction because there is something remaining that is not right. Though we see the value of our emotions, we still think they are not good enough as they are—we *must* transform them into something more positive. Either way, it is necessary to change our emotions before we can deal with them directly. In the third stage, however, no change is needed. The essence of the emotions is not only the path—it is the result.

THE THREE VIEWS AS STEPPING-STONES TO WISDOM

All three of these views, together with their methods, have a vital purpose. If you regard them as stages within a larger scheme—rather than as separate choices—then the process of working with your emotions becomes very profound. If you separate them as three distinct choices, then your path will be incomplete. The most beneficial viewpoint is to see them as sequential stages through which you progress, with the first stage becoming the stepping-stone to the second, and the second stage becoming a stepping-stone to the third.

In the first approach, we focus on the negative aspects of emotions, and we make every effort to thoroughly comprehend their potential to cause harm to ourselves and others. This leads us to see why we must abandon engaging in the emotions without any sense of mindfulness or discipline. This understanding prepares us to view our emotions from a new perspective. We see how they can be either positive or negative, depending on how we relate to them. We find this viewpoint in Western psychology as well, where emotions are not regarded as being necessarily negative but are considered to be positive factors in personal growth.

In any situation, we always have two choices: we can look at its positive side or its negative side. If we are looking at the character of an individual, for example, we can choose to focus on his or her strengths or weaknesses. If we are judging the usefulness of a medication, we can focus either on its ability to reduce high blood pressure or on its side effects, such as muscle pain and dizziness. Or take a sharp knife—is it positive or negative? It is neither. It is a matter of how it is used. A sharp knife can cut vegetables that help to feed hundreds of people, but it can also cut off a finger or end a person's life. There is a positive side and a negative side to everything. In the second stage, we view emotions like a sharp knife, with an emphasis on their positive potential.

In the third stage, we view the emotions as being utterly pure and thoroughly positive. At this point, we are seeing the ultimate nature of emotions and not simply their relative, or confused, manifestation. Any display of emotion becomes the display of wisdom mind—an experience of mind's true nature. The question is only whether—and how—we connect with that experience.

As we learn and work with these methods, they become very effective tools for bringing our path to fruition. To be on the path means to work with our minds and to engage in activities that will progressively diminish suffering and increase the good qualities of happiness, wisdom, and compassion. Many methods are taught for working with our mind, and all of these can contribute toward achieving our goal. The practice of sitting meditation, for example, helps us to calm our busy mind so that we experience a greater sense of peace and clarity. Then there are the trainings in compassion, which help to transform our usual, self-centered way of thinking into concern for the welfare of others.

Such practice instructions are straightforward and easy to understand. For sitting meditation, we are taught to simply follow our breath, let go of our thoughts, and relax. If we are practicing generosity, our intention is simply to benefit others by offering whatever we can. If we could just practice according to those instructions, our journey would be quite simple; but, in fact, we spend most of our time struggling to calm our agitated mind, in a state of distraction. Where does our difficulty come from? Why isn't it as simple as it sounds?

The primary obstacle we meet with when we begin to work with our mind is our own ego-clinging. By *ego*, we mean the sense of "I" that we perceive as being "me" or "myself." *Clinging* refers to our ingrained habit of holding to that "I" closely and making it the primary reference point for all our thoughts and actions. According to the Buddhist view, this ego is illusory; it does not truly exist in any permanent or ultimate sense. Yet we cherish this "self" inordinately, and it is just this "I" that feels anger, passion, jealousy, pride, or indifference in relation to other people and things. Thus, all our disturbing and persistent emotions are tied closely to our ego-clinging, and most of our time in meditation is spent trying to pacify those emotions.

In other words, we spend most of our time working with obstacles, rather than working with the path itself. By finding ways to work skillfully with our emotions and ego-clinging, our path becomes much more effective. If we can use our emotions to pacify our emotions—if we can use what we already have to achieve our goal—then the path becomes much quicker.

Since emotions are so varied in type and strength, the ways of pacifying them may be different as well. Some emotions can be pacified through meditation and the conventional path of practice. Other emotional tendencies should be treated in the beginning by mental health professionals. We may need assistance from psychologists or psychiatrists to process emotions in the early stages of working with them. When the emotion is based on an imbalance in the elements of our body, we may need help from physical health professionals. Sometimes different kinds of medicines, exercises, or physical adjustments can be very helpful. In particular, yoga can be very beneficial, especially if practiced in conjunction with other methods of working with the emotions. Yoga can relax our body, so that our mind can follow suit. While meditation can solve some people's emotional problems, others might need the aid of additional methods. We have to find remedies that work for us.

Past Causes and Present Conditions Create Suffering

In order to work with our emotions, we must find out how they operate. From the Buddhist point of view, emotions arise on the basis of two things: causes and conditions. The first, cause, is the karmic cause or seed, which may have been planted in this life or in past ones. The second, conditions, refers to environmental factors in the present that could exert an influence on the ripening of that seed. When the environment contains conditions that support the growth of the seed, then the seed will develop and produce its fruit, or result.

According to the Buddhist view, the particular body that we have right now is a result of karmic seeds. The physical existence of all beings—human, animal or insect, or other—is produced from karmic seeds. Further, there is a fundamental relationship between the physical body and the mind; this means that there is a physical as well as a mental basis for our emotions.

In the field of neuroscience, there are some studies that say the experience of emotions is triggered as a result of the firing of certain neurons and electrical impulses that stimulate particular areas of the brain. From the Buddhist point of view, however, emotional experience does not originate solely on the basis of physical stimuli; it is the product of karmic seeds and supporting conditions, which *include* our physical body and genetic makeup.

These karmic seeds are of two types: common and individual. Common, or group, karma is like the DNA that is shared by all human beings and that makes us all "human" as opposed to another form of being. Beyond that, there is individual karma, which is like the DNA we inherited from our parents and which makes us a particular person. Because of common karma, we share certain experiences with others, like being born in the East or West, in a time of peace or war. Because of individual karma, we possess physical and mental characteristics that are particular to us. We may be tall or short, industrious or lethargic, artistically or athletically inclined. The environment we live in may support values of kindness, liberality, and peace, or it may breed aggression, fear, and chaos. We may find ourselves in harmony or in conflict with our environment.

From the Buddhist perspective, all of this is not random; it is cause and effect, which is the definition of *karma*. The source of karma, ultimately, is the mind: a thought or intention produces an action—a word or deed—which then produces a result. Therefore, the term *karma* is not a statement of religious belief or doctrine; it is more of an acknowledgement of cause and effect.

The scientific studies that look at the physical elements and mechanisms involved in the arising of emotions are producing more and better information every day. However, even when looked at from a purely physical point of view—emotion as a physical event—there is still the functioning of cause, supporting conditions, and effect. The functioning of our brain and nervous system is affected by factors such as the foods we have eaten, how well our respiratory system supplies our blood with oxygen, and the way our particular brain and its pathways are formed.

It is important for us to see the correlation between body and mind. In the Buddhist view, the body is seen as a support for our mental activities. The way body and mind develop and function is directly connected to their karmic causes, in conjunction with present conditions, which exert different degrees of influence. Thus, the functioning of our body and mind in any moment is dependent upon the numerous causes and conditions that preceded that moment.

Accordingly, emotions do not arise haphazardly or randomly, without causes or conditions. They do not arise suddenly out of nowhere, as we often think. When we perceive an emotion as arising abruptly or unexpectedly, it is because we do not see its causes and conditions, which can evolve from subtle habitual tendencies, or karmic seeds, that have lain dormant in our minds like "sleeper cells." When they become activated, the emotion "suddenly" appears.

The Buddha, in the Abhidharma teachings, called these dormant tendencies "small growers" or "subtle expanders," which means that they start from very subtle causes and conditions and then grow into something very large. At the moment we perform any action, whether it is positive or negative, that action makes an imprint in our mindstream. That imprint is like a seed; it carries the potential to ripen and yield a result. We develop habitual tendencies when we perform certain actions repeatedly. If we become angry and speak harsh words once, then when someone irritates us in the future, we may be more likely to react in the same way. Over time, we may develop a predisposition to speak harshly, even with less provocation.

When present conditions in our environment also support this tendency, for example, if we are undergoing stress at work, having difficulty with relationships, or struggling with an illness, then that latent tendency can expand suddenly. It can be triggered by something small—a moment of frustration or impatience—but then all these factors can combine to supersize it—like they do at McDonald's. This is simply the action of karma, the coming together of many causes and conditions, which produces a certain result.

If we are going to rid ourselves of the destructive aspect of the energy of emotions, we cannot work just on the conditions that are present in our physical and psychological environment. We must work on transforming both the causes originating from the past and the present circumstances in our lives that condition our minds and enmesh us in negative habitual patterns. In many cases, systems of psychotherapy work on the level of conditions rather than on the causal level. Such approaches are helpful for gaining enough stability and strength of mind so that we can reach the cause through the practice of meditation. It is helpful, therefore, to recognize that our emotional disturbances develop from both causes and conditions. Conditions are more easily seen, as they exist and function on a more superficial level; causes are underlying influences and exist at a deeper level of mind.

How to Work with Emotions

Having familiarized ourselves with the three stages of working with the emotions, we can now look at a further means for dealing with our emotions in our day-to-day lives. There is a three-step technique that can be applied at any stage of our practice. Whether we are viewing our emotions as poisons, as friends, or as manifestations of enlightened mind—or whether we are renouncing our emotions, transforming them, or taking them as the path—we can employ the three steps of mindful gap, clear seeing, and letting go.

The first step, mindful gap, refers to the practice of distancing ourselves from whatever emotion may be rising. While remaining mindful and aware, we feel the emotion and hold still, without reacting. We can then view the emotion and the experiencer of the emotion as being separate. We feel that there is a gap between the two. It is this gap, attended by mindfulness that provides the ground or psychological space for working with our emotions. When we are able to create a "safe" distance, we can see the emotion more clearly without becoming overwhelmed by it.

The second step, clear seeing, refers to developing our ability to see clearly both the emotion and the landscape in which it occurs. In this way, we see the whole picture. We see not only a specific emotion and its characteristics, but also our emotional patterns and their relationship to our interactions with the people and events in our environment. In this way, we develop a more profound understanding of our emotions and their internal and external causes and conditions.

The third step, letting go, refers to the methods by which we physically and mentally release emotional energy. While there are several approaches to this, including physical exercise, working with the breath, and relaxation techniques, the primary method is letting go through awareness. The very fact of being aware is already a process of letting go. If we have properly applied the first two methods of mindful gap and clear seeing, then at this level, we begin to let go of our fixation or grasping onto the emotion itself.

As we learn these three steps, we develop our capacity to relinquish the emotions, to transform them, and finally to recognize their ultimate nature of wisdom.

Not Our Bodies, Not Ourselves: Life Lessons from a Cadaver ꙮ

Hannah Tennant-Moore

The starting point of Buddhism is a simple but profound truth: impermanence. We may pay lip service to the truth of impermanence, but there's nothing we work harder to avoid or deny, particularly our own impermanence (also known as death). Here, Hannah Tennant-Moore brings a modern sensibility to a traditional meditation on impermanence and attachment.

Since my sister began medical school last fall, she has spoken constantly about an obese female corpse she refers to as "my cadaver": "She's so fat, it's hard to find the nerves and muscles. You have to do a lot of poking around." Or, "When we first opened her up, there was still shit in her intestines. Can you believe that? She died two years ago!"

Although I was amused (and occasionally disgusted) by my sister's eagerness to share every new detail about this dissected body,

I was also bothered by her apparent remove. After all, this had once been a person. It reminded me of the "Reflection on the Repulsiveness of the Body" from *The Foundations of Mindfulness (Satipatthana Sutta)*, in which the Buddha taught his followers to contemplate what we're made of: "the contents of the stomach, feces, bile, phlegm, puss, sweat, solid fat, tears, fat dissolved, saliva, mucus, synovial fluid, urine." And when he had a captive audience at the cemetery, his descriptions got really vivid: monks were to meditate on "a body dead one, two, or three days: swollen, blue, and festering" and "blood-besmeared skeletons . . . eaten by crows, hawks, vultures, dogs, jackals, or by different kinds of worms." The list goes on and on. Monks were instructed to consider that their own bodies would someday meet the same fate.

It wasn't the gruesomeness—in either these descriptions or my sister's—that I objected to, but the revulsion they expressed. I was particularly put off by the fact that these meditations were used as a tool to fight lust, being a rather lustful nineteen-year-old myself when I first read them. "Okay, I get it," I thought. "The body is impermanent; the body you're now attracted to will someday be a stinking mass of rotting flesh—but do we have to find it repulsive?" I could see nothing wrong with praising and enjoying the body.

I went to visit my sister at school for the first time recently, and naturally she wanted to give me a tour. She showed me the lecture hall, the interfaith meditation room, her large wooden locker filled with dirty scrubs. "Oh, and the cadavers," she remembered brightly, as if it were just another lab or classroom. The room was cold—to keep the bodies from rotting—and windowless. There were about twenty of them, all covered in dirty white plastic. A couple of charred bones floating in the Ganges were the closest I'd ever been to a dead body. At first, I had the feeling that we were not alone in the room, which is what most of us have come to expect from a body—that it equals a person. I felt the urge to pray. I felt the urge to flee. I felt like a voyeur.

And then she lifted the plastic off a body, and suddenly all that went away. It was surprisingly easy to look at, like the plastic model skeleton that was wheeled from classroom to classroom in elementary school—as inhuman as that, but a thousand times more interesting. A surgeon's cut ran from the skull to the perineum, which allowed my sister to show me the parts. She peeled open the thick, rubbery flaps of skin and lifted up a baseball-sized heart. She dug around in the tissue of the upper arm until she found a nerve, which looked like a thick pink rubber band. "Isn't this amazing?" she said. "This is how you know to move your hand." It was hard to find the interesting parts among the excessive fatty tissue. "Jeez, this one's even fatter than my cadaver," my sister observed helpfully, so we moved along to another one.

She showed me brains, blackened lungs, ovaries, biceps. The intricacy and self-sufficiency of it all was what struck me most—that we're carrying around all these various parts, nestled in just the right places, carrying out their specific tasks as we go blindly about our business. These bodies were machines; however miraculous, they had nothing to do with the lives that had once inhabited them. This was true even for the body that had a kind, grandfatherly face, perfectly preserved, with white eyelashes and papery skin—I could tell what he once looked like, but he was nowhere near that room.

This viewing came at a time when I was excessively concerned with body image, having just moved to Southern California, where tank tops and miniskirts are standard attire year-round and first dates often involve a bathing suit. It helped me realize in a concrete way that how we look is not who we are. Ultimately, we have very little control over what happens to our bodies—what they look like, how much pain they're in, how long they last.

After an hour of viewing the insides of corpses, it was clear to me how narrow my first reading of the cemetery contemplations and reflections on the body had been. In urging his followers to meditate on skeletons and bloody remains, the Buddha was advocating consciousness, not disdain for the body. When we are aware of all the intricate processes and parts that make up our bodies, we are less likely to identify the overall image as "me." Disdain for our bodies is, in fact, born not of detachment but of identification. When we identify with our bodies, we're filled with complaints—you might wake up one morning feeling confident and well equipped to face the day, until you step on the scale and see you've gained a few pounds; or you might be giddy with excitement for a date until you discover what the humidity has done to your hair.

Of course, the flash of dharma I received while viewing the cadavers didn't prevent me from asking my sister six times if my butt looked too big in a pair of jeans the next day, but at least I was laughing at myself as I did it. I don't plan to stop wearing clothes I find attractive, or brushing my hair, or looking at myself in the mirror before I go out. This isn't sixth-century B.C.E. India, and I'm not a nun; using my body consciously has a different meaning for me than it did for the Buddha's first followers. For instance, being aware of the physical processes involved in lust does not necessarily require me to head to the nearest burial ground every time I feel attracted to somebody. But it does make it more difficult to throw myself into an unhealthy sexual situation. I can say to myself, "Okay, this is just my body having a reaction. It doesn't mean I want to live happily ever after with this person. It doesn't mean I should take off all my clothes." Similarly, it's difficult to lavish hundreds of dollars and hours and small miseries on beautifying the body if you retain awareness of the rotting flesh it will someday be.

This distance not only allows us to forgive our bodies for their inevitable flaws, but it can also lead us to better care for them. One of the corpses I saw had lungs of blackened soot: a smoker. His heart was a cantaloupe instead of a peach, from pumping so hard to get air to his lungs. His face was sweet, but deep inside, his organs had turned black and swollen. How we treat our bodies does matter, because it matters how we treat everything. In his *Instructions for the Cook,* Dogen asks us to see a lettuce leaf as the Buddha's body—to bring the same level of attention and care to making a salad that we would use to interact with the Buddha. We are asked to honor the Buddha's body, which means honoring the leaf, which means honoring our own bodies—zits, fat butts, and all.

At the end of a med student's first year, she attends a ceremony in which the students thank the families and loved ones of the bodies they spent the past year slicing apart, shifting around, and dousing with chemical preservatives. The ceremony seemed tacky to me when my sister first told me about it—an oddly personal end to an experience expressly geared at being impersonal. But after seeing the bodies and witnessing firsthand my sister's relationship to them—a mix of awe and understanding—the ceremony made sense. You don't have to feel love or attachment to something to honor it. Perhaps the med students related to the cadavers in much the same way the Buddha related to his own body—grateful for the experience it afforded them, but free of sentimental attachment. Why not offer thanks for a gift that will never belong to you?

Pain But Not Suffering ⏪

Bhikkhu Bodhi, Darlene Cohen, Shinzen Young, and Reginald Ray

As long as we have bodies, we will have physical pain; Buddhism promises no escape from that. What we can change is how we experience pain. Four well-known teachers offer us Buddhist techniques to discover the true nature of pain, lessen its ability to cause us mental suffering, and learn its valuable lessons.

BUILT-IN BUDDHA

Bhikkhu Bodhi

When I write about living with pain, I don't have to use my imagination. Since 1976 I have been afflicted with chronic head pain that has grown worse over the decades. This condition has thrown a granite boulder across the tracks of my meditation practice. Pain often wipes a day and night off my calendar, and sometimes more at a stretch. The condition has cost me a total of several years of productive activity. Because intense head pain makes reading difficult,

it has at times even threatened my vocation as a scholar and transla-
tor of Buddhist texts.

In search of a cure, I have consulted not only practitioners of
Western medicine, but also herbal physicians in remote Sri Lankan
villages. I've been pierced countless times by acupuncture needles.
I've subjected my body to the hands of a Chinese massage therapist
in Singapore, consumed Tibetan medicine pills in Dharamsala, and
sought help from exorcists and chakra healers in Bali. With only
moderate success, I currently depend on several medications to keep
the pain under control. They cannot extricate it by the root.

I know firsthand that chronic bodily pain can eat deeply into the
entrails of the spirit. It can cast dark shadows over the chambers of
the heart and pull one down into moods of dejection and despair. I
cannot claim to have triumphed over pain, but in the course of our
long relationship, I've discovered some guidelines that have helped
me to endure the experience.

First of all, it is useful to recognize the distinction between physical pain and the mental reaction to it. Although body and mind are
closely intertwined, the mind does not have to share the same fate as
the body. When the body feels pain, the mind can stand back from it.
Instead of allowing itself to be dragged down, the mind can simply
observe the pain. Indeed, the mind can even turn the pain around
and transform it into a means of inner growth.

The Buddha compares being afflicted with bodily pain to being
struck by an arrow. Adding mental pain (aversion, displeasure, depression, or self-pity) to physical pain is like being hit by a second
arrow. The wise person stops with the first arrow. Simply by calling
the pain by its true name, one can keep it from extending beyond the
physical and thereby stop it from inflicting deep and penetrating
wounds upon the spirit.

Pain can be regarded as a teacher—a stern one that can also be
eloquent. My head pain has often felt like a built-in buddha who
constantly reminds me of the first noble truth. With such a teacher,
I hardly need to consult the sermon in Deer Park at Benares. In
order to hear the reverberations of the Buddha's voice declaring

that whatever is felt is included in suffering, all I have to do is attend to the sensations in my head.

As a follower of the dharma, I place complete trust in the law of karma. Therefore, I accept this painful condition as a present-life reflection of some unwholesome karma I created in the past. Not that I would advise someone who develops a painful illness to immediately resign themselves to it. Although it may be the inevitable fruit of some past karma, it might also be the result of a present cause that can be effectively eliminated by proper medical treatment. However, when various types of treatment fail to help with an obstinate and defiant condition, one can be pretty sure there is a karmic factor. Personally, I don't lose sleep trying to figure out what this past karma might have been, and I would advise others against succumbing to such obsessive concerns. They can easily lead to self-deluding fantasies and superstitious practices. In any case, by trusting the law of karma, one can understand that the key to future good health lies in one's hands. It is a reminder to refrain from harmful deeds motivated by ill will and to engage in deeds aimed at promoting the welfare and happiness of others.

Chronic pain can be an incentive for developing qualities that give greater depth and strength to one's character. In this way, it can be seen as a blessing rather than as a burden, though of course we shouldn't abandon the effort to discover a remedy for it. My own effort to deal with chronic pain has helped me to develop patience, courage, determination, equanimity, and compassion. At times, when the pain has almost incapacitated me, I've been tempted to cast off all responsibilities and just submit passively to this fate. But I've found that when I put aside the worries connected with the pain and simply bear it patiently, it eventually subsides to a more tolerable level. From there, I can make more realistic decisions and function effectively.

The experience of chronic pain has enabled me to understand how inseparable pain is from the human condition. This is something that we in America, habituated as we are to comfort and convenience, tend to forget. Chronic pain has helped me to empathize with the billions living daily with the gnawing pain of hunger; with the millions of women walking miles each day to fetch water for their families; with those in third-world countries who lie on beds in poorly equipped, understaffed hospitals, staring blankly at the wall.

Even during the most unremitting pain—when reading, writing, and speaking are difficult—I try not to let it ruffle my spirits and to maintain my vows, especially my vow to follow the monastic path until this life is over. When pain breaks over my head and down my shoulders, I use contemplation to examine the feelings. This helps me see them as mere impersonal events; as processes that occur at gross and subtle levels through the force of conditions; as sensations with their own distinct tones, textures, and flavors.

The most powerful tool I've found for mitigating pain's impact is a short meditative formula repeated many times in the Buddha's discourses: "Whatever feelings there may be—past, present, or future—all feeling is *not mine, not I, not my self.*" Benefiting from this technique does not require deep samadhi or a breakthrough to profound insight. Even using this formula during periods of reflective contemplation helps to create a distance between oneself and one's experience of pain.

Such contemplation deprives the pain of its power to create nodes of personal identification within the mind and thus builds equanimity and fortitude. Although the technique takes time and effort, when the three terms of contemplation—"not mine, not I, not my self"—gain momentum, pain loses its sting and cracks opens the door to the end of pain, the door to ultimate freedom.

ONE BUTTON AT A TIME

Darlene Cohen

When I became crippled by rheumatoid arthritis, I was completely overcome by unremitting pain, terror, and despair. Unable to walk, too weak to lift a phone, I thought bitterly of how much time I had wasted pursuing everlasting peace of mind. For seven years, over thousands of hours of zazen and maybe thirty sesshins, I had sat on a black cushion pursuing enlightenment in order to cope with just such an occasion—all to no avail. But I was wrong about the failure of practice, and within months of being struck by the condition, I knew it.

First of all, though ravaged by pain and disease, my body was deeply settled. While my mind had been plotting my rise to power at the San Francisco Zen Center, my body had been developing the tremendous stability associated with regular sitting practice. So even though I was overwhelmed and consumed by the pain, I was able to surrender completely to the physicality of my existence, moment after moment. Left alone to explore my consciousness without distraction, I discovered that wherever I looked, there were experiences other than pain waiting to be noticed: here is bending, here is breath, here is sun warming, here is unbearable fire, here is tightness. All these perceptions were fresh and fascinating.

The consciousness that sitting practice cultivates is open to many kinds of experience, not all of them necessarily pleasant. If at any given moment I am aware of ten different elements—my bottom on the chair, the sound of cars passing outside, the thought of the laundry I have to do, the hum of the air conditioner, an unpleasant stab of sharp knee pain, cool air entering my nostrils, warm air going out—and one of them is pain, that pain will dominate my life. But if I am aware of a hundred elements, those ten plus more subtle sensations—the animal presence of other people sitting quietly in the room, the shadow of the lamp against the wall, the brush of my hair against my ear, the pressure of my clothes against my skin—then pain is merely one of many elements of my consciousness, and that is pain I can live with.

With such a mind, life becomes richly textured. Consciously putting a cup on a table and feeling the flat surfaces meet becomes a rare, satisfying, "just-right" kind of experience. Washing dishes is not just about getting the dishes clean; it's also about feeling the warm, soapy water soothing my arthritic fingers. Doing laundry, I can smell its cleanness and luxuriate in the simple movements of folding, a counterpoint to my complex life.

For people in pain, tapping into this wisdom beyond wisdom is simply how to survive. When we have nothing left to hold on to, we must find comfort and support in the mundane details of our everyday lives, which are less than mundane when they're the reason we're willing to stay alive. This is the upside of impermanence: the shining uniqueness of beings and objects when we begin to notice their comforting presence. When preferences for a particular experience fade, the myriad things come forward to play, shimmering with suchness. Obviously, flowers and trees do this, but so do beer cans and microwaves. They're all waiting for our embrace. It is enormously empowering to inhabit a world so vibrant with singularity.

Thirty years after first being devastated by pain, I never enter a room without noticing what sources of comfort and ease will sustain me: not only the recliner and the pillow, but also the light streaming in from the window, the handmade vase on the table, even the muffled drone of the air conditioner—all of it created for the pleasure of human beings. By bringing into my conscious life objects that offer their kind companionship—my toothbrush and my dishes, my spoon and my car—I feel their tangible support as well as their sometimes charming idiosyncrasies. Awareness of this support can be simultaneous with resistance to my pain and the search for ways to stop it. These tracks don't hinder each other; they are both active, engaged encounters.

For instance, I have difficulty dressing. My arthritic shoulders, elbows, and fingers flinch from the stretching, tugging, and tying required to dress myself. Velcro might solve my problem, but it's out of the question; I'm not and never have been a utilitarian dresser. Rather, I'm the sort who is thrilled by the fine art of asymmetrical hems, darts, double-stitched denim seams, linings in jackets, and bias-cut skirts. My throat catches at a flutter of silk in the breeze. My underwear is adorned with lace and embroidered flowers. Instead of hurrying to dress and becoming frustrated by how difficult it is to pull up socks, put on shoes, and button blouses, I make it a well-loved morning ritual: I lay out all the clothes on the couch and sit in the warmth of the morning sun as I put on each lovely article one at a time, noting the temperature change associated with covering my body, admiring the darts and seams and insets that search out its topography.

Most of my physical tasks have taken on this ceremonial quality. If we can't be speedy and productive, if something as simple as putting on clothes takes all of our attention and focus, we must find our home in the activity itself as its goal recedes into the future. The practice of doing each thing for its own sake, the staple of Zen training, had mostly eluded me as a Zen student striving for enlightenment and better housing at Green Gulch Farm. But now, as I live in the vibrancy of the sensual present, clearly seeing each moment as my most viable source of solace and delight, I prefer to stay right here. I have lost any sense that there is something special or tragic about my circumstances. Day in and day out, they are just my life.

PURE EXPERIENCE

Shinzen Young

Is there something we can do with pain besides cope through distraction, denial, wishful thinking, or numbing anesthetics? Is there a universal strategy that can be applied to all pains, regardless of their type, intensity, or causes? Is there a psychologically healthy way of making pain meaningful, a simple, systematic way to harness its energy in the service of life?

If there is, this would be very good news. We could then use the unavoidable discomforts of day-to-day life to foster personal growth. It would certainly be comforting and empowering to know that if we encounter major pain that cannot be relieved by any of the standard methods, there is another option available. Meditation represents such an option.

In order to understand the nature of pain and its relationship to the spiritual path, we must first discuss pleasure. Any pleasure we have can be experienced completely or not. When it is experienced completely, it yields satisfaction. Completeness has nothing to do with the intensity, type, or duration of the pleasure. Completeness requires just two elements: an unbroken contact with the pleasure and the absence of interference with it.

Absence of interference means that the pleasure is not mixed with grasping, either conscious or subconscious. Grasping is a tension or viscosity that impedes the natural flow of the pleasure. It's a kind of tightening around pleasure's arising and passing. To experience pleasure without grasping is to experience it with equanimity—not aloof withdrawal, but radical self-permission to feel the pleasure. Pleasure not mixed with grasping could be called pure pleasure. Pure pleasure purifies consciousness and permanently raises our base level of appreciation for life.

The situation with pain is perfectly parallel to that of pleasure. Any given pain can be experienced either completely or incompletely. When it is experienced completely, it is not experienced as suffering; it does not become a problem. Does it hurt? Yes. Does that eclipse the perfection of the moment? No. Complete pain means pure pain, pain not mixed with resistance, at either the conscious or subconscious level of neural processing. Resistance is inner friction that interferes with the natural flow of pain. Not resisting pain is to have equanimity with the pain, radical self-permission to feel the pain. Pure pain purifies. The "matter" of the pain becomes converted into energy that massages and softens the very substance of the soul.

Let's try to make this process more tangible. In the undistracted meditative state, if pain arises, you can clearly observe the interaction of the pain and your resistance to it. For example, an uncomfortable sensation may arise in your knee as you're meditating. At the same time, you may observe that in reaction to the pain, you are clenching and tightening other parts of your body, while in your mind a stream of judgments and aversive thoughts are erupting.

The sensation in your knee is the pain. The tension is your bodily resistance. The judgments are mental resistance. The resistance can be distinguished clearly from the pain itself. As you consciously relax the tension and drop the judgments, even though the pain level is the same, it seems to be less of a problem. Later, when the resistance returns, you notice that the pain has again become a problem. So once again you drop the judgments and stop the clenching, and the sense of suffering diminishes, even if only slightly. But you are making your first steps in learning how to experience pain skillfully.

Subsequent steps involve letting go of progressively more subtle mind and body resistance, until the deep subconscious resistance begins to break up. At that point, the pain starts to flow. It feels like you're being massaged and nurtured. You experience the pain working on your consciousness at a very deep level. It is as though your consciousness were dough and the pain wave were kneading that dough, working out the lumps and kinks, transforming it at a molecular level into something soft, pliant, and malleable. With continued practice, this skill becomes internalized and integrated into your being. When you encounter discomforts in the course of daily life, you automatically let go into equanimity.

Is it necessary to experience discomfort in order to deepen one's spiritual practice? Absolutely not! The skills that allow us to experience pleasure with heightened satisfaction are the same ones that allow us to experience pain with diminished suffering. Skill with pleasure leads to skill with pain, and vice versa, because what we're really learning is how to feel. If discomfort arises during meditation, we can take measures to relieve it or we can explore it. The choice is ours. If we encounter pain in daily life that cannot be relieved, then we have no choice, since the only alternative to experiencing it skillfully is to experience it as abject suffering.

In this life we must sometimes spend time in purgatory, an uncomfortable place of spiritual purification. If we understand how to meditate, then the purgatory won't turn into hell, a terrifying place of meaningless suffering. From the perspective of spiritual growth, there's a big difference between hell and purgatory. Either way, the idea of voluntarily staying with pain may still seem a little radical. Please remember that we are talking about working with small, manageable doses of subjective discomfort that do not objectively harm the body. And yes, this is a radical thing to do. From Latin, *radical* means addressing an issue at the root, the most basic level.

When we sit and meditate, we may sometimes be subject to discomforts, aches and pains, sleepiness, bodily sensations of agitation and impatience, itches, and awkwardness from the posture. These discomforts are real but quite manageable. In the meditative state, we can experience them with more mindfulness and equanimity than we do in daily life. In meditation, the mind and body go through a natural change, a deep learning process that affects the unconscious levels of neural processing. The deep mind learns a healthy way to deal with pain. As a result, when we encounter real pain in the real world, we discover that we are not suffering the way we used to. By not suffering, I mean that the pain does not obscure the perfection of the moment, does not distort our perception or behavior, does not alienate us from our spiritual source or from our fellow beings.

The Three Bodies of Pain

Reginald A. Ray

The Mahamudra lineage of Vajrayana Buddhism in Tibet teaches us how to approach physical pain from within the context of ultimate awareness. This body of oral instructions begins with the direct pointing out of unborn mind, or ultimate awareness. The lineage holder's transmission opens the practitioner to the unborn mind as a matter of his or her immediate, direct experience. Such awareness is empty of anything definite or solid, brilliantly illuminated like sun-drenched space, and pregnant with supercharged possibility.

Through meditating again and again on this natural state, we are able to let go into it for increasingly extended periods of time. It is from within this "ordinary mind," or *rigpa*, that we can begin to make a nonego-based relationship with our relative experience, including physical pain. It involves approaching pain just as unborn awareness itself would see and work with it. When we do this, we are able to discover the way in which physical pain, far from being any kind of problem, actually has the possibility to liberate us into the three enlightened bodies of the Buddha: *dharmakaya, sambhogakaya,* and *nirmanakaya.*

Physical Pain as Dharmakaya

When physical pain arises, we are instructed to rest within the natural state. Then we look directly into the physical pain. This is not "us" looking from ego's dualistic, self-centered consciousness. Rather, it is us having surrendered our vantage point, letting awareness itself hold or reflect the physical pain that is arising. So it is a looking that occurs from within the primordial awareness.

Resting there, we ask ourselves, what is the essence of this physical pain? We are allowing the experience of pain to register within the field of awareness and checking to see what it is. Does physical pain have any substance, any heart, any essence that would mark it as "physical pain"? What we may discover is that what we thought of as pain—which from within dualistic consciousness seemed so real and problematic—actually has no defining feature at all. It is empty of anything that would mark it as physical pain. This is known as discovering physical pain as dharmakaya.

Lama Thubten Yeshe had a serious and painful heart ailment from which he eventually died. He used to comment that using the Mahamudra instruction to work with physical pain eliminated all the feeling of "problem" or even of "pain." He said, "You won't ever have to go to the doctor to get pain medication." He wasn't saying that we shouldn't be treated for medical conditions, but that through these practices, we eliminate the identity of pain itself, which causes us to be so closed down to it and so preoccupied by the "problem" it presents.

When His Holiness the Sixteenth Karmapa was dying of cancer in a hospital in Zion, Illinois, his deteriorating physical condition suggested to the attending medical staff that he should be in agonizing, incapacitating, absorbing physical pain. Yet all reports depicted him as fully present to others, concerned only about how everyone else was doing. I have often thought that he must have been embodying a high level of mastery, discovering physical pain as dharmakaya.

There is a Mahamudra exercise you can do in order to train in this approach to physical pain, even if you are not within its grip at the moment. Rest your mind in the natural state and then assume a posture—such as squatting slightly—that will shortly cause physical distress. As the discomfort builds, you will find yourself beginning to think about it. Then return to the natural state, and when you are resting there, check to see if there is anything you can locate and define as pain. If you are injured or ill, then you already have the physical pain that you need to do this practice. By doing this practice, you can use physical pain to experience the freedom and fulfillment of the dharmakaya.

Physical Pain as Sambhogakaya

Physical pain, seen from within the natural state, is not simply empty of any essence; it is also charged with unusual vividness and clarity. When there is nothing in particular going on in our relative experience and we rest our minds in the natural state, the field of awareness will be empty and open, but it will not necessarily have much charge to it. However, if there is some strong relative experience going on with us, such as physical pain, when we return to the natural state, we will find the awareness greatly heightened.

When our relative experience—in this case, physical pain—is very strong, we may find it more difficult to let go into the emptiness of the unborn mind. That's because relative experience, particularly when it is especially intense, functions as an almost irresistibly seductive reference point. Whether that intensity is experienced as negative or positive is immaterial; it gives our ego-consciousness something strong to feed on and maintain itself. Given that situation, it can be more difficult for us to let go and release into the formlessness of our primordial mind.

But if we do let go when we are experiencing physical pain, we may discover that the intensity of our awareness is greatly heightened. It can feel strong and immovable, almost monolithic. We may find unique possibilities of letting go of any grasp on the boundaries of awareness or even on awareness itself. It is as if the awareness can more easily burn through any possibilities of holding on that may arise. Discovering this intensity of awareness is known as discovering physical pain as the sambhogakaya.

Physical Pain as Nirmanakaya

One of the central discoveries made by Vajrayana practitioners is that nothing occurs in our life without rhyme or reason. In other words, any relative experience appears with complete timeliness, accuracy, and appropriateness to our immediate situation. Until we have attained the liberation that does not decline, we are caught somewhere each moment of our lives. Though we are not aware of it (if we were, we would cease to be caught), we are always hanging on to our reference points, to our limited self, in some way. We cannot free ourselves by ourselves; we need outside intervention.

According to the Vajrayana, what appears within our experience at such moments always provides the needed intervention. Whatever occurs is a catalyst of freedom; it exactly addresses our bondage as it exists right now. In a most apt and personal way, it cuts through the place where we are caught. This is the meaning of "sacred outlook" or "pure appearance" in Vajrayana: every phenomenal experience that arises exactly addresses our entrapment, cuts through it, and liberates us on the spot. The challenge, of course, is to recognize the liberation and surrender to it, instead of reconstituting our "I" unconsciously and immediately.

The appearance of physical pain is no exception. When we experience short- or long-term pain, it always addresses our particular situation. In this sense, it is truly a blessing. The arrival of pain cuts through the unique bondage of this moment, liberating us into dharmakaya. At the moment of freedom, we see just how much expectation we've been having, how much we've been identifying with some relative situation or experience. Being cut through in this way can be experienced as horrific, humorous, frightening, sad, inspiring, and so on. But in any case, it leaves us with an appreciation of the sacredness of the experience of pain as an incursion of supreme wisdom in our lives.

Open, Fearless, and Creative

Discovering pain as the dharmakaya and as the sambhogakaya are practices that are initially developed on the meditation cushion. After we have trained in these practices in formal meditation, we can then apply them anytime and anywhere. Discovering physical pain as the nirmanakaya is a practice that can be engaged in directly in the postmeditative state simply by looking—again, from within nonconceptual mind—at the impact of the pain we may be feeling.

When we approach physical pain through these Mahamudra instructions, we find that far from being trapped and defeated, we are able to work with it in an increasingly open, fearless, and creative way. Finally, our growing familiarity with, and skill in relating to, our pain in Mahamudra practice can lead us into and through the process of dying.

Washing Out Emptiness

Sallie Tisdale

In our own impermanent body, with all its sicknesses, imperfections, and secretions, we face our deepest fears and aversions. Drawing on the writings of Zen master Dogen and on her own experience as a nurse, Sallie Tisdale challenges us not to look away from the realities of the body, but to practice in this most intimate realm.

After my mother-in-law's recent funeral, my husband, Bob, and his two sisters, Bonnie and Val, took her ashes to the bank of her favorite creek and sprinkled them in. They hiked back with ash-dusted hands.

"I hate to wash," said Val, rubbing her mother's powdered body into her palm. "It's Mom, you know?" I could see the dusty gray ash on her knuckles.

"Were there any big pieces?" I asked.

"A few chunks," she answered, as she turned toward the sink.

Val teaches veterinary medicine. Her sister is a nurse like me, and none of us is squeamish. We do things at work that most people find hard to imagine, and all of us wash our hands with great frequency. I work with cancer patients. Not infrequently, people ask, "How can you stand your job?" They mean different things by this question. Some mean the pain, the deaths, but many simply mean the bodies themselves—sick and weak bodies, and all the fluids bodies produce and we try so hard to hide. Part of my job is to help people deal with matters we are all trained to think of as intensely private. I know that bodies leak and smell; I know that bodies fall apart and turn to ash in our hands.

As Buddhists, we work to accept the impermanence and inevitable decay of the physical body. But it's not enough to accept it as a fact; we can believe in this and still not want it in plain sight. Nagarjuna said, "Change makes all things possible." It is only because of change that suffering can end—and it is because of change that our bodies fall apart, like all compounded things. We cannot have one without the other, but we try.

It's one of the blessings of my work, this intimacy with the authentic, unmasked body, with *the body* as an object in a world of vibrant, shifting forms. But it isn't enough. I can talk bluntly about funk and decay all I want, but unless I can squarely face my own body as it is, I'm missing the point. We fear bodily fluids as vectors of disease, but this is actually a modern concern. Our real fear is a deeper and more primeval one—a fear of taint, of corruption. Bodily fluids are vectors of change, harbingers of all that we can't truly control.

The natural function of our fluids is to invade the world. The word *effluvium* is from Latin; it means "flowing out." Our fluids leave us and spread themselves into public space through odor and sight and touch. Every day, my body produces effluence that needs to be managed in some way. Can I manage it without flinching? Feces, vomit, sweat, sputum, blood, semen, urine, saliva, and tears—none of us can escape these things. In fact, if there is anything that can teach us we are more alike than different, it is the sickbed and the toilet. For Buddhists in particular, they are places of great spiritual practice.

People in most cultures are trained from an early age to be somewhat private with their bodily functions and averse to those of others. There is a lot of wisdom in this, instinctive feelings about privacy and sanitation. This kind of aversion, more of a polite avoidance, has an important place in community. But *aversion* is also a Buddhist technical term, pointing us to a deep koan. It includes a continuum of reaction from mild distaste to deep disgust. It is resistance, obstruction, and desire all at once. Aversion is a form of clinging—in this case, clinging to what is not, a desire for change from the way things are. One form of aversion we all know is that of holding on to our ignorance, refusing to accept the whole of reality—picking and choosing what we prefer, and turning away from the rest.

The physical control we maintain over our bodies is an aspect of internal control. It is an expression of all our ideas about what constitutes "self" and what is truly "other." Small children may be proud of their bowel movements, of this interesting thing they have produced. Their natural and innocent inclination is to share what their bodies make—until they are told, by tone of voice and facial expression and command, not to do so. Part of what we are training children to do is keep the body to itself, to hold on to the fiction that the body can be controlled—that it is not the poorly bound sack of fluid that we secretly feel it to be. Westerners are often toilet-trained to a level of fastidiousness so intense it becomes a kind of loathing.

Those who are free or open about toilet functions may be seen as coarse or deliberately offensive. To be simply relaxed about one's toileting—to be, that is, unashamed—is seen as a kind of licentiousness. It is traditionally a mark of people outside the pale of a society, that they are freer with their bodies and the bodies of others than people in the mainstream. Little social respect is given to those who care for the bodies of others. In the caste system of India, only the untouchables handled corpses. The fact that the Buddha's disciples made robes from the clothes of the dead and sat with corpses were some of the Buddha's most radical acts.

I have reared three children and now have three small grandchildren by my eldest son. Their mother has strong feelings about privacy around toileting, and even at the age of three, my granddaughter is quite reserved in the bathroom. But at the same time, she is as fond of her own smell as most people are. Smell—effluence—is one of the ways we bond with people we love. The territory of the body is the territory of relationship. We like the perfume of the nest, the smells and flavors we associate with home, with our tribal identity. These may be as different as shared food or a parent's cologne, but they are always the flavors of bodies themselves.

In a sense, all of Buddhist practice takes place here, in this most intimate realm: here, in the family, shoulder to shoulder with fellow workers, beside each other on the cushion. Even alone in a cave, there is no way out of the sense object we call the body. We meet each other face-to-face, and so have all our teachers and ancestors met each other. In this way have all the buddhas taught. Hand to sweating hand.

The medieval Japanese Zen master Eihei Dogen described at length the proper way to brush one's teeth. He tells a story from the *Kengu-Kyo* (*The Sutra of the Wise and the Stupid*) about the Buddha brushing his teeth with a willow twig. When he threw the twig to the ground afterward, it grew into a great tree under which he preached the dharma. For Shakyamuni, to clean his teeth with complete attention and wholeheartedness was itself the foundation of the Bodhi seat. By brushing his teeth, he made a place from which he could speak the dharma. Dogen notes the cause and effect at work here, but more than that, he is pointing us at the irrevocable nature of the body as the vessel for the Truth.

Buddhist practice requires us, as it were, to encounter the body with the body itself. That sometimes means looking deliberately at what we don't want to see. It means smelling what leaks out of ourselves and each other, and noticing what thoughts arise with the smells. It means noting our reactions, both physical and otherwise. It means noticing our aversions and turning toward them with curiosity and attention.

Dogen was fond of referring to people as "skin bags." He never tired of reminding us what fragile vessels we are. His own teacher,

Rujing, had, at his own request, been Head of Toilets. Dogen developed a great respect for the varied meanings of hygiene and its power in practice.

Dogen's particular wisdom shines most brightly at the precise intersection of the vast view and the blunt act, and in his years of teaching, he sometimes focused intently on taking care of the body. In the fascicle *Senjo,* devoted to the topic of washing, he wrote, "At just the moment when we dignify body-and-mind with training, eternal original practice is completely and roundly realized. Thus the body-and-mind of training manifests itself in the original state." The very next sentence refers to cutting one's fingernails.

Dogen wrote detailed instructions on how to clean oneself after a bowel movement, how to cut one's nails, shave one's head, use a towel, brush one's teeth, and wash one's face. A certain amount of his instruction is simply the necessary teaching of the untutored and the kind of attitude required for people to live in close quarters in harmony. Some of the advice is painfully relevant today. For one who is in the toilet, he writes, "Do not chat or joke with the person on the other side of the wall, and do not sing songs or recite verses in a loud voice. Do not make a mess by weeping and dribbling, and do not be angry or hasty. Do not write characters on the walls, and do not draw lines in the earth with the shit-stick."

Shakyamuni's life and teaching was based squarely in the management of the body in daily life, and so Dogen's work is based on a great foundation of teaching about the body. He cites a number of Vinaya texts, several sutras, and Chinese texts on monastic behavior. He grounds the details not only in his current place and time, but in history, in the ancestors themselves as the body of the Way. "The buddhas have toilets," he wrote, "and this we should remember."

Dogen's instructions can be minute, covering every aspect of movement into and out of the zendo, into and out of robes, the precise way to fold a towel over one's arm while walking. He is teaching a level of mindfulness that can be seen as infinite—infinite in its nuance and infinitely deep in its meaning. By forcing us to consider the most commonplace details, he forces us to consider how details become the vessel of enlightenment. His tone is matter-of-fact when he is describing how to brush one's teeth and just as matter-of-fact when he is describing how brushing the teeth is awakening itself. For Dogen, the acts themselves are layered with dharma, marbled with dharma—for the deeper mind cannot be separated from using the toilet and folding a towel.

Dogen criticizes those who don't care about hygiene or reject the possibility of using care of the body as a vehicle in practice. But he also criticizes those who seek after purity, who want to skirt past the messy nature of the human. An earlier ancestor, the famous Chinese woman known as Kongshi Daoren, wrote in a poem on a bathhouse wall, "If nothing truly exists, what are you bathing? Where could even the slightest bit of dust come from? ... Even if you see no difference between the water and the dirt, it all must be washed completely away when you enter here."

Dogen reminds us that we are neither pure nor impure. Awakening is the state of seeing past the false opposites of emptiness and form, purity and profanity. So brushing teeth and having a bowel movement are not acts that can lead us to purity—they are themselves purity. They are complete in themselves. And even so, it isn't enough just to wash—we have to discover what it is to be this naturally pure form. "Without washing the inside of emptiness, how can we realize cleanness within and without?" Such apparent paradox is part of the endless repeated pairing of Buddhism: wisdom and activity, each incomplete alone. Such couplings are the skin and bones of the Buddha's body, and they are found in our skin and bones. They are the inside of our emptiness.

Aversion is one of a pair; to be averse to one thing implies being drawn to its opposite. But if we are averse to the body, toward what are we drawn? What else is there for us here? "Remember," Dogen writes, "purity and impurity is blood dripping from a human being. At one time it is warm, at another time it is disgusting." The opening of the wound may be hard, but the flowing of the blood is very easy.

Dogen cautions us not to be drawn into a life solely of the mind or spirit, away from the reality of the body, but to be working always at a true and total presence in the self, here and now—the self, in his words, that is always "flashing into existence."

If we see the body and its fluids as tainted, we ourselves become tainted—not by the fluids, but by the fear. To be truly untainted is to be free of fear—that is, free of self-concern and self-regard. Impurity lies in fleeing reality on any level, physical, metaphysical, or in between. Both the acts and their meanings, the commonplace acts and the multiplied meanings, must be taken together. This way we are able to step outside both and embrace both. The opposites of pure and impure disappear. Completely present, we emerge into true purity.

One of the blessings of long relationships is seeing the changes in the body of another and embracing them. We watch our friends and family grow gray and wrinkled and stooped, and this is a gift, a strange kind of nakedness. We watch our own faces change and blur in the mirror, and we are watching endless, endless change. We are watching eternity.

At the end of our lives, we will find ourselves in the hands of others. I go to work. I cause pain, I relieve pain. I clean up vomit and feces and blood. I dig in, and sometimes I get disgusted, from somewhere down near the brain stem and the gut. I keep a straight face. I see how afraid people are of being judged in just that way, how devastating it is for them to confront the way their bodies crumble. They are so afraid that I will turn away, that they are no longer worthy because they are crumbling. But we are all crumbling, all the time.

Now and then, I think about Dogen dying, soiling his bed, being nursed by Egi, one of his female students. I imagine nursing my own teacher someday. I think of the Buddha dying from food poisoning, puking in his deathbed. I think of myself washing him, his undefended, old body: his skin as fragile as fine paper, tearing at a rough touch, so thin I can see the pulse of blood along the veins of his hand. I imagine his wasted, bony body, the tendons on his neck standing out plain and clear as he gently takes his last breaths.

I think of Dogen and Shakyamuni and all the rest after this last breath—after their bowels relaxed and ran, and their bladders emptied, and their eyes clouded over. I think of the flies arriving, and laying their eggs, and what happened after that.

Prince of the Ascetics: A Short Story

Charles Johnson

This book is a collection of human stories—of human pain,
goodness, and searching—as Buddhism itself is really a human story.
It's the story of a young seeker who lived twenty-five hundred years ago.
It's the story of all those since who have made the same journey he did
and those of us still making it now. To conclude this year's edition of
The Best Buddhist Writing, *the novelist and essayist Charles Johnson goes*
back to the beginning and tells the story of the Buddha's enlightenment
through the eyes of one of his closest companions.

Once upon a time, my companions and I lived in the forest near the village of Uruvela on the banks of the Nairanjana River. We were known far and wide as five men who had forsaken worldly affairs in order to devote ourselves completely to the life of the spirit.

For thousands of years in our country, this has been the accepted way for the Four Stages of Life. First, to spend the spring of one's youth as a dedicated student; the summer as a busy householder using whatever wealth he has acquired to help others; the fall as an ascetic who renounces all duties at age fifty and retires into the forest; and the winter season experiencing the peace and wisdom found only in the *Atma* (or "Self"), which permeates all parts of the world as moisture seeps through sand. My brothers in this noble fourth stage of tranquility, which we had just entered, were Kodananna, Bhadiya, Vappa, and Assajii. We had once been family men, members of the Vaishya (trader) caste, but now owned no possessions. We lived, as was right, in poverty and detachment. We wore simple yellow robes and fasted often.

Wheresoever we walked, always in single file, Vappa, a small man with a snoutlike nose, took the lead, sweeping the ground before us with a twig-broom so we would not crush any living creatures too small to see. When we did not leave our ashram to make alms-rounds for food in Uruvela, we satisfied our hunger with fruit, but not taken off trees; rather we gathered whatever had fallen to the ground. Each day we wrote the Sanskrit word *ahum,* or "I," on the backs of our hands so that we rarely went but a few moments without seeing it and remembering to inquire into the Self as the source of all things. People throughout the kingdom of Magadha affectionately called us Bapu ("father") because they knew that we had just begun the difficult path described in the Vedas and Upanishads. The scriptures say that a fast mind is a sick mind. But we, my brothers and I, were slowly taming the wild horses of our thoughts; learning the four kinds of yoga; banishing the ego, that toadstool that grows out of consciousness; and freeing ourselves from the twin illusions of pleasure and pain.

But one day it came to pass that as we made our monthly rounds in the summer-gilded village, begging for alms, the merchants and women all looked the other way when we arrived. When Assajii asked them what was wrong, they apologized. With their palms upturned, each explained how he had already given his monthly offering to a stunning young swami, a mahatma, a powerful sadhu who was only twenty-nine years old and had recently crossed the river Anoma that divided our kingdom from the land of the Shakya tribe. They said that just being in his presence for a few moments brought immeasurable peace and joy. And if that were not shocking enough, some were calling him *Munisha,* "Prince of the Ascetics."

"How can this be?" My heart gave a slight thump. "Surely you don't mean that."

A portly merchant, Dakma was his name, who was shaped like a pigeon, with bright rings on his fingers, puffed at me, "Oh, but he *is* such. We have never seen his like before. You—*all* of you—can learn a thing or two from him. I tell you, Mahanama, if you are not careful, he will put you five lazybones out of business."

"Lazybones? You call *us* lazybones?"

"As your friend, I tell you, this young man gives new meaning to the words sacrifice and self-control."

Needless to say, none of this rested happily on my ears. Let it be understood that I, Mahanama, am not the sort of man who is easily swayed, but whatever serenity I had felt after my morning meditation was now gone, and suddenly my mind was capricious, like a restless monkey stung by a scorpion, drunk, and possessed by a demon all at the same time.

"This sadhu," I asked helplessly, "where might we find him?"

Sujata, the unmarried daughter of a householder, with kind, moonlike eyes, stepped forward. "He lives at the edge of the forest by the river where the banyan trees grow. I have never seen *any* man so beautiful. Everyone loves him. I feel I could follow him anywhere..."

Now I was in a mental fog. There was a dull pounding in my right temple as we trekked forthwith at a fast pace back into the forest. Vappa was sweeping his twig-broom so furiously—he was as angry and upset as I was—that billowing clouds of dust rose up around us, and we must have looked, for all the world, like a herd of enraged, stampeding elephants. Soon enough we tracked down the brash young man responsible for our alms bowls being empty.

To my surprise, and yet somehow not to my surprise, the villagers had not lied. We found him meditating naked, except for a garland of beads, in a diagonal shaft of leaf-filtered light from the banyan tree above him. Straightaway, I saw that his posture in meditation was perfect, his head tilted down just so, leaving only enough space that an egg could be inserted between his chin and throat. He was twenty years younger than me, no older than one of my sons, his body gaunt and defined, his face angular, framed by a bell of black hair. He looked up when we approached, introduced ourselves, and pressed him to explain how he could have the nerve to install himself in *our* forest. In a sad, heavy way he exhaled, holding me with eyes that seemed melancholy, and said, "I seek a refuge from suffering."

"Who," asked Bhadiya, cocking his head to one side, "are your teachers? What credentials do you have?"

"I have studied briefly with the hermit Bhagava. Then with Alara Kalama and Udraka Ramaputra, who taught me mastery of the third and fourth stages of meditation. But," he sighed, "neither intellectual knowledge nor yogic skills has yet led me to the liberation I am seeking."

I felt humbled right down to my heels. Those two venerated teachers were among the greatest sages in all India. Compared to them, my own guru long ago was but a neophyte on the path.

Twilight was coming on as he spoke, the blue air darkening to purple the four corners of the sky. A whiff of twilight even tinctured the shadows as he unfurled what I surmised was a bald-faced lie, a fairy tale, a bedtime story so fantastic only a child could believe it. Until a year ago, he said, he had been a prince, whose loving father, Shuddodana, had sheltered him from the painful, hard, and ugly things of the world. The palace in which he was raised, with its parks, lakes, and perfectly tended gardens, gave you a glimpse of what the homes of the gods must look like. He was raised to be a warrior of the Shakya tribe, had a hundred raven-haired concubines of almost catastrophic beauty, and ate food so fine and sumptuous that even its rich aroma was enough to sate a man's hunger. He said he would have continued this voluptuous life of pleasure and privilege, for he had all that this world could offer, but one day while he and his charioteer, Channa, were out riding, he saw a man old and decrepit. On a different day he saw a man severely stricken with illness. On the third day he saw a corpse being carried away for cremation. And when he recognized that this fate awaited *him,* he could not be consoled. All satisfaction with the fleeting pleasures of his cloistered life in the palace left him. But then, on a fourth trip, he saw a wandering holy man whose equanimity in the face of the instability and impermanence of all things told him that *this* was the life he must pursue. And so he left home, abandoning his beautiful wife, Yoshodhara, and their newborn son, Rahula, and found his lonely way to our forest.

Once he had breathed these words, my companions begged to become his disciples. Kodananna even went as far as to proclaim that if all the scriptures for a holy life were lost, we could reconstruct them from just this one devoted ascetic's daily life. He had seduced them with his sincerity for truth-seeking. I, Mahanama, decided to remain with my brothers, but to be frank, I had great misgivings about this man. He came from the Kshatriya caste of royalty. Therefore he was, socially, one *varna* ("caste") above us, and I had never met a member of royalty who wasn't smug and insensitive to others. Could only *I* see his imperfections and personal failures? How could he justify leaving his wife and son? I mean, he was not yet fifty, but he had forsaken his responsibilities as a householder. True enough, his family was well taken care of during his absence, because he was a pampered, upper-caste, rich boy, someone who'd never missed a meal in his life but now was slumming among the poor, who could shave his waist-long beard, his wild hair, take a bath, and return to his father's palace if one day the pain and rigor of our discipline became disagreeable. I, Mahanama, have never had an easy life. To achieve even the simplest things, I had to undergo a thousand troubles, to struggle and know disappointment. I think it was then, God help me, that I began to hate every little thing about him: the way he walked and talked and smiled; his polished, courtly gestures; his refined habits; his honeyed tongue; his upper-caste education— none of which he could hide. The long and short of it was that I was no longer myself. Although I consented to study with him, just to see what he knew, I longed, so help me, to see him fail. To slip or make a mistake. Just *once,* that's all I was asking for.

And I *did* get my wish, though not exactly as I'd expected.

To do him justice, I must say our new teacher was dedicated and more dangerous than anyone knew. He was determined to surpass all previous ascetics. I guess he was still a warrior of the Shakya tribe, but instead of vanquishing others, all his efforts were aimed at conquering himself. Day after day he practiced burning thoughts of desire from his mind and tried to empty himself of all sensations. Night after night he prayed for a freedom that had no name, touching the eighty-six sandalwood beads on his *mala* for each mantra he whispered in the cold of night, or in rough, pouring rain. Seldom did he talk to us, believing that speech was the great-grandson of truth. Nevertheless, I spied on him, because at my age I was not sure any teacher could be trusted. None could meet our every expectation. None I had known was whole or perfect.

Accordingly, I critically scrutinized everything he did and did not do. And what struck me most was this: it was as if he saw his body, which he had indulged with all the pleasures known to man, as an enemy, an obstacle to his realization of the highest truth, and so it must be punished and deprived. He slept on a bed of thorns. Often he held his breath for a great long time, until the pain was so severe he fainted. Week after week he practiced these fanatical austerities, reducing himself to skin, bone, and fixed idea. My companions and I frequently collapsed from exhaustion and fell behind. But he kept on. Perhaps he was trying to achieve great merit or atone for leaving his family or for being a fool who threw away a tangible kingdom he could touch and see for an intangible fantasy of perfection that no one had ever seen. Many times we thought he was suicidal, particularly on the night he made us all sleep among the dead in the charnel grounds, where the air shook with insects, just outside Uruvela. During our first years with him, he would eat a single jujube fruit, sesame seeds, and take a little rice on banana leaves. But as the years wore on, he—being radical, a revolutionary—rejected even that, sustaining himself on water and one grain of rice a day. Then he ate nothing at all.

By the morning of December seventh, in our sixth year with him, he had fallen on evil days, made so weakened, so frail, so wretched he could barely walk without placing one skeletal hand on Bhadiya's shoulder and the other on mine. At age thirty-five, his eyes resembled burnt holes in a blanket. Like a dog was how he smelled. His bones creaked, and his head looked chewed up by rats, the obsidian hair that once pooled round his face falling from his scalp in brittle patches.

"Mahanama," he said. There were tears standing in his eyes. "You and the others should not have followed me. Or believed so faithfully in what I was doing. My life in the palace was wrong. This is wrong too."

The hot blast of his death breath, rancid because his teeth had begun to decay, made me twist my head to one side. "There must be . . ." He closed his eyes to help his words along. ". . . some Way between the extremes I have experienced."

I kept silent. He sounded vague, vaporish.

And then he said, more to himself than to me, "Wisdom is caught, not taught."

Before I could answer, he hobbled away, like an old, old man, to bathe, then sit by himself under a banyan tree. I believe he went that far away so we could not hear him weep. This tree, I should point out, was one the superstitious villagers believed possessed a deity. As luck would have it, the lovely Sujata, with her servant girl, came there often to pray that she would one day find a husband belonging to her caste and have a son by him. From where we stood, my brothers and I could see her approaching, stepping gingerly to avoid deer pellets and bird droppings, and if my eyes did not deceive me, not recognizing him in his fallen state, she thought our teacher was the tree's deity. Sujata placed before him a golden bowl of milk-porridge. To my great delight, he hungrily ate it.

I felt buoyant and thought, "Gotcha."

Vappa's mouth hung open in disbelief. Bhadiya's mouth snapped shut. Kodananna rubbed his knuckles in his eyes. They all knew moral authority rested on moral consistency. Assajii shook his head and cried out, "This woman's beauty, the delights of food, and the sensual cravings tormenting his heart are just too much for him to resist. Soon he will be drinking, lying, stealing, gambling, killing animals to satisfy his appetite, and sleeping with other men's wives. Agh, he can teach us nothing."

Disgusted, we left, moving a short distance away from him in the forest, our intention being to travel the hundred miles to the spiritual center of Sarnath in search of a better guru. My brothers talked about him like he had a tail. And while I cackled and gloated for a time over the grand failure of our golden boy, saying, "See, I *told* you so," that night I could not sleep for thinking about him. He was alone again, his flesh wasted away, his mind most likely splintered by madness. I pitied him. I pitied all of us, for now it was clear that no man or woman would ever truly be free from selfishness, anger, hatred, greed, and the chronic hypnosis that is the human condition. Shortly after midnight, beneath a day-old moon in a dark sky, I rose while the others slept and crept back to where we had left him.

He was gone, no longer by the banyan tree. Up above, a thin, rain-threaded breeze loosed a whirlwind of dead leaves. It felt as if a storm was on its way, the sky swollen with pressure. And then, as I turned to leave, seeking shelter, I saw faintly a liminal figure seated on kusha grass at the eastern side of a bodhi tree, strengthened by the bowl of rice milk he had taken and apparently determined not to rise ever again if freedom still eluded him. I felt my face stretch. I wondered if I had gone without food so long that I was hallucinating, for I sensed a peculiar density in the darkness, and the numinous air around him seemed to swirl with wispy phantoms. I heard a devilish voice—perhaps his own, disguised—demanding that he stop, which he would not do. Was he totally mad and talking to himself? I could not say. But for three watches of the night he sat, wind wheeling round his head, its sound in the trees like rushing water, and once I heard him murmur, "At last I have found and defeated you, *ahumkara,* or 'I-maker.'"

At daybreak, everything in the forest was quiet, the tree bark bloated by rain, and he sat, as if he'd just come from a chrysalis, in muted, early-morning light, the air full of moisture. Cautiously, I approached him, the twenty-fifth buddha, knowing that something new and marvelous had happened in the forest that night. Instead of going where the path might lead, he had gone instead where there was no path and left a trail for all of us. I asked him, "Are you a god now?"

Quietly, he made answer. "No."

"Well, are you an angel?"

"No."

"Then what are you?"

"Awake."

That much I could see. He had discovered his middle way. It made me laugh. These rich kids had all the luck. I knew my brothers and I would again become his disciples, but this time, after six long years, we'd finally be able to eat a decent meal.

Author's note: The final six lines of dialogue are from the spiritual teachings of the late Eknath Easwaran.

Contributors

CAMERON BARNETT was thirteen years old when he and his mother, JoAnn, attended Thich Nhat Hanh's 2006 family retreat at Plum Village in France.

MARTINE BATCHELOR was ordained as a Buddhist nun in Korea in 1975 and studied Zen Buddhism under the guidance of the late Master Kusan at Songgwang Sa monastery until 1985. She edited the books *Women on the Buddhist Path* and *Buddhism and Ecology*, and is the author of *Meditation for Life* and *Way of Zen* and, mostly recently, *Let Go: A Buddhist Guide to Breaking Free of Habits*, excerpted in this edition of *Best Buddhist Writing*. She co-leads meditation retreats worldwide with her husband, the well-known author and Buddhist scholar Stephen Batchelor. They live in France.

BHIKKHU BODHI, an American Buddhist monk, was ordained in Sri Lanka in 1972. He has translated several important works from the Pali canon, including the *Sumyatta Nikaya (The Connected Discourses of the Buddha)*. He currently lives at Bodhi Monastery in Lafayette, New Jersey.

SYLVIA BOORSTEIN, PHD, is a cofounding teacher at Spirit Rock Meditation Center in Woodacre, California, and a senior teacher at the Insight Meditation Society in Barre, Massachusetts. She is a practicing psychotherapist and the best-selling author of such books as *Pay Attention, for Goodness' Sake* and *That's Funny, You Don't Look*

Buddhist. She and her husband, Seymour, divide their time between Sonoma County, California, and their home in France.

MICHAEL CARROLL is the founding director of Awake at Work Associates, a consulting group that works with individuals and organizations to rediscover balance and well-being in the workplace. He worked for more than twenty years as a human resources professional and is an authorized teacher in the Shambhala Buddhist lineage. His clients include such organizations as Procter & Gamble, AstraZeneca, Starbucks, Lutheran Medical Center, and the National Board of Medical Examiners.

PEMA CHÖDRÖN is an American Buddhist nun whose root teacher was the renowned meditation master Chögyam Trungpa Rinpoche. Since his death in 1987, she has studied with Trungpa Rinpoche's son, Sakyong Mipham Rinpoche, and her current principal teacher, Dzigar Kongtrul Rinpoche. Pema Chödrön is acharya for Gampo Abbey in Nova Scotia, the first Tibetan monastery in North America established for Westerners. Her many popular books include *The Places That Scare You, When Things Fall Apart,* and *Start Where You Are.*

CHOKYI NYIMA RINPOCHE, eldest son of the late Tulku Urgyen Rinpoche, is abbot of Ka-Nying Shedrub Ling, one of Nepal's largest Buddhist monasteries. In 1981 he founded the Rangjung Yeshe Institute, where international students in Nepal can study Tibetan Buddhism, and later started Rangjung Yeshe Publications, which makes Dzogchen teachings and translations available in English. Among his books are *Medicine and Compassion: A Tibetan Lama's Guidance for Caregivers* and *Present Fresh Wakefulness: A Meditation Manual on Nonconceptual Wisdom.*

DARLENE COHEN is a longtime member of the San Francisco Zen Center and an ordained Zen priest. While living at Green Gulch

Farm, Zen Center's temple in Marin County, she developed rheumatoid arthritis, and this led her to explore the potential of meditation
practice to address chronic pain and catastrophic situations. She is
the author of *Turning Suffering Inside Out: A Zen Approach to Living
with Physical and Emotional Pain.*

His Holiness the Dalai Lama is the spiritual and temporal
leader of the Tibetan people and winner of the Nobel Peace Prize.
Unique on the world stage today, he is a statesman, spiritual teacher,
and deeply learned theologian. In talks and teachings throughout
the world, he advocates a universal "religion of human kindness"
that transcends sectarian differences.

Aidan Delgado is an Iraq veteran, peace activist, and Zen Buddhist. While in Iraq, he declared himself a Buddhist conscientious
objector and relinquished his weapons. After completing his one
year tour of duty, he returned to the United States and became a
member of Iraq Veterans Against the War and the Buddhist Peace
Fellowship. Delgado currently lives in Sarasota, Florida, where he
plans to attend law school and perhaps run for political office.

The Dzogchen Ponlop Rinpoche is a meditation master and
scholar in the Kagyu and Nyingma schools of Tibetan Buddhism.
He is president of Nalandabodhi, a network of meditation centers;
founder of the Nitartha Institute, a course of Buddhist study for
Western students; and publisher of *Bodhi* magazine. He is the author
of *Wild Awakening: The Heart of Mahamudra and Dzogchen*, and,
most recently, *Mind Beyond Death.*

R. J. (Richard) Eskow is a writer, musician, and consultant
specializing in politics, health issues, and communications. He is
a former Fortune 500 senior executive who has worked on global
policy reform in the former Soviet states and health needs in the
Third World. He is especially interested in the intersection between

spiritual activity and social involvement. Eskow is a regular contributor to *The Huffington Post* and maintains his own blogs, A Night Light and The Sentinel Effect.

NORMAN FISCHER is founder and teacher of the Everyday Zen Foundation, whose mission is to open and broaden Zen practice through what he calls "engaged renunciation": living a fully committed religious life that does not exclude family, work, and a passionate interest in the contemporary world. Fischer practiced and taught at the San Francisco Zen Center for twenty-five years and served as abbot from 1995 to 2000. His latest collection of poetry is *I Was Blown Back*, and in 2008 he published *Sailing Home: Using Homer's Odyssey to Navigate Life's Perils and Pitfalls*, his reflections on Homer's *Odyssey* as a map of the human inner journey.

NATALIE GOLDBERG is the author of eleven books, including the best-seller *Writing Down the Bones* and, most recently, *Old Friend from Far Away: The Practice of Writing Memoir*. Her paintings are displayed at the Ernesto Mayans Gallery in Santa Fe, New Mexico. With filmmaker Mary Feidt, she recently completed the documentary *Tangled Up in Bob*, about Bob Dylan's childhood on the Iron Range in northern Minnesota. Goldberg has been a Zen practitioner for over thirty years and teaches workshops and retreats on writing as a spiritual practice.

JOSEPH GOLDSTEIN has played a key role in the establishment of the Vipassana tradition in North America. He is a cofounder and guiding teacher of the Insight Meditation Society and is also a founder of the Forest Refuge, a center for long-term meditation practice. Goldstein is the author of the influential *One Dharma: The Emerging Western Buddhism* and, mostly recently, *A Heart Full of Peace*, excerpted here.

STEVE HAGEN was a student of the late Dainin Katagiri Roshi, from whom he received dharma transmission in 1989. He is head teacher at Dharma field Meditation and Learning Center in Minneapolis and author of the bestsellers *Buddhism Plain and Simple* and *Buddhism Is Not What You Think*.

THICH NHAT HANH is a Zen teacher, poet, and founder of the Engaged Buddhist movement. A well-known antiwar activist in his native Vietnam, he was nominated for the Nobel Peace Prize by Martin Luther King, Jr. In 2005 he returned to Vietnam for the first time since his exile in 1966. The author of more than forty books, Thich Nhat Hanh resides at Buddhist practice centers in France and Vermont.

LIN JENSEN is Senior Buddhist Chaplain at High Desert State Prison in Susanville, California, and founder of the Chico Zen Sangha in Chico, California. A member of the Buddhist Peace Fellowship, he practices active nonviolence by sitting solitary daily peace vigils on Chico's downtown sidewalks. He is the author of *Bad Dog! A Memoir of Love, Beauty, and Redemption in Dark Places* and *Pavement: Reflections on Mercy, Activism, and Doing "Nothing" for Peace*, excerpted here.

CHARLES R. JOHNSON is a novelist, scholar, and essayist who holds the S. Wilson and Grace M. Pollock Professorship for Excellence in English at the University of Washington in Seattle. He has been the recipient of many awards, including a Guggenheim Fellowship and a MacArthur Foundation grant. His novels include *Dreamer* and *Middle Passage*, for which he won a National Book Award.

SISTER CHAN KHONG was a biology student at Saigon University when she met Thich Nhat Hanh in 1959 and took him as her spiritual teacher. She helped him to found the famed School for Youth and Social Service and was one of the original six members of the Order of Interbeing, at which time she was given the name Sister Chan Khong, meaning "True Emptiness." From 1969 to 1972 she worked with Thich Nhat Hanh in exile in Paris organizing the

Buddhist Peace Delegation. Since then, she has played a central role in all of Thich Nhat Hanh's many achievements.

JAMES KULLANDER holds a master of divinity degree from Union Theological Seminary in New York City and is editor-in-chief at Omega Institute in Rhinebeck, New York. He has published essays and commentaries in a variety of print and online publications and is working on a book based on the essay published here. His in-depth interviews with Pema Chödrön, Marion Woodman, and Sister Joan Chittister published in *The Sun* magazine are part of an ongoing compilation of interviews with the women who have most influenced him.

FRANCES MOORE LAPPÉ is the author or coauthor of sixteen books, including the 1971 bestseller *Diet for a Small Planet*. With her daughter, Anna Lappé, she leads the Small Planet Institute, a collaborative network based in Cambridge, Massachusetts, devoted to research and popular education to bring democracy to life. In 2007, the Institute released Lappé's newest book, *Getting a Grip: Clarity, Creativity, and Courage in a World Gone Mad*.

CYNDI LEE is the founder and director of OM yoga in New York City. A practitioner of Tibetan Buddhism and hatha yoga, she is known as a nurturing teacher with an offbeat and playful style. Lee has written several books, including *Yoga Body, Buddha Mind* and *OM Yoga: A Guide to Daily Practice*.

NOAH LEVINE is a counselor, Buddhist teacher, and author of the national bestseller *Dharma Punx*. Son of the acclaimed Buddhist teacher Stephen Levine, he holds a masters degree in counseling psychology and has studied in both the Theravada and Mahayana Buddhist traditions. Levine teaches meditation workshops and retreats nationally, and leads groups in juvenile halls and prisons.

JOHN DAIDO LOORI, ROSHI is abbot of Zen Mountain Monastery in Mt. Tremper, New York, which under his direction has grown to be one of the leading Zen monasteries in America. He received transmission in both the Rinzai and Soto lines of Zen and is a dharma heir of the late Taizan Maezumi Roshi. He is also an award-winning photographer and videographer with a unique approach to integrating art and Zen practice.

JOANNA MACY, PHD, is a scholar of Buddhism, general systems theory, and deep ecology. Her wide-ranging work addresses the psychological and spiritual issues of the nuclear age, the cultivation of ecological awareness, and the fruitful resonance between Buddhist thought and contemporary science. Her group methods, known as the Work That Reconnects, have been adopted in classrooms, churches, and grassroots organizing, helping people to transform despair and apathy into constructive, collaborative action. Among her many books is the classic *World as Lover, World as Self*; a new chapter from the 2007 updated edition is excerpted here.

SUSAN MOON is a writer, teacher, and former editor of *Turning Wheel* magazine. She is the author of *The Life and Letters of Tofu Roshi*, a humor book about an imaginary Zen master, and editor of *Not Turning Away: The Practice of Engaged Buddhism*. The mother of two grown sons, she has been a Zen student since 1976 and is a member the Everyday Zen sangha.

DAVID NICHTERN is composer, musician, and senior teacher in the Shambhala Buddhist lineage. He is director of Buddhist studies and practice at OM yoga and leads yoga and meditation retreats around the world with his wife, Cyndi Lee. Nichtern is the founder of Dharma Moon records, an award-winning composer/guitarist/producer, and the composer of the hit song "Midnight at the Oasis."

REGINALD A. RAY, PHD, is a professor of Buddhist studies at Naropa University and cofounder of the Dharma Ocean Foundation in Crestone, Colorado. He is the author of *Touching Enlightenment: Finding Realization in the Body* and *Indestructible Truth: The Living*

Spirituality of Tibetan Buddhism. Over the last thirty years, Ray has studied with many accomplished masters of Tibetan Buddhism and Zen, most notably his root teacher, Chögyam Trungpa Rinpoche. In recent years, he has also worked with indigenous teachers from North and South America and Africa.

RIGDZIN SHIKPO (Michael Hookham) is dharma director of the Longchenpa Foundation, a lay organization in Great Britain presenting the Dzogchen teachings of the Nyingma school of Tibetan Buddhism. Shikpo met his principal teacher, Chögyam Trungpa Rinpoche, in 1965, and received detailed instruction from him on the preliminary and main practices of the Dzogchen tradition. He also received guidance from the late Dilgo Khyentse Rinpoche, and in 1993 completed a three-year retreat under the direction of Khenpo Tsultrim Gyamtso Rinpoche. Shikpo's emphasis is on presenting the Dzogchen teachings in English using methods and language appropriate to Western students.

HANNAH TENNANT-MOORE is a Brooklyn-based freelance writer and former editor of *The Santa Barbara Independent*. Her work has appeared or is forthcoming in *The Gay and Lesbian Review Worldwide*, *The Sun*, and *Tricycle*. She is a winner of *Turning Wheel* magazine's Young Writers Award and is currently working on a book of essays about dating in Generation Y.

SALLIE TISDALE is the author of seven books, including *Women of the Way*, *The Best Thing I've Ever Tasted: The Secret of Food*, and *Talk Dirty to Me: An Intimate Philosophy of Sex*. She also writes for *Harper's*, *Antioch Review*, and other journals. Tisdale is a lay teacher at Dharma Rain Zen Center and works part time as a palliative care nurse.

TRALEG KYABGON RINPOCHE received both the traditional education of an incarnate Tibetan lama (*tulku*) and a comprehensive Western education, with a particular interest in psychology and comparative religion. He is the president and spiritual director of

Kagyu E-Vam Buddhist Institute in Melbourne, Australia, and E-Vam Institute in upstate New York. His books include *Mind at Ease: Self-Liberation through Mahamudra Meditation* and *The Practice of Lojong: Cultivating Compassion through Training the Mind*, excerpted in this volume.

KATE LILA WHEELER writes fiction, journalism and personal essays and teaches meditation. She lives in Somerville, Massachusetts, with her husband and dog. Currently she is working on the last draft of a novel, *Holy Woman*, with support from a fellowship at the Radcliffe Institute. Her previous two books of fiction are *When Mountains Walked* and *Not Where I Started From*.

YONGEY MINGYUR RINPOCHE, a son of the renowned Dzogchen master Tulku Urgyen Rinpoche, is a young teacher in the Karma Kagyu school of Tibetan Buddhism. He teaches extensively in the West, bringing together traditional Buddhist practice and contemporary culture and science.

SHINZEN YOUNG is a Vipassana meditation teacher and the author of *Break Through Pain: A Step-by-Step Mindfulness Meditation Program for Transforming Chronic and Acute Pain*. He has worked for thirty years coaching people through a wide spectrum of chronic and acute pain challenges. Young leads meditation retreats in the mindfulness tradition throughout North America.

Credits

Cameron Barnett, "Retreat at Plum Village." From the Summer 2007 issue of *The Mindfulness Bell*.

Martine Batchelor, "Grasping." From *Let Go: A Buddhist Guide to Breaking Free of Habits* by Martine Batchelor, copyright © 2007 by Martine Batchelor. Reprinted with permission from Wisdom Publications, 199 Elm Street, Somerville, MA 02144 USA. www.wisdompubs.org.

Bhikkhu Bodhi, Darlene Cohen, Shinzen Young, and Reginald Ray, "Pain But Not Suffering." From the Spring 2007 issue of *Buddhadharma: The Practitioner's Quarterly*.

Sylvia Boorstein, "A Little Lower Than the Angels: How Equanimity Supports Kindness." From *Happiness Is an Inside Job: Practicing for a Joyful Life* by Sylvia Boorstein, PhD, copyright © 2007 by Sylvia Boorstein. Used by permission of Ballantine Books, a division of Random House, Inc.

Michael Carroll, "The Mindful Leader." From *The Mindful Leader: Ten Principles for Bringing Out the Best in Ourselves and Others* by Michael Carroll, © 2007. Reprinted by arrangement with Shambhala Publications Inc., Boston, MA. www.shambhala.com.

Pema Chödrön, "Choosing Peace." From the November 2007 issue of the *Shambhala Sun*.

Thich Nhat Hanh, "Nothing to Do, Nowhere to Go: Practices Based on the Teachings of Master Linji." From *Nothing to Do, Nowhere to Go: Commentaries on the Teachings of Master Linji* by Thich Nhat Hanh, copyright © 2007 by Unified Buddhist Church. Reprinted with permission from Parallax Press. www.parallax.org.

Lin Jensen, "Hitting the Streets." From *Pavement: Reflections on Mercy, Activism & Doing "Nothing" for Peace* by Lin Jensen, copyright © 2007 by Lin Jensen. Reprinted with permission from Wisdom Publications, 199 Elm Street, Somerville, MA 02144 USA. www.wisdompubs.org.

Charles R. Johnson, "Prince of the Ascetics: A Short Story." From the 2007 edition of *StoryQuarterly*.

Sister Chan Khong, "Learning True Love." From *Learning True Love: Practicing Buddhism in a Time of War* by Sister Chan Khong, copyright © 2007 by Unified Buddhist Church. Reprinted with permission from Parallax Press. www.parallax.org.

James Kullander, "My Marital Status." From the December 2007 issue of *The Sun*.

Frances Moore Lappé, "Natural Abundance." From the January 2008 issue of the *Shambhala Sun*.

Cyndi Lee and David Nichtern, "Yoga Body, Buddha Mind." From the March 2007 issue of the *Shambhala Sun*.

Noah Levine, "Learning Forgiveness." From *Against the Stream: A Buddhist Manual for Spiritual Revolutionaries* by Noah Levine, copyright © 2007 by Noah Levine. Reprinted by permission of HarperCollins Publishers.

John Daido Loori, "The Great Way." From *Finding the Still Point: A*

Yongey Mingyur Rinpoche, "The Joy of Living." From *The Joy of Living: Unlocking the Secret and Science of Happiness* by Yongey Mingyur and Eric Swanson, copyright © 2007 by Yongey Mingyur and Eric Swanson. Used by permission of Harmony Books, a division of Random House, Inc.

About the Editor

MELVIN MCLEOD is editor-in-chief of the award-winning *Shambhala Sun*, North America's oldest and most widely read Buddhist magazine. The *Shambhala Sun* offers accessible, authentic Buddhist teachings and examines all aspects of modern life from a contemplative perspective. He is also editor-in-chief of *Buddhadharma: The Practitioner's Quarterly*, an in-depth, practice-oriented journal for Buddhists of all traditions. A former correspondent for the Canadian Broadcasting Corporation, he is a student of the late Chögyam Trungpa Rinpoche and Khenpo Tsultrim Gyamtso Rinpoche.